D1228899

INDONESIA
The Challenge of Change

INDONESIA
The Challenge of Change

edited by

Richard W. Baker
M. Hadi Soesastro
J. Kristiadi
Douglas E. Ramage

ST. MARTIN'S PRESS
New York

Published by
Institute of Southeast Asian Studies
30 Heng Mui Keng Terrace
Pasir Panjang Road
Singapore 119614
Internet e-mail: publish@iseas.edu.sg
World Wide Web: http://www.iseas.edu.sg/pub.html

First published in the United States of America in 1999 by
St Martin's Press
Scholarly and Reference Division
175 Fifth Avenue
New York, N.Y. 10010

Library of Congress Cataloguing-in-Publication Data

Indonesia: the challenge of change / edited by Richard W. Baker ...
[et al.].
  p.   cm.
Includes bibliographical references and index.
ISBN 0-312-22261-0
  1. Indonesia—Economic conditions—1945- 2. Indonesia—Politics
and government—1966– 3. Indonesia—Social conditions. I. Baker,
Richard W.
HC447.I55635 1999
338.9598—dc21   98-50388
                                                                      CIP

ISBN 981-3055-78-2 (softcover, ISEAS, Singapore)
ISBN 981-3055-79-0 (hardcover, ISEAS, Singapore)

For the USA, Canada, and Hong Kong this hardcover edition (ISBN 0-312-22261-0)
is published by St Martin's Press, New York.

Typeset by International Typesetters Pte Ltd
Printed in Singapore by Seng Lee Press Pte. Ltd.

CONTENTS

List of Tables   ix
List of Figures   xi
Acknowledgements   xiii
List of Contributors   xv
Preface   xix

INTRODUCTION   1

SECTION I: THE ECONOMY   11
1. **Growth and Private Enterprise**   13
    Didik J. Rachbini
        Structural Change   13
        Investment Trends   14
        Fund Mobilization, Credit Policies, and the
            Financial Sector   20
        The Changing Face(s) of Private Enterprise   28
        Government and Private Enterprise   33
        Conclusion   36

2. **Public Enterprises under the New Order**   41
    I Ketut Mardjana
        Public Enterprises at the Start of the New Order   42
        The Constitutional Debate   44
        Public Enterprise and the Oil Boom   45
        Multiple Objectives, Management Problems   45
        The Post-Oil Boom Period   47
        Reform Strategies   49
        Counter-Trend: Strategic Industries   51
        The Policy Debate   52
        One Goal, Two Approaches   53
        Conclusion   54

SECTION II: GOVERNMENT AND POLITICS   59
3. **Formal Political Institutions**   61
    Ramlan Surbakti
        The Powerful Presidency   62
        The Subordinate Cabinet   65
        The Powerless Parliament?   68
        The Dependent Courts   71
        Economic Growth and Governmental Processes   73
        Conclusion   78

4. **The Bureaucracy and Reform**   **81**
T. A. Legowo
    The Making of the New Order Bureaucracy   81
    Institutional Development   83
    The Need for Reform   86
    Forms of Reform   90
    Further Steps in Bureaucratic Reform   94
    Conclusion   97

5. **The Armed Forces**   **99**
J. Kristiadi
    ABRI's Perception of Its Mission, Function, and Role   99
    Growth and the Military Budget   101
    Changing Social Dynamics and ABRI's Role
       and Mission   107
    ABRI and Democratization   109
    Personnel Recruitment   110
    Conclusion   113

6. **Economic Growth and the Performance of**
   Political Parties   **115**
M. Djadijono
    Leadership Selection and Internal Party Management   116
    Characteristics of Party Programmes   121
    The Parties and the Parliament   125
    Political Party Autonomy: The Financial Factor   126
    Growth, Parties, and Politics: Indicators and Prognoşis   130

SECTION III: MIXED INSTITUTIONS   137
7. **Trade Unions and Labour Unrest**   **139**
Sukardi Rinakit
    Employment and Structural Changes in the Economy   140
    Trade Union Problems   142
    Political Background of Trade Union Management   143
    Government Control of SPSI   144
    Alternatives to SPSI   147
    Causes of Labour Strikes   147
    Case Study: Strike at Tangerang   150
    Conclusions   154

8. **Education: Access, Quality, and Relevance**   **159**
Onny S. Prijono
    Access to Education   160

The Quality Gap   163
Relevance: Mismatch between Graduates and
        Labour Force Needs   165
Government Initiative:"Link and Match" and the
        "Dual System"   169
Enterprise and Education   170
Education as a Commodity   173
Conclusion   175

9.   **Mass Media: Between the Palace and the Market**   **179**
     Dedy N. Hidayat
     Economic Development and the Growth of the
             Media Industry   180
     Political Affiliation, Organizational Structure,
             and Personnel   182
     Changing Structure of the Media Industry   184
     Vertical Political Integration   187
     Development, the Media, and Democracy   189
     Diversity, Democracy, and the Market   193

SECTION IV: OTHER INSTITUTIONS   199
10. **Social Organizations: Nahdlatul Ulama and
     Pembangunan**   **201**
     Douglas E. Ramage
     Social Organizations and Their Roles in
             Indonesian Society   201
     NU's Organizational Structure   202
     NU's Purpose and Objectives   203
     Political Background of NU   203
     Adaptation to Pembangunan   204
     Changes in Institutional Behaviour   205
     Political Factors   206
     Economic Factors   207
     Thinking about the Future, or How NU Copes with
             "Modernity"   209
     Impact of Issues Generated by Economic Change on NU   211
     Conclusion   213

11. **Non-Governmental Organizations and the
     Empowerment of Civil Society**   **217**
     Muhammad AS Hikam
     NGOs under the New Order   220
     Three Case Studies: 222

Legal Aid Institute (LBH)   222
Democracy Forum (Fordem)   224
Indonesian Environmental Forum (Walhi)   227
Conclusion   229

12. **Policy Advisory Institutions: "Think-Tanks"**   **233**
Dewi Fortuna Anwar
Constraints and Limitations on Think-Tanks   233
Think-Tanks in Jakarta: 235
Indonesian Institute of Sciences (LIPI)   235
Centre for Strategic and International
Studies (CSIS)   237
Institute for Economic and Social Research,
Education, and Information (LP3ES)   239
Centre for the Study of Development
and Democracy (CESDA)   241
Institute for Strategic Studies in Indonesia (ISSI) 241
Centre for Policy and Implementation
Studies (CPIS)   242
Centre for Information and Development
Studies (CIDES)   243
Other Think-Tanks   245
Typology of Think-Tanks   246
Conclusion   249

CONCLUSION   255
Richard Baker and M. Hadi Soesastro
Government Institutions: Not Keeping Pace   255
Mixed Institutions: Mixed Records   259
The Private Sector: Dynamic Responses   264
New Institutions: Filling Gaps   268
Implications and Prospects   269

Bibliography   273

Index   293

LIST OF TABLES

Table 1.1 Indonesian Growth Rates, 1979–95 14
Table 1.2 Approved Foreign Investment, 1967–96 16
Table 1.3 Realized Foreign Investment, by Sector, 1967–97 (April) 17
Table 1.4 Approved Domestic Investment, 1967–96 19
Table 1.5 Realized Domestic Investment, by Sector, 1967–97 (April) 21
Table 1.6 Fund Mobilization through *Tabanas* and *Taska* Programmes, 1971–91 23
Table 1.7 Credit of Twenty Largest Customers of State Banks, 1994 26
Table 1.8 Capitalization of the Jakarta Stock Exchange, 1989–97 28
Table 1.9 Successful Indigenous Businessmen Over Several Periods 29
Table 1.10 Comparison of Private Conglomerates and State Enterprises, 1993 32
Table 1.11 Activity of Private Conglomerates in Strategic Business Sectors 34

Table 2.1 Public Enterprises (BUMN): Numbers, Sales, and Assets, 1993 43

Table 3.1 Laws Passed by the Indonesian Parliament (DPR), by Period, 1966–95 69

Table 4.1 Military Officers in Ministerial and Governor Positions, 1968–93 82
Table 4.2 Number of Central Government Offices, 1968–93 83
Table 4.3 Number of Civil Servants, 1980–92 84
Table 4.4 Expenditure on Civil Servants, 1969/70–1993/94 85
Table 4.5 Transfer of Government Functions to Regions 93
Table 4.6 Sources of Income of District Governments 1988/1989 and 1991/1992 94

Table 5.1   Military and National Budgets, 1969/70–1993/94   102
Table 5.2   Academic Qualifications of Candidates for the
             Indonesian Armed Forces Academy, Academic
             Years 1993/94 and 1994/95   111

Table 6.1   Cases of Public Confrontation with State
             Security Authorities, 1995   132

Table 7.1   Indonesia's Employment Structure, 1971–90   141
Table 7.2   Labour Strikes, 1971–94   148
Table 7.3   Causes of Labour Strikes, 1987–94   148
Table 7.4   Manufacturing Labour Wages in Asia, 1991
             and 1993   149
Table 7.5   Tangerang Worker Sample: Gender and Work Status   151
Table 7.6   Tangerang Worker Sample: Views on Worker-
             Management Communication, by Education Level   153
Table 7.7   Tangerang Worker Sample: Views on Worker-
             Manager Communication, by Income Level   153

Table 8.1   Labour Demand and Supply, by Education Level,
             1988–2003   166
Table 8.3   Projected Labour Supply and Demand for University
             Graduates, 1994/95–1998/99   168

LIST OF FIGURES

Figure 2.1   National Capital Formation, Indonesia, 1978–90   48
Figure 2.2   Growth of Assets, Sales, and Profits of State
             Enterprises under BPIS, 1989–91   55

Figure 4.1   The Structure of Indonesia's State Administration   87

ACKNOWLEDGEMENTS

The Editors acknowledge the sponsorship of two organizations that made this research possible: the Centre for Strategic and International Studies (CSIS) and the East-West Center (EWC).

The Centre for Strategic and International Studies is an independent research organization in Jakarta, Indonesia. Established in 1971, CSIS' main activities consist of policy-oriented studies on both domestic and international affairs.

The East-West Center is a public, non-profit educational institution located in Honolulu, Hawaii. It was established in 1960 by the United States Congress to foster mutual understanding and co-operation among the governments and peoples of the Asia-Pacific region.

In addition, the Editors thank *The Jakarta Post* and their photographer, Mulkan Salmona, for permission to use the photo (STRA00064.JPG, 23-4-1998 at 19.47p.m.) that appears on the front cover of this book.

Finally, the editors would like to express their deep appreciation to all who contributed to the project and made the publication of this volume possible: to the authors for making the time in their crowded agendas to prepare the case studies; to the other participants in the project workshops, as well as several anonymous reviewers who read drafts of the manuscript for their many valuable comments and suggestions; and to the Managing Editor of the Institute of Southeast Asian Studies, for the support and persistence in seeing the book through to final publication. Of course, the responsibility for the overall design of the project and for the conclusions drawn in the book remains ours.

THE CONTRIBUTORS

Dewi Fortuna Anwar is Assistant for Foreign Affairs to the State Secretary, State Secretariat, Indonesia. She previously served as the Head of the Regional and International Affairs Division at the Centre for Political and Regional Studies of the Indonesian Institute of Sciences (LIPI) and a Research Executive at the Center for Information and Development Studies (CIDES), Jakarta. She obtained a Master's degree in International Relations from the School of Oriental and African Studies (SOAS) at the University of London, and earned a Ph.D. from Monash University, Australia.

Richard W. Baker is an International Relations Specialist at the East-West Center, Honolulu. He holds a B.A. degree in Politics and Economics from Yale University and a Master of Public Affairs degree from the Woodrow Wilson School at Princeton University. From 1967 to 1987 he was a career officer in the United States Foreign Service, including assignments in Indonesia in 1972–76. He was a co-director of the study that produced this book, and principal editor of the book.

M. Djadijono is a member of the research staff in the Department of Political Affairs of the Centre for Strategic and International Studies, Jakarta. He is a graduate of the Faculty of Political Science of the University of Indonesia.

Dedy N. Hidayat is a lecturer in the Faculty of Social and Political Sciences at the University of Indonesia. He is also a media consultant and is a researcher at the Institute for Mass Communication Research and Development, Jakarta. He graduated from the University of Indonesia in 1980 with a degree in Communications; he was also an editor of the student newspaper. He studied for his Master's degree in Journalism under a Fulbright grant at the E.W. Scripps School of Journalism at Ohio University. He holds a Ph.D. in Mass Communication from the University of Wisconsin.

Muhammad AS Hikam is a Research Fellow at the Center for Economic and Development Studies of the Indonesian Institute of Sciences (LIPI), Jakarta. He holds a B.A. in Literature from Gadjah Mada University, Yogyakarta, and a Ph.D. in Political Science from the University of Hawaii.

J. Kristiadi is Deputy Executive Director of the Centre for Strategic and International Studies, Jakarta. He was previously Head of the Department of Political Affairs. He earned both B.A. and Ph.D. degrees in Political Science from Gadjah Mada University, Yogyakarta. He was one of the organizers of the study that produced this book.

Tommi A. Legowo is Head of the Department of Political and Social Change at the Centre for Strategic and International Studies, Jakarta. He is a graduate of the Faculty of Social and Political Sciences at Gadjah Mada University in Yogyakarta. He obtained his Master's degree in Political Theory from the Department of Government, University of Essex, Colchester, England.

I Ketut Mardjana heads the Division of Planning and Foreign Relations of the Research and Development Agency in the Department of Finance of the Government of Indonesia. He holds a Ph.D. from the Faculty of Business and Economics of Monash University, Melbourne, Australia.

Onny S. Prijono is Head of the Department of Socio-Cultural Affairs at the Centre for Strategic and International Studies, Jakarta. She graduated from the University of Indonesia, and holds a Master's degree in International Development Education from Stanford University.

Didik J. Rachbini is Director of a newly-established research institute, INDEF (Institute for Development of Economics & Finance), in Jakarta. He is also a lecturer in the post-graduate programme of the University of Indonesia, and Dean of the Faculty of Economics of Mercu Buana University, Jakarta. He received his Bachelor's degree (Ir.) from the Bogor Agricultural Institute (Institut Pertanian Bogor — IPB), and earned M.S. and Ph.D. degrees in Development Studies from Central Luzon State University, the Philippines.

Douglas E. Ramage is Representative of the Asia Foundation for Indonesia and Malaysia. He holds a B.A. from the University of Maryland and earned his Ph.D. from the University of South Carolina; his dissertation was on political discourse in Indonesia. From 1993 to 1995 he was a Fellow at the East-West Center in Honolulu. He was one of the organizers of the study that produced this book.

Sukardi Rinakit is a member of the research staff of the Department of Socio-Cultural Affairs of the Centre for Strategic and International Studies, Jakarta. He holds a B.A. in criminology from the University of Indonesia, and a Master's degree in Southeast Asian Studies from the National University of Singapore. From 1990 to 1995 he was secretary at the Research and Development Institution of the All-Indonesia Workers' Union.

M. Hadi Soesastro is the Executive Director of the Centre for Strategic and International Studies, Jakarta. He holds a Diploma in Engineering from the Rhine-Westphalia Technical Institute in Aachen, Germany, and obtained his Ph.D. from the Rand Graduate School, Santa Monica, California. He has lectured at a number of universities, and in 1988–89 was a visiting professor at the East Asian Institute, School of International and Public Affairs, Columbia University. He was a co-director of the study that produced this book.

Ramlan Surbakti is a lecturer in the Faculty of Political and Social Sciences, as well as the Head of the Post-Graduate Program in Political Science, at Airlangga University, Surabaya. He holds a B.A. in Government from Gadjah Mada University in Yogyakarta, an M.A. in Political Science from the Ohio State University, and a Ph.D. from Northern Illinois University.

PREFACE

This study is the product of a collaboration between two research institutions, the Centre for Strategic and International Studies (CSIS) in Indonesia and the East-West Center in the United States.

The genesis of the project was a proposal from the East-West Center in 1994 to conduct a broad-ranging survey of institutional change in Indonesia resulting from the rapid economic growth experienced during the period of the New Order government. CSIS agreed to co-sponsor the study, and in mid-1994 the editors met to identify the specific sectors to be examined and appropriate experts in each area to conduct the case studies. A preliminary workshop was held in Jakarta in December 1994 at which draft papers were presented and discussed by a group including the authors as well as a number of other analysts and authorities in the various fields. A follow-up workshop in April 1995 conducted a similar review of revisions of the studies. Subsequently the editors worked with the individual authors to complete the studies, the case study reports were put into comparable formats, and then the concluding chapter was prepared based on the papers and the workshop discussions.

The title originally proposed for this work was "Riding the Miracle", which the project organizers believed appropriately captured both the exhilaration and the elements of challenge and uncertainty involved in the processes of change under way in Indonesia. However, shortly after the manuscript was completed in mid-1997, Indonesia effectively fell off the economic growth wave. Ripple effects of economic problems in Thailand and speculation against the Thai baht triggered a run on the Indonesian rupiah in July and a rapid worsening of monetary and financial conditions that reached crisis proportions by the end of 1997. In 1998 the mounting economic crisis produced a wave of violent incidents and political protests that culminated in the sudden resignation of President Soeharto in May. In the months that followed, the successor government under former Vice President B.J. Habibie struggled to reverse the continuing economic decline and to respond to public demands for political reform.

A number of the underlying institutional problems identified in this study contributed directly to the gravity of the 1997–98 crisis and to Soeharto's ultimate downfall. The crisis in turn served to dramatically increase awareness, both within and outside Indonesia, of the depth and seriousness of these issues. It also provided new opportunities and incentives to address some of the long-standing problems. Thus the subject matter of the project has taken on increased interest and importance, and the editors are hopeful that the study can contribute to a better understanding of the fundamental issues behind the ongoing crisis.

While it was impracticable at such a late stage to update the individual case studies to directly incorporate the events of 1997–98, the Introduction and Conclusion were re-written to highlight some of the connections between the issues discussed in the study and the crisis that was still unfolding as the book went to press. The new title also better reflects the changed circumstances and focus of attention.

The editors would also like to note that all but one of the case studies were authored by Indonesian specialists on the institutions or sectors in question, and the group included a number of younger scholars. Therefore the study provides a collection of essentially Indonesian insights on the critical trends and issues affecting their nation, one that is clearly destined to play a major role in the future of Southeast Asia and the larger Asia-Pacific region. We hope that these Indonesian perspectives will enrich the international scholarly dialogue on these subjects.

INTRODUCTION

The subject of this study is institutional change — specifically, how twelve different institutions, including the bureaucracy, the armed forces, the media, and private and public enterprise, have been responding to the process of change. The changes brought about by growth, and the differing reactions to them across a society, are major factors in determining the further evolution and future stability of the society. These questions are particularly salient in a period of major political change, and Indonesia has now entered such a period.

The resignation of President Soeharto in May 1998 due to a grave economic crisis and mounting political protests led to a sudden transfer of leadership to Dr B.J. Habibie, Soeharto's Vice-President. This leadership change was more significant and has involved more uncertainty for Indonesia than would be the case in most countries because it is only the second such transition in Indonesia's fifty years of independence.

The increasing tension level in the country had been dramatically illustrated by the political conflict and violence that erupted during the run-up to the May 1997 national parliamentary election. In June 1996, the government instigated the removal of the leader of the opposition Indonesian Democratic Party, Megawati Sukarnoputri, the daughter of Indonesia's charismatic first president who was seen by many as a possible challenger to Soeharto. This confrontation eventually triggered a major and destructive riot in Jakarta in late July. The July incident was followed over the succeeding months by a chain-reaction series of disturbances in numerous cities and towns throughout Java and elsewhere in the archipelago as well. This was an unprecedented level of violence for the previously closely-controlled electoral process under the New Order.

Not long after the parliamentary election, an even more serious development threatened the most fundamental achievement of the New Order, its record of rapid economic development. An almost totally unanticipated series of events beginning in July 1997 threw Indonesia's economy into a tailspin. The value of the rupiah fell by more than 80 percent as of early 1998, production declined precipitously and many companies faced imminent bankruptcy, inflation rose into double digits, and the economic growth rate became negative for the first time in thirty years. Another wave of violent incidents wracked the archipelago, reflecting economic hardships, fears of price rises and shortages of basic commodities, and heightened ethnic antagonisms especially against Indonesia's Chinese minority.

The depth of the economic crisis of 1997–98 indicated a general loss of confidence in the Soeharto government as well as uncertainty about the succession issue and therefore about the country's whole future direction. The crisis was all the more traumatic because it occurred so suddenly and against the background of almost three decades of spectacularly successful economic growth.

The New Order's Economic "Miracle"

Indonesia's "New Order" government, led by then General Soeharto, succeeded the "Old Order" government of the country's founding President Sukarno in March 1966. The new regime took over after a period of political chaos and widespread violence including mass killings following the abortive communist coup of 30 September 1965. It inherited a country that was in a state of economic collapse. Nearly two decades of slow deterioration in economic conditions had been followed by five years of a rapidly increasing downward spiral. By early 1966 production was at a virtual standstill, physical infrastructure was disintegrating, and hyper-inflation was rendering the nation's currency essentially worthless. Most of the population of some 100 million people was living in a state of abject poverty, with the rural population at near subsistence levels.

Over the next three decades, the New Order government compiled what can only be classified as an extraordinary record of economic rehabilitation, growth, and transformation. National income increased sixfold in real terms. The growth rate was 7 per cent or more per year between 1967 and 1981, and after falling to just over 3 per cent in the 1980s due to declining oil prices and other structural problems, in the 1990s growth rates again approached and at times exceeded 7 per cent.[1] By 1996 Indonesia's Gross Domestic Product (GDP) was over US$200 billion.

More importantly, the per capita income of Indonesia's nearly 200 million people grew at some 4.5 per cent annually after 1965, and as of the mid-1990s it was four times greater in real terms than it had been in 1965. In U.S. dollars, the average Indonesian's annual income increased from around US$50 in 1965 to approximately US$1,000 in 1995 (and nearly US$1,200 in 1996).[2] Using a more complex measure developed by the World Bank that attempts to compensate for differences in purchasing power between countries and thus provide a more realistic basis for comparing actual standards of living, in 1995 Indonesia's per capita income stood at nearly US$4,000 (World Bank 1997, p. 129).

The growth in Indonesia's per capita income was the result of a combination of strong growth in the economy and a simultaneous fall in the rate of population growth, from 2.4 per cent per year in the 1970s to under 1.8 per cent in the 1990s. The reduction in the population growth rate was itself partly the result of deliberate government policy, in the form of a concerted nation-wide family planning effort that accelerated the decline in population growth which historically has tended to follow periods of significant economic growth.

Finally, overall income growth was also accompanied by a remarkable degree of equity. This is an area in which both the statistical measures and the accuracy of the basic data are the subjects of debate. Nevertheless, available welfare indicators show that the poorer segments of the Indonesian population benefited significantly from the overall economic growth. In 1970 it was estimated that 60 per cent of the population — some 70 million people — lived in absolute poverty (defined by the World Bank [1993b] as a lack of the basic necessities of clean water, food and shelter). By 1990 the poverty rate had fallen to 16 per cent or 29 million people, and as of the mid-1990s was estimated at 11 per cent or 21 million people (*Far Eastern Economic Review* [hereafter cited as *FEER*], 3 April 1997, p. 5).

According to the World Bank,[3] income inequality also declined in Indonesia between 1965 and 1990. Other World Bank statistical measures[4] indicate that at the end of the 1980s income distribution in Indonesia was comparable to, or more equitable than, that of most other Southeast Asian countries — and surprisingly even appeared to be slightly better than that of some much wealthier developed countries such as Australia and France. The reduction of inequality in Indonesia again to some degree reflected direct action by government, through policies such as the introduction of high-yield crops and assistance programmes targeted on poor rural villages.

None of this is to say that poverty was on the verge of being eliminated in Indonesia by the middle of the 1990s. Millions of people remained very poor, and large numbers were still living near the line of absolute poverty. Further, the gap in living standards between rich and poor, particularly in the urban areas, had become more visible than in the early years of the New Order, and absolute differences in incomes between the cities, particularly Jakarta, and most rural areas and regions had also been increasing (Bresnan 1993, pp. 286–87). Nor does it say that Indonesia had achieved an average per capita income level anywhere near those of the advanced industrialized economies. Even at the purchasing power parity estimate of US$4,000 in 1995, the income of the average Indonesian remained far below the U.S. level of more than US$25,000 per capita. But it does indicate that Indonesia had in a very short time climbed from the ranks of the poorest countries to a solid position among the lower-middle income countries, and the general view — including among development experts — was that the prospect was for a continuation of this pattern of rapid growth through the mid-term future. This impressive achievement led the World Bank to include Indonesia among the eight "high performing Asian economies" that were the subject of its landmark 1993 report, *The East Asian Economic Miracle* (World Bank 1993*b*).

From Boom to Bust

The economic crisis that began in July 1997 brought the growth record of the preceding three decades — as well as talk of a continuing economic miracle — to an abrupt halt. As previously noted, the economic collapse also brought with it an increase in social unrest and incidents of violence, and a general loss of confidence in the Soeharto government that ultimately led to Soeharto's dramatic resignation on 21 May 1998.

A number of specific factors contributed to the severity of the economic crisis. These included pure coincidence, since the initial run on the rupiah in July was in part the result of the ripple effect of a foreign exchange crisis in Thailand that impacted the currencies of all the countries of Southeast Asia. The specific problems in the Indonesian economy that made the rupiah vulnerable were a large, boom-fuelled private corporate debt, much of which was in short-term credits for long-term projects such as real estate development and little of which was hedged against exchange rate losses, and the general weakness and lack of transparency in the Indonesian banking and financial systems.

For its part, the Indonesian Government's initial reaction to the rupiah crisis was strong and relatively impressive. It almost immediately floated the rupiah to conserve foreign exchange reserves, it raised domestic interest rates to encourage foreign capital inflows, and in September 1997 it eliminated or postponed numerous government projects in order to reduce the government budget deficit. When pressure against the rupiah continued, in October the government requested the help of the International Monetary Fund (IMF). By the end of the month an agreement had been negotiated with the IMF that would provide some $23 billion in international financial support in return for a series of structural reforms by the Indonesians.

However, the reform package required some very difficult actions by the Soeharto government, actions that would be painful both for the general population and for powerful interest groups with direct ties to the president. When the package failed to stop the rupiah's slide, Soeharto began dragging his heels on the reforms. The delays in implementation in turn further reduced confidence in the government on the part of the general business community and the IMF and led to further declines in the value of the rupiah. This eventually necessitated two renegotiations of the IMF agreement in the first part of 1998.

The government's inability to deal with the economic crisis triggered a new series of incidents in various parts of the extended archipelago during the first months of 1998, as well as a wave of student demonstrations and protests. Over time, other elements of the population including key opposition political figures joined the student movement, and this fuelled an escalation in the protestors' demands including direct calls for Soeharto to step down. Although Soeharto and his hand-picked vice presidential candidate, his long-time research minister B.J. Habibie, were formally elected to a five-year term of office without opposition by a tame and largely appointed People's Consultative Assembly in March, the underlying conditions continued to deteriorate. The killing by security forces of four university students in Jakarta on 12 May sparked a two-day riot marked by massive looting and burning of shopping districts, with over 1,000 deaths, and precipitated the final unraveling of support for the president. Soeharto's sudden announcement of his resignation on 21 May left his new, ill-prepared vice president to deal with a combination of economic collapse and political revolution.

At a more fundamental level, behind the immediate causes and chronology of the crisis lay a series of long-term problems and issues that had built up over the course of the 30-plus years of the New Order government. On the economic side the problems included pervasive corruption, crony capitalism and nepotism, and the associated monopoly arrangements that raised costs for the economy as a whole and reduced Indonesia's international competitiveness. The economic issues were connected with and reinforced by a highly centralized and relatively closed political and decision-making structure, which greatly inhibited the advocacy of alternative courses of action or genuine public debate. In addition, a variety of other structural and institutional problems compounded the difficulties of dealing with the new demands created by a high-growth, increasingly globalized economy. Although many of these issues had long been identified by Indonesians and foreign observers alike, they were deep-seated and resistant to easy solutions and, in the context of the continuing economic boom, had been put off or given only secondary priority. The crisis of 1997-98 served to focus new attention on these problems and to give them new urgency.

This study addresses many of these structural issues as well as other challenges posed by a period of rapid economic change across the spectrum of the institutions of Indonesia's economy, government, and society.

The Challenge of Change

Rapid and dramatic economic growth, particularly when sustained over a number of years, inevitably causes vast changes throughout a society. It alters the basic economic structures and processes themselves. It brings about changes in social structure and values, through rising levels of education and skill as well as greater exposure to and consciousness of differences within the society and between it and the outside world. Political dynamics and power relationships also change. Growth affects the number and size of interest groups within the society, the nature and levels of demand for goods and services, and the ability and desire of various groups to seek access and influence over decision making. In the case of Indonesia, the growth of an increasingly educated, affluent middle class has been one of the major results of economic change.

Advancing economic levels also require increasing sophistication and complexity in a society's institutional structure — economic, social, and political — and bring with them new challenges for the leaders and managers of these institutions. Old institutions must adapt to new conditions, and new institutions and organizational forms are spawned. Finally, rising economic levels inevitably affect relationships among the various sectors and institutions in a society, and contacts with the outside world tend to expand as well, bringing in yet more new influences. All of these changes can evoke both positive and negative reactions within the society, further complicating the process of adaptation. This study examines this process in the specific case of Indonesia since 1965.

The Study

There is an impressive and rapidly growing body of literature, much of it by non-Indonesian observers, on the Indonesian experience during the New Order era. The World Bank study of economic growth has already been mentioned. Other recent significant works include Adam Schwarz' *A*

Nation in Waiting (1994) on political dynamics, John Bresnan's *Managing Indonesia* (1993) on policy-making by the New Order government, and *Indonesia's New Order: The Dynamics of Socio-economic Change* (1994), edited by Hall Hill, on social and economic change. Works on specific sectors include the annual *Indonesia Assessment* series sponsored by the Indonesia Project of the Australian National University, whose 1990s editions have covered such topics as higher education, labour, population, and the finance sector, and Philip Eldridge's *Non-Government Organizations and Democratic Participation in Indonesia* (1995) on NGOs. Numerous other books and articles are available on Indonesia's contemporary society, economy, and politics by leading scholars in these fields.

This study does not attempt to retrace the ground already well covered in these various works. Rather, it attempts to assess the effects of economic growth and the challenges posed by these changes on twelve basic institutions or sectors of Indonesian life and society. The institutions cover a broad range, including economic sectors, government structures and bodies, and social organizations. Inevitably, there are some omissions from the list (for example, neither agriculture nor the rural sector as a whole are covered), but it does provide a representative and manageable sample.

The case studies are organized as follows. We begin by surveying the major sectors of the economy — private and public enterprises. We then move to the government sector, including the overall government structure, the bureaucracy, the armed forces, and the political parties. Next we look at three other institutions which, together with the political parties, reflect a mixture of government management and control and broader societal forces: trade unions, the education system, and the mass media. Finally, we consider the impact of economic change on one very traditional institution, the mass social organization, and two relatively new types of institution, non-governmental organizations and policy advisory "think-tanks".

Some of the institutions in the case studies are more narrowly defined than others. For example, the armed forces and the political parties are quite specific institutions, while private enterprise and education are much more general categories. Nor are all of the categories strictly mutually exclusive. For example, the category of political structure and processes (Chapter 3) could be considered to encompass the other governmental institutions discussed in the subsequent three chapters — the bureaucracy, the armed forces, and the political parties. However, each of the other three groups has its own unique characteristics and occupies an important position within the overall government structure, and so it was considered worthwhile to give them separate, more detailed examination.

In each chapter, the author assesses the ways in which the institution in question has been affected by economic growth — that is, the degree to which it either has been changed by, or has adapted itself to, the changing economic conditions. These analyses lead to the identification of various issues and challenges to the institutions that have been posed by the process of sustained, rapid economic growth and its associated changes. Where appropriate, there is also a discussion of efforts that have been or might be made to deal with the major challenges, and an assessment the success or failure of the efforts to date.

Each of the case studies inevitably reflects its author's particular interests and expertise, and none is or could be a completely exhaustive review of all the dimensions of change in that sector. However, the individual perspectives of the authors help highlight the variety of circumstances and responses in the different sectors to the country's changing economic environment.

Findings: The Adaptation Gap

The final chapter compares the results of the case studies, to identify common threads and larger issues that may affect the country's future. The overall conclusion — significant if not especially surprising — is that there are substantial differences in the ways in which the various Indonesian institutions and sectors have met the challenges of change. These varying reactions in turn suggest differing prognoses for the respective institutions as the process of change continues.

The most striking specific finding is that there has been a particular gap between the responses to change of the government and political institutions in Indonesia and those of the more independent sectors of the society. Many government and government-connected institutions have been rather passive or even defensive in their responses, adapting to changing external circumstances only to the degree necessary to continue performing their functions or to sustain their position. The institutions less directly controlled by government have tended to be far more pro-active, trying to harness the forces of change; in some cases the institutions themselves are the direct product of changing conditions. Further, the case studies suggest that the discontinuity between a change-resistant government and political structure and a more dynamic private sector and civil society has been increased over time.

The discontinuity between government and other sectors of Indonesian society is clearly one of the underlying factors that caused and exacerbated the economic-political crisis of 1997–98. It also constitutes one of the most fundamanetal challenges facing the next generation of Indonesia's national leadership, whether this be the current government under B.J. Habibie or some other group that may emerge from the election process now scheduled for 1999.

Notes

[1] Data on Indonesia's economy, population, and growth rates vary widely and can be subject to wide margins of error. There is no common set of figures for any of these series, even among the international financial institutions such as the International Monetary Fund (IMF), the World Bank, and the Asian Development Bank. However, there is universal agreement on the basic fact of Indonesia's successful economic growth record under the New Order government, and there is general congruence among the various sets of data as to the orders of magnitude and the major trends in the growth rates. The figures cited here represent best estimates drawn from a variety of sources. These include the World Bank (1993*b* and other regular publications), Asian Development Bank and IMF publications, Bresnan (1993, pp. 284–88), Schwarz (1994, pp. 57–59), Mills (1995), and data from the Indonesia's Central Bureau of Statistics as well as various Indonesian government documents including President Soeharto's report to the March 1998 People's Consultative Assembly. However, they should not be considered either original or definitive.

[2] In the United States, it would cost nearly US$250 in 1995 dollars to purchase the equivalent of US$50 dollars' worth of goods in 1965; this supports the rough estimate that Indonesians' real per capita income in 1995 (US$1,000) was four times that of 1965.

[3] The Bank bases this conclusion on changes in the so-called "Gini coefficient", a standard statistical measure of income inequality (World Bank 1993b, pp. 2–4, 72–74).

[4] This measure is the ratio of the income shares of the richest fifth and the poorest fifth of the population (World Bank 1993*b*, p. 31).

SECTION I

The Economy

1

Growth and Private Enterprise

Didik J. Rachbini

One of the most significant results of economic progress in Indonesian life over the past three decades has been the expansion of private economic enterprises and the emergence of the private sector as a major element of the overall economy. Indeed, the private sector has been the major driving force in Indonesia's continuing economic growth. This chapter examines the changes in the size and structure of the private sector, as well as some of the issues associated with the increased role and success of private enterprise.

The chapter is organized as follows. First, the overall structural changes in the Indonesian economy during the New Order period are summarized. Then, trends of investment in Indonesia are analysed; the private sector grew both through foreign investment and increasingly the expansion of domestic investment. The next section describes the role of financial institutions and changing government policies in this sector. The fourth section discusses the composition of the domestic private business sector. The changing fortunes of different groups of indigenous businessmen as well as Chinese-Indonesian ("*non-pribumi*") businessmen are charted. The chapter concludes with comments on the issue of conglomeration and the continuing problems of the small business sector and of equity in Indonesia.

STRUCTURAL CHANGE

In the two decades between 1971 and 1991, Indonesia's economy was structurally transformed, from dominance by the primary sector (agriculture) to the secondary and tertiary sectors (industry, and trade and services). Table 1.1 shows the differing growth rates of the major sectors during this period. Although agriculture grew at a moderate rate, and the country achieved self sufficiency in rice production in 1984, the share of

TABLE 1.1
Indonesian Growth Rates, 1979–95
(percent)

	1979–89	1987	1988	1989	1990	1995
Agriculture	3.7	1.8	2.2	3.5	3.9	4.0
Manufacturing Industry	12.7	7.1	9.0	12.1	12.9	11.3
Other Sectors	7.2	6.3	6.7	8.4	8.5	–
GDP (Without Oil Economy)	6.8	5.8	7.3	8.1	8.1	9.0
GDP Total	5.7	5.0	5.6	7.4	7.4	8.1

Sources: The World Bank and BPS (Central Bureau of Statistics).

agriculture in GDP decreased from 44.8 per cent to 19.1 per cent. Manufacturing increased from 8.4 per cent to 21.3 per cent, and the mining and manufacturing sectors combined increased from 16 per cent to 35 per cent. Meanwhile, the share of trade and other service sectors in GDP also increased, from 38.8 per cent to 45.6 per cent.

Within the industrial sector, revenues from oil and natural gas exports were a major source of economic growth in the 1970s and through the early 1980s, but manufacturing (non-oil) exports replaced oil and gas as the leading exports in the latter 1980s and 1990s. Manufacturing experienced extraordinary double-digit growth at some stages during this period, becoming the dominant sector within today's Indonesian economy.

INVESTMENT TRENDS

Since 1967, when a new foreign investment law was passed by the parliament,[1] new investment has played a significant role in Indonesia's economic growth. A major element of the government's overall economic strategy to recover from the collapse of the mid-1960s and resume growth was to stimulate investment. Because the extended political crisis had so damaged potential domestic investment sources, foreign investment was viewed as playing a particularly important role in meeting the recovery and growth objectives.

The foreign investment law was consistent with a broader thrust of the New Order government's development planning team (the so-called "technocrats" headed by Professor Widjoyo Nitisastro) to open the Indonesian economy. However, the policy of welcoming foreign investment was also intended to increase domestic investment, through joint venture activities as well as the encouragement of independent initiatives by domestic investors. (The 1967 foreign investment law was followed a year later by passage of a corresponding new domestic investment law.[2]) The policy of encouraging domestic investment can be considered to have been basically successful, as total domestic investment since 1967 has been approximately one and one half times the total of (non-oil) foreign investment.[3]

Foreign Investment

The 1967 foreign investment law represented a dramatic shift in national policy after nearly two decades in which the former government had effectively closed Indonesia's economy to foreign investment, particularly from Europe and the United States.

As indicated in Table 1.2, response by investors to the new law was initially slow, with only 12 projects being approved in the first year. However, the number of applications and approvals grew rapidly, averaging 55 new projects per year between 1968 and 1974. The numbers then dropped dramatically, to less than 25 approvals per year between 1975 and 1984. The initial drop was due primarily to reaction to the so-called "Malari" incident of 1974.[4] The economic impact of the slowdown in foreign investment was magnified by the drop in the price of oil in the early 1980s, from more than US$20 per barrel to less than US$10 per barrel. After the government instituted a set of new policies designed to attract foreign investment in 1985, applications and approvals grew rapidly again, jumping to nearly 100 approved projects in 1986 and reaching nearly 800 projects in 1995. As of 1996, 4,753 foreign investment projects had been approved with a total value of US$160,679 million (Table 1.2). As of April 1997, investments valued at about US$51 billion had been completed (Table 1.3).[5]

Table 1.3 shows the sectoral distribution of realized foreign (non-oil) investments. The largest share was in the secondary or industrial/manufacturing sector, with almost 70 per cent of total realized investment as of April 1997. Chemicals was the leading subsector, with 24 per cent of all investment (and rapidly growing, having increased from a 14 per cent share in 1994). Metals was next, with approximately 17 per cent of the total, followed closely by paper, at 14 per cent. The textile subsector has also seen significant foreign investment, mostly from Japan, with nearly

TABLE 1.2
Approved Foreign Investment, 1967–96

Year	Number of Projects		Value (US$ million)	
	New	Cumulative	New	Cumulative
1967	12	12	207	207
1968	35	47	264	472
1969	37	84	128	599
1970	83	167	167	76
1971	62	229	287	1,053
1972	47	276	163	1,216
1973	69	345	324	1,540
1974	53	398	542	2,082
1975	24	422	1,145	3,227
1976	22	444	221	3,448
1977	20	464	167	3,615
1978	23	487	207	3,822
1979	13	500	249	4,071
1980	20	520	1,074	5,145
1981	24	544	707	5,852
1982	31	575	2,417	8,269
1983	46	621	2,470	10,740
1984	23	644	1,096	11,836
1985	45	689	853	12,690
1986	93	782	848	13,537
1987	130	912	1,520	28,958
1988	145	1,057	4,411	33,368
1989	294	1,351	4,714	38,082
1990	432	1,783	8,751	46,833
1991	376	2,159	8,778	55,611
1992	305	2,464	10,323	65,934
1993	329	2,793	8,144	74,078
1994	449	3,242	23,724	97,803
1995	799	4,041	39,915	137,717
1996	712	4,753	22,962	160,679

Notes: Data exclude investments in oil and gas and the non-bank financial sector.
Annual investment amounts are from both new investments and expansion of previous investments.
Totals may not add due to rounding.

Source: Processed from BKPM (Investment Co-ordinating Board) data.

TABLE 1.3
Realized Foreign Investment, by Sector, 1967–97 (April)

Sector	Number of Projects	Value (US$ million)	Share (%)
Primary	365	4,104	8.0
1 Food Crops	31	173	0.3
2 Estate Crops	61	769	1.5
3 Livestock	20	144	0.3
4 Fisheries	81	168	0.3
5 Forestry	48	261	0.5
6 Mining	124	2,589	5.0
Secondary	3,092	35,463	68.9
1 Food	231	1,792	3.5
2 Textiles	673	2,834	5.5
3 Wood	189	467	0.9
4 Paper	87	7,034	13.7
5 Pharmaceuticals	77	164	0.3
6 Chemicals	622	12,363	24.0
7 Non-Metals	121	1,965	3.8
8 Basic Metals	103	3,592	7.0
9 Metal	879	5,027	9.8
10 Other	110	226	0.4
Tertiary	937	11,866	23.1
1 Electricity, Gas & Water	11	2,615	5.1
2 Construction	170	412	0.8
3 Trade	157	509	1.0
4 Hotels & Restaurants	144	4,057	7.9
5 Office Buildings	45	1,161	2.3
6 Housing	73	1,329	2.6
7 Transportation	73	848	1.6
8 Other	264	935	1.8
Total	4,394	51,433	100.0

Notes: Data exclude oil and gas; banks; insurance and rentals.
Columns may not add due to rounding.
Source: Processed from BKPM (Investment Co-ordinating Board) data.

6 per cent of the total (down from 8 percent in 1994 despite a nearly 45 per cent increase in total investment during that time). The second largest sector for foreign investment was services, with 23 percent of the total. (Foreign investment in the services sector grew rapidly in recent years, having nearly tripled in absolute value and increased its share from 17 per cent since 1994.)

By location, foreign non-oil investment in Indonesia has been Java-centred. Over 60 per cent of the total value of foreign investment, both approved and realized, has been for projects located in Java and Madura.[6] Foreign investment has been concentrated in Java in large part due to the availability of infrastructure (electricity, roads, transportation, and telephone service) to support those industries.

The geographic concentration of investment is in fact still more intense. Eighty-five per cent of the realized projects on Java and Madura, representing 72 per cent of the total investment value in these provinces (and 45 per cent of the national total), are found in Jakarta and neighbouring West Java province. The majority of these are located in the so-called "Jabotabek" area, the region immediately surrounding Jakarta.

In terms of origin, investments from Japan are the largest both in numbers, with nearly 20 per cent of all approved projects as of 1996, and in value, with approximately 15 per cent of total approved foreign investment. Singapore was in second place, at 10 per cent by value. Hong Kong and the United Kingdom were next, with 9 per cent each, followed by Taiwan and the United States which were both just under 5 per cent (BPS August 1996).

Domestic Investment

Domestic investment under the new investment law also started slowly, but it expanded even more rapidly than foreign investment (see Table 1.4). Twenty-six investment projects, with a total value of Rp38 billion, were approved by the national Investment Co-ordinating Board (BKPM) in 1968, but by the end of the first five-year development plan (Repelita I) in 1974, total approved domestic investment had reached Rp1,195 billion. This total tripled during Repelita II (1974–79) and then grew another six times during Repelita III (1979–84). This represented double digit growth, or better, in every year since 1968. From 1968 through 1996, cumulative approved domestic investments totaled Rp443,988 billion (approximately US$239 billion).

TABLE 1.4
Approved Domestic Investment, 1967–96

Year	Number of Projects		Value:	Rp (billion)		US$ (million)
	New	Cumulative	New	Cumulative	Growth (%)	New
1967	–	–	–	–	–	–
1968	26	26	38	38	–	128
1969	73	99	34	72	88	103
1970	176	275	113	184	157	310
1971	214	489	186	370	101	474
1972	268	757	386	756	104	930
1973	299	1,056	269	1,025	36	649
1974	134	1,190	170	1,195	17	410
1975	78	1,268	159	1,354	13	382
1976	75	1,343	409	1,763	30	985
1977	155	1,498	484	2,246	27	1,165
1978	188	1,686	679	2,925	30	1,563
1979	166	1,852	655	3,580	22	1,051
1980	159	2,011	2,817	6,397	79	4,493
1981	164	2,175	2,292	8,689	36	3,627
1982	205	2,380	3,616	12,305	42	5,467
1983	333	2,713	6,476	18,781	53	7,122
1984	145	2,858	2,109	20,890	11	2,056
1985	245	3,103	3,736	24,626	18	3,364
1986	315	3,418	4,412	29,038	18	3,439
1987	570	3,988	10,450	39,487	36	6,357
1988	843	4,831	14,202	53,689	36	8,425
1989	863	5,694	19,594	73,283	36	11,069
1990	1,324	7,018	56,511	129,794	77	30,666
1991	804	7,822	41,078	170,871	32	21,062
1992	436	8,258	29,342	200,213	17	14,455
1993	548	8,806	39,450	239,664	20	18,902
1994	823	9,629	53,289	292,953	22	24,662
1995	775	10,404	69,853	362,806	24	31,065
1996	619	11,023	81,182	443,988	22	34,659

Notes: Data exclude investments in oil and gas and the non-bank financial sector.
Annual investment amounts are from both new investments and expansion of previous investments.
Totals may not add due to rounding.
Sources: Processed from BKPM (Investment Co-ordinating Board) data
(US$ exchange rates from IMF, *International Financial Statistics*).

Following the pattern of foreign investment, the dominant share of realized domestic non-oil investment was in the secondary (industrial/manufacturing) sector, with over 65 per cent of total investment value as of April 1997 (see Table 1.5). The second largest sector is services (21 per cent), and the primary sector is third (14 per cent).

Within the industrial/manufacturing sector, the chemicals subsector received the most domestic investment, and as with foreign investment this subsector expanded extremely rapidly in recent years (from a negligible level of domestic investment in the early 1990s). The textiles subsector was second, with 19 per cent of the total (also representing an expansion of its share in recent years, up from 11 percent in 1994). Because of its comparative advantages of low labour cost plus experience, the Indonesian textile industry has been competitive in the international market. Textiles and wood (which have enjoyed a rapidly expanding international market since the 1970s, especially in Japan) are Indonesia's largest non-oil exports. Over the last two decades, the textile industry had also been absorbing hundreds of thousands of new workers. Non-metals mining and the paper and pulp industry were in third and fourth place, with 16 and 15 per cent of the sector total, respectively. Although Indonesia still imports pulp, the pulp and paper industry has been growing strongly because of the large domestic market.

By location, also following the pattern of foreign investment and for the same reasons, domestic private investment in Indonesia has been Java- and Jakarta-centred. Over 60 per cent of all approved and realized domestic investments, by value, were located in Java and Madura (see note 6 for sources). Jakarta and West Java accounted for approximately 70 per cent of the investments in Java and Madura by all measures (approved and realized, by number and by value), and approximately 45 per cent of the overall national total by value. The major portion of the Jakarta and West Java investments again are in the "Jabotabek" area surrounding Jakarta. The most modern industries are particularly represented in this group. With both foreign and domestic private investment heavily clustered in Java, there has been a significant and growing gap in the level of industrialization between Java and the rest of Indonesia.

FUND MOBILISATION, CREDIT POLICIES, AND THE FINANCIAL SECTOR

Bank Indonesia (the central bank) has played a major role in promoting the private business sector. The central bank has three primary functions: to

TABLE 1.5
Realized Domestic Investment, by Sector, 1967–97 (April)

Sector	Number of Projects	Value (US$ million)	Share (%)
Primary	1,877	27,049	13.6
1 Food Crops	70	845	0.4
2 Estate Crops	724	16,894	8.5
3 Livestock	139	1,370	0.7
4 Fisheries	360	3,730	1.9
5 Forestry	425	2,507	1.3
6 Mining	159	1,705	0.9
Secondary	7,690	129,904	65.3
1 Food	1,094	10,068	5.1
2 Textiles	1,820	24,427	12.3
3 Wood	1,023	7,844	3.9
4 Paper	467	19,295	9.7
5 Pharmaceuticals	95	518	0.3
6 Chemicals	1,365	31,271	15.7
7 Mining (Non-Metal)	463	21,267	10.7
8 Basic Metals	259	7,645	3.8
9 Metal	995	7,268	3.7
10 Other	109	301	0.2
Tertiary	2,143	41,979	21.1
1 Electricity, Gas & Water	8	875	0.4
2 Construction	133	1,415	0.7
3 Trade	16	168	0.1
4 Hotels & Restaurants	702	15,561	7.8
5 Office Buildings	98	4,920	2.5
6 Housing	252	7,463	3.8
7 Transportation	744	8,081	4.1
8 Other	190	3,495	1.8
Total	5,587	198,932	100.0

Notes: Data exclude oil and gas; banks; insurance and rentals.
Columns may not add due to rounding.
Source: Processed from BKPM (Investment Coordinating Board) data.

act as the monetary authority, to control the banking system, and to support business activities through credit policy. From 1969 to 1983 (the pre-deregulation period), the central bank exercised very direct control over the financial sector, setting interest rates, mobilizing funds, and allocating credit. The government used these instruments to support both state enterprises and private businesses. Government influence over business finance in this period was further enhanced by the dominant role of the state banks in providing investment credits, as private banks were generally limited to short-term activities which made it difficult for them to give credit in large amounts.

Fund Mobilization

At the end of the 1960s, Bank Indonesia introduced two national saving programmes, known as *Tabanas* and *Taska*,[7] as a means of mobilizing funds from the society for national development. Over two decades, these programmes succeeded in recruiting millions of participants, from both urban and rural areas. However, in terms of capital accumulation, they were only able to raise relatively small amounts (Table 1.6).

As of 1991, the total funds accumulated through the *Tabanas* and *Taska* programmes was Rp1,600 billion, only two to four per cent of the amount needed to meet national investment needs. With 17.8 million participants, this meant that the average account was only Rp100,000 per participant, which is a very small amount of money. This demonstrated that the funds available from average citizens and the traditional economy (including small businesses) were very limited.

In the absence of a broad-based source of savings, capital mobilization was mostly accomplished through state institutions (banks and state enterprises), foreign capital, and large domestic enterprises. State enterprises, such as the state oil company Pertamina, accumulated capital through their control over sectors such as the exploitation of oil and natural gas. Larger, established private businesses could acquire capital through such means as state-granted concessions to exploit forests, monopolies over certain strategic commodities (wheat flour, soybeans, cement, etc.), and links with state companies. These advantages enabled some enterprises to enjoy extraordinarily rapid short-term growth.

When state and corporate savings are added to individual savings, total national savings increased quite rapidly from the beginning of the 1970s. In 1971 savings totalled only Rp5 billion. This figure increased to Rp226 billion in 1979, Rp754 billion in 1984, and in 1990 total savings reached

TABLE 1.6
Fund Mobilization through *Tabanas* and
Taska Programmes, 1971–91
(participants in thousands; amounts in Rp million)

Year	*Tabanas* Participants	Amount	*Taska* Participants	Amount	Total Participants	Amount
1971	867	5	20	36	887	5,025
1972	2,389	26	18	99	2,407	25,779
1973	2,871	33	12	84	2,882	32,549
1974	3,450	44	9	74	3,459	44,058
1975	4,111	70	9	114	4,120	70,245
1976	5,430	109	11	158	5,441	109,305
1977	6,864	154	9	138	6,873	153,730
1978	7,459	191	7	120	7,466	192,000
1979	7,996	217	6	122	8,002	213,000
1980	8,829	292	5	122	8,879	292,000
1981	9,481	384	13	168	9,493	384,000
1982	9,952	446	16	307	9,968	446,000
1983	11,004	532	16	331	11,069	532,000
1984	12,425	670	16	452	12,441	670,000
1985	14,712	936	18	357	14,730	936,000
1986	16,380	1,218	16	449	16,395	1,218,000
1987	16,729	1,286	16	646	17,806	1,331,000
1988	–	–	–	–	20,406	1,569,000
1989	–	–	–	–	19,028	1,793,000
1990	–	–	–	–	20,250	1,892,000
1991*	–	–	–	–	17,865	1,623,000

Note: * As of June.
Sources: Bank Indonesia reports, 1971/72, 1977/78, and 1989/90;
Statistics of the Indonesian Economy and Finance, January 1993;
BPS, Economic Indicators, December 1993.

Rp8,129 billion. Bank deposits experienced comparable growth, from Rp34 billion in 1969 to Rp29,866 billion in 1990. Total bank funds are greater still, and have grown at double-digit levels every year since the late 1960s, from Rp100 billion in 1969 to Rp30,806 billion in 1988. This growth of the availability of funds was a significant factor in the expansion of business enterprises, both public and private.

Credit Policies: 1969–83

Consistent with its mission to support business activities, before 1983 Bank Indonesia pursued an essentially expansionary credit policy. This included providing subsidized credits to the state banks (so-called "liquidity credits") to fund government projects. To achieve monetary stability and an acceptable balance of payments, the Department of Finance and Bank Indonesia maintained a "credit ceiling" policy. Credit ceilings were set for each economic sector, and sectors were prioritized in line with the national development plan. State bank funds were allocated according to the priorities.

However, the combination of subsidized government credits and the credit ceiling policy resulted in significant market distortions, and was eventually recognized as constituting excessive state intervention in the economy. Government subsidies on credits to favoured sectors helped fuel inflation, which averaged 18 per cent a year in the 1970s (McLeod 1993, p. 99). As a result of the credit ceiling policy, the state banks came to hold excess reserves, both domestic and foreign. They had little incentive to raise funds from the public, economic institutions, or business. Growth of funds in the state banks slowed, as the banks focused on allocation of funds into various investments rather than mobilization of funds (Djanin 1992, p. 99).

Reforms: *Pakjun 1983* and *Pakto 88*

The significant drop in the price of oil in the early 1980s faced Indonesia with a severe financial crisis. With increasing foreign debt payments, and a low level of non-oil exports, government resources were severely reduced. In response, the government introduced a series of monetary policy reforms, the overall purpose of which was to fill the gap between investment needs and savings levels. Through deregulation and debureaucratization, the reforms also sought to remove barriers to the effective working of the market mechanism in the monetary system.

The reform package of June 1983, called *Pakjun 1983*, contained three major elements. First, interest rates were decontrolled, to improve incentives in the banking system to make investments, and therefore to increase the demand for deposits and the mobilization of funds. Second, the credit ceiling system was abolished, to allow flows of credit to respond to market forces and remove the distortions and unproductive uses (or non-use) of funds that had occurred under the sectoral allocation policies. Third, Bank Indonesia reduced the subsidies on the liquidity credits provided to state banks, and obligatory deposits by state enterprises in state banks were reduced, in order to force the state banks to operate on a more efficient and businesslike basis. The government also reduced the number of government investment projects financed by liquidity credits, to reduce inflation as well as the distorting effect of government direction of state bank funding decisions.

In October 1988, a second reform package referred to as *Pakto 88* implemented a sweeping deregulation of the banking sector. These reforms opened up licensing for new banks, the establishment of branches, and joint ventures. The reserve requirement was also lowered.

Pakto 88 was a major turning point, and led to an impressive change from state domination of the banking sector to a more liberalized system of banking in which the private sector played an increasingly significant role. This was reflected in the rapid growth both of the numbers of private banks throughout the country and of the private banks' share of total deposits. In the five years between 1988 and 1993, the number of private commercial banks in Jakarta doubled, from 104 to 213. The number of branches rose from 876 to 3382. Before *Pakto 88*, the state banks' share of total funds and credit was about 70 per cent, while that of the private banks was only 30 per cent. By the middle of the 1990s, the share of the private banks was about 50 per cent. For the 1994–99 national development plan period, the government projected that the private sector would provide over 70 per cent of total investment.

Impacts of Competition

The new competition from private banks stimulated the state banks to expand their own branches, funds and credit schemes. In 1988, the seven state banks together had only 852 branches; this number increased to 1018 in 1990 and 1066 in 1993. The expansion in the numbers of banks and branches in turn produced growing competition in mobilising funds from the society, business sector, and other economic institutions. Total funds in banks and credit in circulation both increased significantly after 1988. From only Rp44 trillion in 1988, by September 1994 total credit was estimated to have reached about Rp170 trillion. (However, the ratio of funds to GDP in Indonesia in the early 1990s was only 20.8 per cent, which was lower than the Philippines' 25.2 per cent, Singapore's 84.9 per cent, and Thailand's 87.0 per cent, so there clearly remained substantial opportunities for raising funds for investment in Indonesia.)

Combined with Bank Indonesia's tighter monetary policies which were designed to reduce inflation, attract foreign investment, and maintain a stable exchange rate, the newly intense competition in the banking sector helped fuel significant increases in interest rates. In order to attract funds, private banks offered higher interest rates for deposits. In 1991, three years after *Pakto 88*, private banks were offering 22–24 per cent annual interest for savings or deposits. This led to parallel rises in lending interest rates, to some 25-28 per cent per year. The higher cost of funds had a dampening effect on domestic investment in many sectors.

Concentration

During the period when the state banks dominated the banking system, the state banks were also closely linked to a number of large private companies. The state banks became known as the "treasurers", or credit providers, for certain specific companies. These same companies were given other state facilities as well, such as licenses, monopoly power for certain commodities, and tariff protection. With this official support, these companies were able to rapidly expand their business activities, both vertically and horizontally, and many of them evolved into large conglomerates.

The dominant role of the state banks in supporting the growth of the conglomerates can be seen from the limited number of customers holding large amounts of credit from these banks (Table 1.7). As of 1994, the top 20 customers held over 40 per cent of the total credits provided by the six large state banks. The five largest customers of the state banks received about Rp9.7 trillion, nearly 14 per cent of the total; and the single largest customer received Rp3.8 trillion from a consortium of Bapindo, BBD and BDN, over 10 per cent of the total credit provided by these three banks.

TABLE 1.7
Credit of Twenty Largest Customers of State Banks, 1994
(Rp billion)

Bank	Total Credit	20 Largest Customers	20 Customers (as % of total)
BAPINDO	8,546	4,747	55.5
BBD	15,846	5,144	32.5
BDN	13,051	7,226	55.4
EKSIM	7,428	3,773	50.8
BNI	11,515	4,052	35.2
BRI	15,314	5,215	34.0
Total	71,700	30,157	42.1

Source: State bank reports.

(The others of the top five received, respectively, Rp2.0 trillion, Rp1.45 trillion, Rp1.25 trillion, and Rp1.11 trillion.)

Another indicator that state bank credits were often provided on the basis of privilege and connections rather than sound economic underpinnings is the high level of non-performing loans in the portfolios of the state banks. In 1994, according to the governor of Bank Indonesia, 13.5 per cent of all outstanding state bank loans were categorized as either "doubtful" or "bad" (Hendrobudiyanto 1994, p. 167); in 1995 this figure rose to 16.6 per cent (*Far Eastern Economic Review* (22 May 1997, p. 54).

These practices created a huge gap between the general public and the large majority of enterprises on one side, and a few big companies with privileged access to economic opportunities and resources on the other side. As a result, in the 1990s the dominance and privileged status of the conglomerates became a political issue.

The Stock Exchange and Private Capital

A comparatively recent development with significant potential for the future of the private sector of the economy has been the emergence of the stock exchange as a major factor in investment finance. Other than the state-dominated banking system, before the 1980s Indonesia hardly had a capital market worth the name. The post-1983 deregulation of the financial sector included, in 1984, opening the previously sleepy Jakarta Stock Exchange (JSE) for trading in government bonds. Further steps in deregulating the capital market followed in 1987 and 1988. Combined with the general dynamism of the economy, the result of deregulation of the capital market was an explosive growth in the JSE in the 1990s (see Table 1.8). From a total capitalization of only Rp4.3 trillion in 1989, the market grew in double or triple figures every subsequent year, reaching Rp237 trillion by mid-1997 which was over fifty times the level of 1989. Despite considerable volatility in its index, and the inevitable problems of establishing appropriate regulatory and oversight mechanisms to ensure proper disclosure on the part of listed firms and adequate protections for investors, the JSE was set to play a significant role in financing the country's further economic growth.

Not only did the capital market grow exponentially in the 1990s, but the role of domestic investors in the market was increasing. Initially the JSE was largely a vehicle for foreign portfolio investment in Indonesian enterprises. However, the share of domestic investment in the exchange rose dramatically in the mid-1990s, from only 28 per cent in 1995 to 41 per

TABLE 1.8
Capitalization of the
Jakarta Stock Exchange, 1989–97
(Rp trillion)

Year	Capitalization	Growth (%)
1989	4.3	–
1990	14.2	229
1991	16.4	16
1992	24.8	51
1993	69.3	179
1994	103.8	50
1995	152.2	47
1996	215.0	41
1997 (May)	237.0	–

Source: Jakarta Stock Exchange.

cent as of March 1997 (*FEER*, 22 May 1997, p. 54). Direct participation in the stock market is still limited to a very small group of investors. But with growing numbers of members of the middle class having investable savings, and an increasingly active set of intermediary vehicles such as mutual funds and corporate pension funds, it seemed likely that domestic private sector investment could be the dominant force in the Indonesian capital market.

THE CHANGING FACE(S) OF PRIVATE ENTERPRISE

The Private Sector in the 1950s and 1960s

In the first years after independence, the government tried to develop the indigenous (*pribumi*) private business sector through the so-called *Benteng* (Fortress) Programme which provided a variety of government facilities including licences and credit to *pribumi* entrepreneurs. Within a decade, a number of large indigenous-led businesses emerged, headed by such figures as Abdul Ghani Aziz, Agoes Dasaad, Ahmad Bakrie, Eddy Kowara, and Hasjim Ning. Twenty-three businessmen have been identified as being directly and indirectly the major beneficiaries of the *Benteng* Programme (see Table 1.9).

As of the 1960s, however, only eighteen out of the twenty-three were still major figures in Indonesian business. Others, such as Aslam and Markham, did not survive in the New Order. In the New Order period

TABLE 1.9
Successful Indigenous Businessmen Over Several Periods

Benteng Programme (1949–59)	Guided Economy (1959–65)	New Order (1965–)
Abdul Ghani Aziz	Abdul Ghani Azis	Bakrie
Agoes Dasaad	Agoes Dasaad	Eddy Kowara
Ahmad Bakrie	Ahmad Bakrie	Fritz Eman
Aslam	Aslam	Hasjim Ning
Eddy Kowara	Eddy Kowara	Nitisemito
Fritz Eman	Fritz Eman	Pardede
Haji Sjamsoedin	Hasjim Ning	Soedarpo
Hasjim Ning	Markham	Sastrosatomo
Herling Laoh	Moh. Tabrani	
Koesmoeljono	Nitisemito	
Mardanus	Omar Tusin	
Moh. Tabrani	Panggabean	
Nitisemito	Pardede	
Omar Tusin	Rahman Tamin	
Pardede	Sidi Tando	
Rahman Tamin	Soedarpo	
Rudjito	Sastrosatomo	
Sidi Tando	Suwarma	
Soedarpo	Wahab Afan	
Sastrosatomo		
Soetan Sjahsam Sosrohadikoesomo		
Usman Zahiruddin		
Wahab Affan		

Source: *Info Bank*, No. 123, March 1990.

since 1965, only seven major *Benteng* Programme beneficiaries (the Bakrie family, Eddy Kowara, Fritz Eman, Hasjim Ning, Nitisemito, Pardede, and Soedarpo) remained among the ranks of leading businessmen. The decline of the *Benteng* Programme indigenous businesses could be attributed both to the unfavourable macro-economic situation as well as to the political changes in the mid-1960s.

The Private Sector under the New Order, 1960s–1970s

Given the relatively low long-term survival rate of *Benteng* Programme beneficiaries, the New Order government concluded that the programme was an unsuccessful approach to growing indigenous businesses. It therefore discontinued the programme. Under the New Order, opportunities (such as licenses, concessions, and credit) were given to businesses largely without distinction between indigenous and non-indigenous businessmen.

Robison (1986, p. 329) has divided the major indigenous capitalists in the New Order period into three main categories:
1. The survivors of the *Benteng* Programme and Guided Democracy periods;
2. Politico-bureaucrats of the New Order government who established private business groups; and
3. New Capitalists who emerged with the patronage of the new centres of politico-bureaucratic power.

Outside of these three categories is the almost unique case of Th. M. Gobel. He was involved in manufacturing in association with a foreign firm, Matsushita. His joint ventures with this Japanese company included the manufacture of such products as radios, televisions, air conditioners, and batteries. Gobel seemed to be a truly independent businessman, without a political patron. He continued to be independent from patronage under the New Order government. One demonstration of this independence was his choice to affiliate with one of the non-ruling political parties (the Islamic-oriented Development Unity Party or PPP).

The political changes of the mid-1960s stimulated many changes in the private business sector. With the decline of old patrons, new actors emerged under new patrons. The new patrons were primarily military officers in politically powerful positions. New business relationships were established, which by the end of the 1960s had created a new set of private business networks. The new networks significantly included a number of Chinese-Indonesian (non-*pribumi*) businessmen, who received concessions in various strategic business activities such as importing, food distribution, and forestry.

One of the most successful of the indigenous *Benteng* survivors under the New Order was Soedarpo Sastrosatomo, whose business base was shipping. Also, the batik textile co-operative GKBI was able to transform its businesses from small batik production to large-scale enterprises. This group maintained close co-operation with the government.

In the beginning of the 1970s, some *pribumi* businessmen had significant positions in the import and distribution of automobiles and machinery. Hasjim Ning was a particularly visible success in this period; his PT Daha, assembler of Fiat automobiles, ranked in the top five automobile enterprises. During the 1970s, however, these firms faced increasing competition from new Japanese products, such as Toyota (represented by Astra International, headed by non-*pribumi* businessman William Soeryadjaya) and Mitsubishi under Ibnu Sutowo, *pribumi* director of the state oil company Pertamina (in Robison's typology, Sutowo was one of the leading politico-bureaucrats). Another significant new player in the automobile sector was Indomobil, one of many enterprises of leading non-*pribumi* businessman Liem Sioe Liong (whose Indonesian name is Sudono Salim). The Japanese automotive enterprises were generally run quite efficiently, and soon came to dominate business in this sector.

Private Business in the 1980s and 1990s

As of the mid-1990s state enterprises continued to play a significant role in the economy, with assets of almost Rp230 trillion (over US$110 billion). However, the most spectacular growth took place in the private enterprise sector, particularly among the rather small group of conglomerates (see Table 1.10). The top 13 of these groups — controlling 1,549 separate companies — have average sales of more than Rp2 trillion (US$1 billion) and total sales of about Rp57.9 trillion. This represents nearly 23 per cent of the total national GDP, just below the 24.4 per cent of sales attributed to all the state enterprises. Familiar names among the top group of conglomerates are Salim, Sinar Mas, Astra, Lippo, Gudang Garam, Jarum, Dharmala, Bob Hasan, Barito Pasific, and Argo Manunggal. Table 1.11 gives an indication of the range of activities of the major conglomerates.

The major conglomerates together have assets valued at about Rp30 trillion (US$15 billion). The largest is that controlled by Sudono Salim, whose total assets have been estimated at about Rp6 trillion (US$3 billion). In one firm alone, PT Indocement, he controls 260 million shares which at a nominal value of Rp10,000 per share would total Rp2.6 trillion. Salim's other large enterprises include Indofood, Bank Central Asia, and Indomobil. These holdings make him one of the richest businessmen in the world (*Prospek,* 16 January 1993). The second richest Indonesian businessman is Prajogo Pangestu, with estimated assets of Rp1.6 to 3 trillion (*Tempo,* 8 January 1994).[8] Prajogo's major source of wealth is his control of licences to exploit millions of hectares of forests. He has also acquired a significant percentage of the shares of Toyota assembler and distributor Astra International.

Below the largest conglomerates are 51 other groups with average individual sales between Rp500 billion and Rp2 trillion (US$250 million

TABLE 1.10
Comparison of Private Conglomerates and State Enterprises, 1993

Category	Number of Owners	Number of Companies	Total Sales (Rp billion)	Sales as % of GDP*
1. *Private Corporations* (grouped by sales, in Rp billion)				
Over 2,000	13	1,549	57,898	22.8
1,000 – 2,000	15	866	22,564	8.9
500 – 1,000	36	1,001	24,117	9.5
100 – 500	200	2,418	37,073	14.6
Subtotal			141,652	55.8
2. *Co-operatives*	33.7 million	39,050**	6,800	2.7
3. *State Enterprises* (BUMN)	n/a	n/a	62,000	24.4
4. *Small Private Sector and Informal Sector*	n/a	n/a	14,000	5.5
Total	n/a	n/a	224,452	88.4

Notes: *   Percent of GDP is not identical with contribution to GDP; precentages are based on 1993 estimate of total Indonesian GDP as Rp 254,000 billion.
     ** Village Cooperatives (KUD): 8,749; Non-KUD: 30,301; member contributions totalled Rp 1,100 billion.
Sources: Various (collected from *Warta Ekonomi*).

to 1 billion). The top 15 groups in this category, with sales of between Rp1 and Rp2 trillion, control about 866 companies and have estimated total sales of Rp22.6 trillion which is over nine per cent of Indonesia's total GDP. Total sales of this cluster (1,867 companies) are about Rp46.7 trillion, or 18.4 per cent of total GDP. Thus the sales of the 64 largest private enterprise groups in Indonesia were the equivalent of over 40 per cent of the country's total economic output.

Another significant development in the 1980s was the rise in the business world of a new generation of young *pribumi* businessmen, many of whom were children of high-ranking military officers. Most prominent among this group were the children of President Soeharto himself.

Soeharto's second son, Bambang Trihatmodjo (estimated personal assets in 1993: US$220.2 million), was particularly successful and is the leading businessman among the children. His Bimantara Group had an estimated 134 subsidiaries. The eldest daughter, Siti Hardijanti Rukmana (known as Tutut, estimated personal assets in 1993: US$190.5 million), had built the Citra Lamtoro Gung Group which has some 62 subsidiaries.

The president's other children were also involved in business. First son Sigit Harjojudanto (estimated personal assets: US$178.6 million) had the Arseto Group with about 15 subsidiaries. The youngest son, Hutomo Mandala Putra (Tommy, estimated personal assets: US$107 million), despite his youth managed within a single decade to build his Humpuss group into a significant business with some 69 subsidiaries. The president's other two daughters, Siti Hedijati Herijadi (Titiek) and Siti Hutami Endang Adyningsih (Mamiek), also own companies, and in the mid-1990s the first of the Soeharto grandchildren made a dramatic entry onto the business scene (Vriens 1995).

GOVERNMENT AND PRIVATE ENTERPRISE

The growth of large enterprises under the New Order has been an integral part of the state effort to stimulate and maintain economic growth. The New Order leadership saw economic stagnation, as in the early 1960s, as the root of political problems and instability. For that reason, the government focused its attention on economic development. A major element of the government's growth strategy was to encourage the stronger enterprises to invest large amounts of capital in economic activities.

Non-*pribumi* entrepreneurs Sudono Salim and Bob Hasan, and Soeharto's cousin Sudwikatmono, were among the first businessmen who responded to the government effort to develop a new business system in the country. The subsequent growth of conglomerates was very closely related to government support. The economic success of this arrangement is indicated by the previously-cited growth statistics for both the overall economy and the conglomerates.

Reliance on government-favoured private enterprises, however, also brought with it certain problems. One of these was the opening for misuse of privileged access to government support. A highly public example of this difficulty was a major scandal in the early 1990s involving the state bank Bapindo. Politically-connected businessman Edy Tanzil received a huge credit (Rp800 billion) from Bapindo for a textile enterprise, Kanindo. The project turned out to be grossly overfinanced, and much of the money

TABLE 1.11
Activity of Private Conglomerates in Major Business Sectors

Sector	Groups	
1. Automotive	Salim William Soeryadjaya	Krama Yudha Bimantara
2. Wood/Timber	Prajogo Pangestu Burhan Uray Susanto Liam	Bob Hasan
3. Finance	Salim (BCA Group) Lippo Sinar Mas (BI) Samsul Nursalim (BDNI) Usman A. (Danamon)	Bank Persero Bank Niaga
4. Edible Oils	Salim Sinar Mas	
5. Crude Palm Oil	Salim Sinar Mas William Soeryadjaya	PTP-PTP (State enterprises)
6. Sugar	Salim Dharmala Prajogo Pangestu	
7. Property/Real Estate	Ciputra Sinar Mas Dharmala Ongko (Indokisar)	
8. Paper & Pulp	Sinar Mas Inti Indo Rayon	
9. Husbandry	Salim	
10. Petrochemicals	Salim Prajogo Pangestu	Humpuss Pertamina

Table 1.11 (continued)

Sector	Groups		
11. Cement	Salim	Hashim D	
12. Animal Feed	Ometraco Dharmala		
13. Wheat Flour	Salim	Berdikari	
14. Cigarettes	Gudang Garam Djarum	Sampoerna Bentoel	
15. Textiles	Argo Pantes Salim Lippo	Pan Brothers GKBI Texmaco PMA Jepang	
16. Construction	Salim (Total) Bangun Persada	Ciputra (Jaya)	
17. Food	Salim (Indofood) ABC (Husain Djojonegoro)		
18. Shipping	Salim Gesuri Soedarpo Sastrosatomo	Bimantara Humpuss	
19. Automotive Components	Astra Salim Pakati Yega Hadi Budiman	Krama Yudha Bakrie	
20. Glass	Subentra (Tan Siong Kie)		
21. Fisheries	Mantrust Djajanti	Sekar Ika Muda	
22. Electronics	Yasonta Astra Amcol	Gobel Lippo	

Source: *Prospek*, no. 15 (16 January 1993), p. 19.

from the loan disappeared, forcing Bapindo to write off the credit as a bad debt.

Another problem with close government-business relations, as previously noted, is the contrast between the privileged status and wealth of a few firms and businessmen, and the economic condition of smaller enterprises that lack government connections as well as the general public. Concerns over economic equity and democratization emerged as a major public issue as early as the beginning of the 1980s. In what was clearly a political response to this concern, on 4 March 1990 President Soeharto invited thirty-one of the richest businessman (almost all non-*pribumi*) to his estate at Tapos in West Java for a highly-publicized meeting at which he called on them to transfer shares in their enterprises to the co-operatives (generally poorer, *pribumi* business efforts). The eventual outcome of this initiative was modest, but it served to highlight the seriousness of the issue in the eyes of the government.

A further issue emerged with the increasing prominence of the group of *pribumi* businesses run by children of high-ranking officials, most conspicuously Soeharto's children. Some of these businesses were regarded as legitimate successes; others were viewed more sceptically. Some analysts attribute Soeharto's daughter Tutut's success primarily to her good fortune in being a member of the president's family. Others argue that some of her companies are run efficiently, and point to the fact that the Lamtoro Gung group has been able to go international, including winning bids for construction projects in Malaysia and the Philippines. The rapid rise of the Humpuss group companies of Soeharto's youngest son Tommy is certainly related to the fact that these companies have received lucrative licenses from the government and state enterprises (especially the state oil company Pertamina) as well as other privileges from the government (Vriens 1995).

By the 1990s, the economic role and favoured status of Soeharto's family had become a political issue in its own right, in addition to the general issues of economic democratization and the appropriate relationship between government and private business.

CONCLUSION

The rapid growth of the Indonesian economy up to the mid-1990s was accompanied by, and directly contributed to, an increasing role for private enterprise. The expansion of the private sector helped to move the Indonesian economy into a stage of continuous industrialization, and private enterprise became the major engine of the country's economic growth. Further, this outcome was in many ways the result of a deliberate effort by the New Order government to encourage and foster the growth of the private sector.

Nevertheless, the role and structure of the private sector remain problematic in a number of respects. Significant participation in economic activities in Indonesia is still limited to the few large entrepreneurs who dominate information, technology, capital, finance, political access, and other resources. And the growth of the private sector has remained closely connected with the state. The New Order government largely abandoned the former Sukarno government's distinction between *pribumi* and non-*pribumi* entrepreneurs and programmes designed to favour *pribumi* business. But most of the successful private businesses, both *pribumi* and non-*pribumi*, continue to be very dependent on connections with the government. Further, a new group of *pribumi* businessmen (and women) has risen to prominence under the New Order, the principal distinction between them and the previous generation of *pribumi* business leaders being the predominance of relatives of Soeharto and other powerful officials.

A second problem in the development of the private sector under the New Order is that small business did not grow significantly. The major private sector contributors to economic growth were the conglomerates and other large enterprises. Small business by contrast is not strong, and has not similarly benefited to date from government programmes and facilities. Without a dynamic and expanding small (and medium-size) business sector, the overall economic structure will be unbalanced and the full potential for economic growth cannot be realized.

Finally, despite the impressive record of economic growth, Indonesia's economy still contains a relatively large segment of traditional agriculture as well as a large informal sector, both of which have been growing very slowly and have low productivity. There has unquestionably been economic progress in the countryside and among the lower income groups in the cities, and until the crisis of 1997–98, the incidence of poverty was steadily decreasing — although the definition of the poverty line is still a controversial matter (Salim 1993, pp. 3–10). However, the poor of Indonesia overwhelmingly work in traditional, informal, and marginal jobs. The lowest economic group has gained relatively far less from the development process than the upper income classes. Thus despite the gains, an equity problem still exists, and the gap in income between the rich and the poor is more visible today than at the start of the New Order period. This poses another serious question for the country's future.

Notes

[1] This was the Foreign Capital Investment Act of 1967 (Act No. 1/1967).

[2] The Domestic Capital Investment Act (Act No. 6/1968).

[3] Through April 1997, cumulative realized foreign investment totalled over US$51 billion, while realized domestic investment was the equivalent of approximately US$82 billion (see Tables 1.3 and 1.5). The dollar domestic investment figure is a rough estimate, calculated using the 1997 exchange rate to convert the rupiah total in Table 1.3. Using annual investment amounts and exchange rates through the period would produce a substantially higher total dollar value for domestic investment and a correspondingly higher ratio of realised domestic to foreign investment for the 1967–94 period. However, the figures for investment approvals in Tables 1.2 and 1.4 for the period of 1990–96 also show domestic investment running at about 1.5 times foreign investment, with domestic approvals totalling just over US$175 billion and foreign approvals just under US$123 billion.

[4] Student leaders, particularly in Jakarta, nearby Bogor, and the capital of West Java, Bandung, launched a campaign of political criticism and protests in 1973, one of the targets of which was domination of the country by Japanese investments. This movement culminated in a riot in Jakarta in January 1974, in which there was extensive damage and looting.

[5] Many approved investment projects (both foreign and domestic) are not completed, for various reasons. As of early 1997 less than a third of the total value of approved foreign investments had actually been realized. Realized domestic investment represented less than half of the total value of investments approved up to that time. However, the two series have run roughly in parallel over time, so the trends and breakdowns by sector and location are very similar.

[6] Data on approved investment projects is taken from BPS December 1996, pp. 65–69; data on realized projects was obtained from the Investment Co-ordinating Board (BKPM).

[7] The *Tabanas* and *Taska* programmes were implemented through the state banks. They had very low requirements (e.g., a minimum first

deposit of only Rp50), in order to encourage the common people to save their money in banks and to promote monitization.

[8]   *Tempo* estimated the assets of Prajogo at about three trillion rupiahs, or about ten times the total agricultural (*Bimas*) credits provided to ten million farmers in Indonesia.

2

Public Enterprises under the New Order

I Ketut Mardjana

Indonesian public enterprises are a large part of the national economy and are intertwined with almost all economic sectors, including strategic industries essential for national development. Public enterprises, or BUMNs,[1] arguably constitute the backbone of Indonesia's economy, especially in the area of infrastructure such as roads, seaports and air ports, transportation, and telecommunications. State enterprises have been the dominant investors in public utilities and services such as the provision of electricity, fuel, and water. Other fields in which public enterprises are engaged include: high technology industries such as aircraft and ship-building; mining industries including tin, coal, gold, nickel, and bauxite; plantation estates producing palm oil, rubber, tea, and sugar cane; trade sectors such as import-export companies, bonded warehouses, and general trading; contracting and construction companies; and, in the financial sector, banking, insurance, and pawnshops. The contribution of public enterprises to total GDP during 1983–89 ranged between 12 and 16 per cent of gross added value, and their contribution to the national budget during 1979–88 ranged between 43 and 59 per cent of corporate taxes.

Public enterprises are also part of the Indonesian political system. Article 33 of the Indonesian Constitution states that: "Branches of production essential to the state and governing the life and living of the public shall be controlled (*dikuasai*) by the state."This article is considered to provide a constitutional basis for BUMNs (Halim 1986, p. 12), legitimizing public enterprises as a policy tool for promoting the welfare of the society. The role of public enterprises is reinforced by the *Wawasan Nusantara*, or Archipelago policy. This policy considers Indonesia as a unity in terms of politics, society and culture, economy, and defence and security.

These arguments provide a legal and ideological justification for the government to use public enterprises in effect as extra arms of government in the implementation of national development programmes. They are used as "agents of development", and as instruments in applying government programmes to ease the economic disparity between the "strong" and "weak" economic groups.[2] They are also required to operate in unprofitable regions. For example, Garuda Indonesia airline, PT Pelni shipping and sea carrier, and Perum Damri interstate bus enterprise are required to operate even in the less-developed regions of the country. In compensation, they receive subsidies for possible losses incurred.

BUMNs come under the control of various departments or agencies, depending basically on the fields in which they operate. Table 2.1 lists the departments or agencies, the numbers of BUMNs they control, and the total sales and total asset value of the BUMNs.

Since the government began facing financial difficulties due to declines in the price of oil in the early 1980s, improvement in public enterprise performance became an important policy objective. Although it has not been easy to formulate specific plans to achieve this end, and it has been even more difficult to implement reforms, there has been a gradual shift from strong political control of Indonesian public enterprises towards a more market-oriented approach. (A notable exception to this trend is the high technology field, which is discussed at the end of this chapter.)

This chapter examines policy changes in the public enterprise system in Indonesia over the thirty years of the New Order government. It considers the situation of BUMNs at the beginning of New Order era, during the oil boom, and in the post-oil boom period. It also examines the various constitutional, economic, and management arguments that have surrounded the subject of public enterprises and the efforts to reform this sector in line with the overall growth and modernization of the economy.

PUBLIC ENTERPRISES AT THE START OF THE NEW ORDER

With the fall of President Sukarno in 1965–66 and the coming to power of the "New Order" government under General Soeharto, Sukarno's Guided Economy policy was replaced with a new, more market-oriented economic concept. Most importantly, private investment, both domestic and foreign, was encouraged. In contrast to the old order government's frequent attacks on private ownership, the New Order government adopted a progressive private sector development programme. Sukarno's self-reliance economic policy (whose slogan, *Berdikari*, meant to "stand on

TABLE 2.1
Public Enterprises (BUMN): Numbers, Sales, and Assets, 1993

Department or Agency	Number of BUMN	Sales (Rp million)	Assets (Rp million)
Industry	28	4,823,058	10,091,817
Agriculture	35	3,761,815	6,503,500
Finance	31	18,054,134	143,847,707
Transportation	17	5,395,131	14,912,945
Public Works	19	3,125,754	3,812,884
Trade	8	1,726,943	775,270
Mines & Energy	7	36,363,086	63,046,767
Tourism, Post & Telecommunications	7	4,219,161	8,728,583
Forestry	6	517,234	775,560
Information	4	17,064	77,762
Health	2	703,209	665,483
Defence & Security	1	87,262	330,702
Education & Culture	1	11,868	35,806
Manpower	1	669,605	1,796,375
Non-Departmental	1	152,152	58,476
Strategic Industry (BPIS)	10	2,758,969	11,641,380
Total	178	82,386,445	267,101,017

Note: The asset value is based on historical cost valuation, which is below actual (market) value.
Source: Department of Finance data, 1993.

one's own feet"), which had been intended to free the economy from foreign intervention, was ended.

In line with its new economic policy, the government also reformed the public enterprise system.[3] In 1966, public enterprises were restructured from one standard type, PN (*Perusahaan Negara*, literally meaning state enterprise), into three forms, *Perjan*, *Perum* and *Persero*,[4] depending on the type of activity of the enterprise. All three classes of enterprise were expected to be self-sufficient in financing their own operations. To accomplish this objective, the cabinet directed that:

1. Subsidies to state enterprises would be stopped, except for limited subsidies to public utilities;
2. In the field of distribution, the government would begin a process of debureaucratizing and deregulation; and
3. Managers of state enterprises would be given full responsibility for the management of their businesses. Government departments were prohibited from using funds of the enterprises under their supervision for

expenses more appropriately borne by the government budget (Wirjasuputra and Rieffel 1972, p. 13).

The period of shifting the economy from the tight central planning policy of the old order government to the more market-oriented policy of the New Order government has been described as a period of de-*étatisme*.[5] This demonstrated the political will of the New Order government to release public enterprises from strong bureaucratic control and to re-establish them as normal business entities.

THE CONSTITUTIONAL DEBATE

As previously noted, the 1945 Constitution provides that essential branches of production are to be controlled (*dikuasai*) by the state. There is a broad consensus that BUMNs are one of the tools through which the government can control vital economic sectors in order to promote the welfare of the people. However, there has also been considerable debate over the practical meaning of the word *dikuasai*. On the one hand, *dikuasai* can be interpreted as meaning supervised and regulated but not necessarily owned by the state. On the other hand, *dikuasai* can also be interpreted as requiring direct management by government through state ownership of the enterprises in these sectors.

These differing interpretations have been advanced for many years. Founding President Sukarno favoured government ownership (Rice 1983, pp. 61–63). First Vice President Hatta, on the other hand, recommended that government ownership should be restricted to firms on which other industries are dependent (e.g., electricity, telecommunications, etc.). Hatta's view was that industries which produce basic goods for the people need only be controlled by government (e.g., through price regulation), without necessarily being publicly owned (Hatta 1954, p. 273).

Underlying Sukarno's policy was the belief that public ownership was politically necessary in order to remove the previous colonial economic structures and avoid new economic oppression of the people, there being very few private businesses run by indigenous Indonesians at that time. In fact, state ownership and state investment helped to shift the balance of economic power from the colonial to a national orientation. Conversely, the encouragement of private investment, both domestic and foreign, under the New Order government suggests the wider acceptance of the interpretation of the word *dikuasai* as not necessarily requiring public ownership (Sadli 1986, pp. 14–15).

PUBLIC ENTERPRISES AND THE OIL BOOM

In practice, the management of public enterprises has tended to change in line with the changing political-economic conditions and considerations of the state. The oil boom of 1973–82, which vastly increased government revenues, led to reverses of the New Order's initial course with respect to public enterprise policy. BUMNs were again heavily burdened with government directives to promote development. Government controls over state enterprises were restored and even made more pervasive. This is called the neo-*étatisme* period (see Wibisono 1988, p. 6).

The increases in government revenue due to the high price of oil resulted in increased budget allocations to assist more rapid economic development. Public enterprises were again looked to as important tools in the implementation of national development. Massive new investments were made in the public enterprise sector, either for replacement or for new establishments. New public enterprises, either with the government as a sole shareholder or as joint ventures, were established in industries such as fertilizers, cement, steel, aluminium, etc. This led to the application of protectionist as well as interventionist policies.

MULTIPLE OBJECTIVES, MANAGEMENT PROBLEMS

The treatment of public enterprises as agents of development and their inclusion in national planning has left the BUMNs responsible for a multiplicity of functions and objectives. This leads to confusion within enterprise management, with the objectives being interpreted in different ways, and causes the enterprises to lose their corporate character. Furthermore, the substantial agenda can make it difficult for enterprises to achieve the specific targets in their charters. The leading daily newspaper *Kompas* commented on this situation as follows:

> The authorities need to clarify the functions and objectives of each public enterprise.... Government regulation No. 3/1983 outlines seven functions and objectives for Indonesian public enterprises, whether as *Perum*, *Perjan*, or *Persero*. These multiple functions and objectives make it difficult to formulate specific strategies and goals for each state enterprise.... This may cause difficulty in measuring public enterprise achievement.... (Author's translation, *Kompas,* 4 August 1986)

Bureaucratic controls also prevent BUMNs from operating independently. For example, the prices of domestic air and land (bus and train) transport, sea transportation fares, electricity, port services (containers, landing space, etc.), road tolls, postal tariffs, cement, fertilizers, pesticides, and petrol are all regulated by the government. The regulation of prices in such industries, and subsidized credit schemes in the banking sector, are intended to protect other industries as well as the majority of the people. These phenomena reflect the social service and development roles of public enterprises, but complicate their efficient and economic management.

Another burden for the BUMNs is the requirement to follow government regulations on purchasing and contracting. More important still, they frequently must follow the investment policies of the government departments, to which they are responsible. Some investments related to public enterprises are actually carried out by the departments. For example, the Transportation Department undertook the development of seaports and airports, and purchased new buses, then transferred these projects to public enterprises involved in these areas. These decisions were made outside of the control of the public enterprises. Other investment projects are conducted by public enterprises but under tight supervision from the departments. Thus there can be a large area of overlap between the responsibilities of BUMNs and their departments.

Planning and investment decisions which are made by the supervising department rather than the public enterprise management often generate excess capacity and idle assets (Premchand and Wijayasuriya 1987). This may reflect differences of view between the departments and public enterprise management. Supervising departments may base their plans on the macroeconomic calculation that a given development would bring about maximum returns for the nation and the people. On the other hand, the public enterprises should plan on the basis of corporate objectives that relate to return on investment and the payback period.

For enterprises, excess capacity means a higher cost per unit of production, lower profits or even losses. However, public enterprises' efforts to increase revenue are bounded by price regulations as well as very long procedures for obtaining licenses to diversify into new lines of business. Government pricing policies take into account not only the costs of production, but also factors such as the impact on inflation, the purchasing power of ordinary people, and more importantly the political implications of prices.

THE POST-OIL BOOM PERIOD

Reductions in state funds caused by declining oil prices in 1983 compelled the Indonesian Government to implement budget austerity measures. Sharper falls in 1986 made conditions even worse. Foreign exchange reserves for financing imports of capital goods and other components for domestic production were reduced. New sources of foreign exchange were needed. These were sought primarily through increased non-oil exports, to compensate and replace the decrease in oil export revenues. At the same time, increased international borrowing was sought to support the development programmes. These measures required structural adjustments within the domestic economy. Reforms to improve efficiency would both increase the competitive position of Indonesian products in international markets and protect the domestic market from undue penetration by foreign goods and services.

Explaining the need for changes in government policy to meet the new challenges, Ali Wardhana, former Finance Minister and former Co-ordinating Minister for Economy, Finance, and Industry, has stated that "protection and government controls, which had been the chosen policy instruments for many years, are inimical to [a] competitive domestic market; they have created the 'high cost' economy that the country is now trying to escape" (Wardhana 1989, p. 208). Similarly, Soesastro (1989, p. 854) argued "in Indonesia the necessity-driven deregulation policy is aimed primarily at a direct assault on the 'high cost', internationally uncompetitive economy".

More recent events in the international economy, particularly the GATT Uruguay Round agreement in late 1993 and APEC's 1994 Bogor declaration on free trade in the region, have further increased the pressures on the Indonesian economy to become more efficient. Liberalization of the world economy directly affects Indonesia's economy, including the public enterprise system, through growing international market competition. The dramatic changes in economic philosophy reflected in the reforms in Eastern Europe and the former USSR, Pakistan, India, and Latin America have also added to the pro-reform atmosphere.

The movement towards reform was also reinforced by the influence of international development and lending agencies, mainly Western development organisations such as USAID, the IMF and the World Bank. They advocate privatisation and a shift away from extensive government intervention towards more emphasis on market control (Toh 1991, p. 22). The international agencies' support for privatisation was reflected in conditions placed on financial aid, technical assistance programmes, and research and development projects.

The increased role of the private sector in Indonesia, which as discussed in the previous chapter was encouraged by the New Order government, also affected public enterprises. Figure 2.1 illustrates the rapid growth of private sector capital formation, especially in the period after 1985, and the corresponding decrease in government capital formation. Interestingly, the contribution of state enterprises shows no significant change through this period, indicating that there was little actual transfer of assets from public enterprises to the private sector through 1990. However, the development of the private sector, by increasing competition in the markets, in turn brought pressure on the public enterprises to become more efficient.

All these factors — government budget constraints, policy debates, international trends and pressures, and the changing domestic economy — led to a renewed effort by the government in the late 1980s and 1990s to reform the public enterprise system.

FIGURE 2.1
National Capital Formation, Indonesia, 1978–90

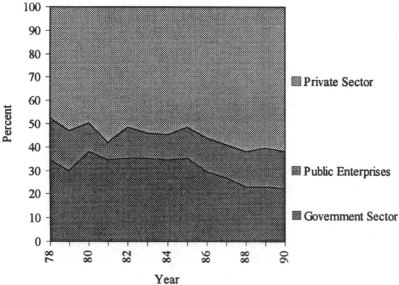

Source: BPS (Central Bureau of Statistics).

REFORM STRATEGIES

The overall intention of the renewed reform effort was to reduce government involvement in the day-to-day operations of public enterprises in order to make them into more genuinely corporate institutions. Specific objectives were to replace centralized controls with greater corporate autonomy, to establish incentive systems instead of administrative requirements, and to create an "enterprise" culture rather than a bureaucratic one.

Privatization has been the preferred choice in many countries to realize these objectives. However, the issue of privatizing public enterprises has been controversial in Indonesia. On the one hand, there is the previously-mentioned argument that public enterprises are mandated by the Constitution. Opposition to privatization has also focused on the economic gap between Chinese-Indonesian conglomerates and indigenous Indonesian businesses, and on the fears of foreign domination of the economy. In this line of thinking, public enterprises are considered as the "fortress for the indigenous" (*benteng pribumi*), and should be retained for this purpose.

The counter-argument is that Indonesian public enterprises, with their broad scope and their monopolistic positions in many sectors, are inherently inefficient, and that this inefficiency weakens national competitive power and impairs the national economy as the whole. Under this rationale, privatization would increase incentives to operate efficiently and eliminate the high transaction costs involved in direct government intervention in management.

In the face of these conflicting considerations, in 1988 the Indonesian Government embarked on a reform programme for BUMNs that allowed for privatisation but placed greater emphasis on structural and management reforms. The programme involved two major approaches. The first aimed to improve relationships between public enterprises and the market through company restructuring. Specific steps included changing the legal status of public enterprises, contracting out, consolidation or merger, splitting up, and joint ventures, as well as the partial or full sale of the assets of some of the stronger public enterprises (either through the market or by direct placement), and even the liquidation of some of the weakest. The second approach sought to change the relationship between government and public enterprises in order to give management a stronger market orientation. Under this approach, managers were to be granted more autonomy in decision making, and in return the salaries and other rewards for managers and directors were to become more dependent on the enterprise's financial performance.

This two-track reform effort was not notably successful. The average level of return on investment (ROI) achieved by public enterprises in 1992 (2.68 percent) was not significantly different from that of 1987, before the reform programme. The privatization element proceeded particularly slowly. Of fifty-two BUMNs scheduled to go public through the sale of shares in 1989 and 1990, only two had actually done so by 1994 — the cement firm PT Semen Gresik in 1991 and the international telecommunications enterprise PT Indosat in 1994.

The combination of the modest results of the structural/management reform programme as a whole, the rapid growth of the Jakarta stock exchange in the mid-1990s, and the successful listing of Indosat on the New York exchange in 1994 led the government to readjust the programme. Increased reliance was placed on privatization through the partial sale of public enterprise shares both in the domestic and international capital markets. This approach was seen as increasing the efficiency of public enterprises in several ways. Listing on stock exchanges carries an implicit assumption — and corresponding encouragement, of compliance by the listed enterprises with the various government regulations, including those increasing enterprise autonomy and responsibility. Moreover, the need to induce investors to buy shares puts pressure on both government and public enterprises to be more transparent and more concerned with efficiency.

Following the successful listing of PT Indosat on the New York Stock Exchange in 1994, the government announced its intention to prepare other public enterprises for listing on local or international exchanges. It identified PT Telkom (domestic telecommunications), PT Jasa Marga (toll road company) and PT Garuda Indonesia (airline) as prime candidates for this programme. PT Telkom has since been successfully listed, along with the state bank PT Bank Negara Indonesia. As of mid-1997, it was anticipated that PT Aneka Tambang (mining), PT Krakatau Steel, PT Jasa Marga, and PT Bank Rakyat Indonesia would be put on the markets in the near future (*FEER*, 22 May 1997, p. 56).

In a related move that itself constituted a significant policy change, in 1994 the government (through Regulation No. 20/1994) permitted foreign investment in public utilities, even allowing complete foreign ownership of these companies. Public utilities had previously been considered one of the core industries covered by the constitutional mandate for public control of vital economic sectors, so the new policy constituted a further demonstration that the government no longer considered that the constitution required direct public ownership of such sectors. Under the new policy, PT Perusahaan Listrik Negara (electric power generation) was among the public enterprises expected to be privatised during 1997 (*FEER,* 22 May 1997, p. 56).

COUNTER-TREND: STRATEGIC INDUSTRIES

At the same time as the renewed efforts at BUMN reform and privatization, however, another policy initiative saw the further use of public enterprises as a tool of national development policy. In 1989 the government consolidated ten state enterprises[6] which were categorized as strategic industries and put them under the control of a new government body, the Strategic Industry Management Board or BPIS (Badan Pengelola Industri Strategis). In operating these state enterprises, BPIS enjoys government privileges and protection. In an atmosphere of rising criticism of protectionism, however, this move generated controversy.

BPIS, chaired by Dr Bacharuddin Jusuf Habibie, then Minister of Research and Technology, has three main tasks: (i) to develop strategic industries that enhance the application of technology in support of national development and self-sufficiency in national security, (ii) to co-ordinate policy implementation in strategic industries, and (iii) to control the management of strategic industries. BPIS is considered as deserving special treatment from the government because of its strategic position in strengthening national development and national resilience. Habibie put it this way:

> It is clear that BPIS will get privileged treatment. This is because BPIS is assumed to be strategic in strengthening national defence. That is why it is led by a minister. Moreover, the supervising board is led by the President himself.... Given this fact, it would be inappropriate if special treatment were not given to this project (Author's translation of Habibie's statement in *Warta Ekonomi* 1, no. 22 [26 March 1990], p. 25).

In addition, Habibie argued that the intention of this long-planned project was to enhance national efficiency and productivity and, in the long run, to transform Indonesia into an advanced industrial country. The development of high technology and strategic industries was seen as a short cut to the achievement of higher value added for Indonesia's industrial production (see Kwik 1993).

THE POLICY DEBATE

The concept that the establishment of strategic industry and technology is necessary to enhance Indonesia's economic development became known as "Habibienomics". By contrast, the overall economic development strategy implemented in the country since 1966, and which was advanced by the development economists (the so-called "technocrats") in the National Development Planning Board (Bappenas), is based on the concept of comparative advantage with an orientation towards free markets, export of labour-intensive products and natural resources. A major debate developed between the Habibie and technocrat camps concerning the most appropriate policies for sustaining rapid economic growth (see Kwik 1993; Juoro 1993; Alam 1993; and Sjahrir 1993, pp. 86–87).

In Habibie's view, the technocrats' comparative advantage strategy, though it may help in expanding the labour force, provides little added value and is not capable of dealing with long-term problems. On the other side, four main criticisms have been advanced against the programme for concerted development of high technology industry and the use of BPIS as the instrument for implementing the programme.

The first criticism is that the establishment of BPIS goes against the deregulation and debureaucratization thrusts of the government's public enterprise reform programme, and that every effort should be made to carry out the high-technology programme through private enterprise. As the economist Sjahrir has commented, "If the private sector is able to handle the ten state enterprises, then they should be promoted. We are committed to deregulation and debureaucratization" (Sjahrir 1990, p. 22). An alternative argument is that such high-tech projects in Indonesia are inconsistent with an overall development strategy aimed at generating employment for rapidly growing numbers of workers (*Tempo*, 12 June 1993).

The second criticism has centred on the costs of the programme. This view stresses that government sponsorship means either a drain on the government budget to fund the public enterprises involved, or the taking out of overseas loans with government guarantees. The Word Bank, in its report *Indonesia: Sustaining Development* (1994a), argues the experience of many countries has shown that high-technology projects sustained by government investment, government subsidies, and other types of protection are ineffective and expensive.

The third criticism is that the new policy has created confusion and uncertainty. Since the concept of strategic industries has not been clearly defined, there is considerable potential for other public enterprises being taken over and merged with BPIS. Habibie stated that a strategic industry is "an industry that, according to the President, could strengthen national resilience" (*Warta Ekonomi* 1, no. 22 [26 March 1990], p. 25), a definition that did little to clarify matters. Other public enterprises which could generally be categorized as operating in a strategic area, and which could therefore possibly be transferred away from their ministries, included the state oil company Pertamina, PT Pelni (shipping), and even state banks.

The fourth criticism has been that this mega-project is a "one man show" (Alam 1990). This is based on the fact that Habibie simultaneously held the positions of Minister of Research and Technology, Chairman of the Agency for Analysis and Development of Technology, head of BPIS, and also Executive Director of PT IPTN, PT PAL, and PT PINDAD. The last three are state enterprises under the supervision of the government institutions that he chaired. With one person holding several related positions, there is an obvious potential for conflicts of roles or interests, and thus for complicating the control process (Sjahrir 1993, p. 86).

Habibie rejected these criticisms. He acknowledged that development of high technology and industry involves government protection and subsidies. However, he believes that this will only be the case in the initial phase. In the long run, he argues, these projects will provide higher added value and increase productivity and efficiency for national development (see Kwik 1993). As to the "one man show" argument, he asserts that, although decisions on these institutions and enterprises come from and through him, all the activities are controllable and are well co-ordinated (*Tempo*, 10 October 1992).

ONE GOAL, TWO APPROACHES

Viewed from the perspective of public enterprise policy, the two approaches pursued by the government — restructuring/privatization and the establishment of BPIS — although following different paths, were both intended to enhance the efficiency and productivity of public enterprises. Restructuring/privatization attempts to instil private management practices into the public enterprise sector by releasing enterprises from strict government control. BPIS seeks to energize strategic industries through direct government action to ensure adequate resources and co-ordination of effort.

Whether, or which of, these two approaches will ultimately be judged as successes or failures could only become clear over a period of years. Habibie's projection that the BPIS industries would not need permanent government subsidies was reinforced — and the pressure on him to succeed was increased — by President Soeharto's statement to Parliament on 16 August 1993 declaring the government's commitment to abolish all types of protection, starting with upstream industries (*Tempo*, 28 August 1993). However, to date there has been little progress in profit accumulation by the BPIS enterprises (see Figure 2.2). Similarly, *Tempo* magazine (28 August 1993) reported that the profits of PT IPTN decreased by 58 per cent, from Rp8.2 billion in 1991 to Rp3.4 billion, in 1992.[7] There seemed to be little likelihood that these projects could be financed by retained earnings in the near-term future.

An academic study by David McKendrick of PT IPTN, the aircraft manufacturing company and one of the ten state enterprises under BPIS, offered an additional preliminary assessment of the government-centred approach. The study's major conclusion was that "the financial costs of IPTN's first ten years of operation were considerably greater than the benefits" (McKendrick 1992, p. 64).[8] McKendrick also pointed to the lack of inter-firm links with IPTN, caused by the insulation of IPTN from public scrutiny and by the unwillingness or inability of IPTN to draw other firms into its circle of activities (McKendrick 1992, p. 63). Thus the claim that the establishment of strategic industries will diffuse technology for economic development obviously has yet to be realized.

CONCLUSION

Indonesia has no single model or policy with respect to public enterprises. The government has attempted to promote greater market linkages to public enterprise, by improving the relationships between public enterprise and the market and between public enterprises and the government, and increasingly through the listing of public enterprises on international and domestic stock exchanges.

At the same time, however, a rather different policy was launched that granted new privileges and protection to advanced technology and strategic industries under the co-ordination of BPIS. This was viewed as a strategy to accelerate Indonesia's economic development in these fields. Government protection and subsidies were considered necessary in the short run, but in the long run the industries under the BPIS were expected to become financially independent.

FIGURE 2.2
Growth of Assets, Sales, and Profits of State Enterprises
under BPIS,* 1989–91

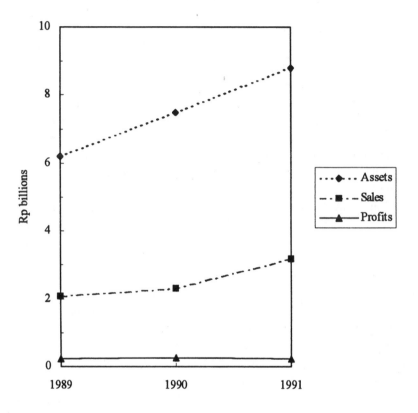

Note: * One enterprise (UP-LEN) not included due to unavailability of data.
Source: Department of Finance.

Both of these policy courses reflected the influence of economic growth. On the one hand, the rapid growth of the private sector and the increasing interaction between the Indonesian economy and the global economy have been a strong motivation behind government efforts to increase the competitiveness of public enterprises through reform, including privatization. On the other hand, the increasing resources generated by successful development, and the challenges of sustaining rapid growth and raising the technological level of Indonesia's economy led to the creation of new public enterprises at various times as well as the policy of centralizing strategic industries under close government control. The future evolution and configuration of Indonesia's public sector enterprises thus remain uncertain, subject both to economic trends and to the outcome of continuing policy debates within the government.

Notes

[1] BUMN is the acronym for Badan Usaha Milik Negara, state-owned public enterprise. These terms are used interchangeably here.

[2] The terms "strong" and "weak" were initially political euphemisms used to identify Chinese-Indonesian or non-*pribumi* and indigenous Indonesian or *pribumi* entrepreneurs. Now, however, many *pribumis* have entered into the category of conglomerate entrepreneurs (see "Pertanda Zaman ..." 1991).

[3] Under the Sukarno Government, between 1958 and 1959 there had been a major increase in the number of Indonesian public enterprises due to the nationalization of Dutch companies as a result of the dispute over West Irian. More than 600 Dutch enterprises were nationalized at that time. Almost half of these were plantation estates, more than a hundred were industrial and mining businesses, while the rest were engaged in trading, banking and insurance, communications, gas and electricity, and construction (Warouw [n.d.], p. 15). In 1959, the government announced the Guided Economy policy, under which the roles of foreign companies were limited as were the roles of Chinese businesses in trade and other economic activities. Allocation, production, investment, and distribution became functions of the central government. Act No. 19 of 1960 reorganized public enterprises into only one type, PN (Perusahaan Negara). Under the reorganization, by 1965 the total number of public enterprises had been reduced to 223 (Wirjasuputra and Rieffel 1972, pp. 4–5).

[4] The new policies were contained in Article 40 of Resolution No.XXIII/MPRS/1966 and the subsequent Cabinet Presidium Instruction No. 21/EK/IN/11/1966. *Perjan* (Perusahaan Jawatan) is a social service corporation of a departmental agency. Its budget is included in a ministerial department's budget, and it is headed and staffed by civil servants. No *Perjan* now exists, since the pawnshop and railway corporations have been converted to *Perum*. *Persero* (Perusahaan Perseroan) is a commercial, limited liability corporation whose shares are wholly or partly owned by the government. *Perum* (Perusahaan Umum) is a public

corporation. This category includes all former PNs that do not meet the conditions required for conversion into *Perjan* and *Persero*. A *Perum*'s capital is wholly government owned, and not divided into shares.

5   The Sukarno period, with its Guided Economy policy, was called a period of *étatisme*, because economic activities were dominated by the state.

6   These state enterprises are: PT IPTN (Industri Pesawat Terbang Nusantara), aircraft manufacturing; PT PAL (Pabrik Angkatan Laut), shipbuilding; PT KS (Krakatau Steel), steel; PT BI (Barata Indonesia) and PT BBI (Boma Bisma Indra), heavy equipment manufacturing; PT INTI (Industri Telekomunikasi Indonesia), telecommunications equipment manufacturing; PT INKA (Industri Kereta Api), railway; Perum Dahana, explosives; PT PINDAD (Perindustrian Angkatan Darat), weapons and ammunition; and UP-LEN (Unit Produksi Lembaga Elektronika Nasional), the national electronics institute's production unit.

7   *Tempo* reported that of the ten state enterprises under BPIS, six enterprises were profitable (PT IPTN, PT KS, PT Dahana, PT INTI, PT INKA, and UP-LEN) and four were unprofitable (PT PINDAD, PT PAL, PT BI, and PT BBI). Three of the six profitable enterprises (PT KS, PT INTI, and PT IPTN) experienced decreasing profits in 1991 and 1992.

8   The benefit-cost ratio of IPTN for 1976–85 was 0.62 (McKendrick 1992, p. 60).

SECTION II

Government and Politics

3

Formal Political Institutions

Ramlan Surbakti

This chapter analyses the relationship between the sustained high economic growth under the New Order and four formal governmental political institutions. These are: the presidency, the cabinet, the Parliament (Dewan Perwakilan Rakyat or DPR) and the Supreme Court (Mahkama Agung). The purpose is to consider the ways in which these institutions — and the governmental processes they are responsible for — changed or altered as a result of rapid economic growth.

From its inception, the New Order was a "developmental" regime, placing high priority on achieving rapid economic development and improved levels of national prosperity and welfare. The New Order also had highly bureaucratic-authoritarian political structures and processes, which the Soeharto government regarded as necessary for economic development. The government argued that political stability is the *sine qua non* for economic growth and that political development follows economic development. The government proclaimed its desire to build a democratic political system based on Pancasila (the five principles of state) and the Constitution of 1945, but this remained subordinate to the goal of economic development.

The remarkable success of the New Order in sustaining high economic growth for nearly thirty years created both direct and indirect pressures on Indonesia's formal political institutions and governmental processes. For example, direct pressures arose from the increasing revenues available to government, the growing number of businessmen and business activities and their influence on government, and rising living standards. Indirect impacts of economic growth included growing demands for access to economic and political opportunity, greater participation in decision making, and increased attention to human rights issues.

This chapter looks first at the direct impacts of sustained high economic growth on the major branches of government (presidency, cabinet,

Parliament, and the Supreme Court). It then considers changes in policy and processes that reflect influences wrought by rapid growth, including popular demands for greater economic equality, deregulation and debureaucratization of the political economy, and democratization.

Changes in governmental structures and processes can be categorized in two types: substantive and cosmetic. Substantive changes refer to comprehensive and long-term changes in the character and nature of political institutions, while cosmetic changes refer primarily to incremental and short-term adjustments that do not necessarily reflect a fundamental reorientation.

THE POWERFUL PRESIDENCY

During the New Order period up to 1998, the most powerful person in Indonesia was President Soeharto, and clearly the president's power and authority had been immensely strengthened since the early years of the New Order. President Soeharto and his government always based their legitimacy, in part, on the government's promise of *pembangunan* (development) — to provide steadily improving standards of living for Indonesians. It is reasonable to assume that as the New Order was increasingly successful at fulfilling its developmental promise, this heightened the power and legitimacy of President Soeharto himself. However, the key question is whether such power was due to the strengthening of the executive branch of government, specifically the *office* of the president, or was due primarily to the personal qualities and political acumen of Soeharto.

Five factors contributed to the powerful presidency in Indonesia during the New Order: constitutional, cultural, personal, political, and economic. First, the Indonesian Constitution of 1945 provides for a very strong chief executive. Nine of thirteen articles in the Constitution dealing with the presidency provide powers *to* the president, namely key executive, legislative, judicial, foreign policy and security powers. Limitations and checks and balances *on* the presidency are not core concerns of the Indonesian Constitution.

Second, cultural factors serve to strengthen the office. Significant numbers of Indonesians, especially the Javanese, perceive the president essentially as a king. On numerous occasions presidential behaviour is more easily understandable in cultural terms as that of a traditional monarch than a modern head of state. For example, the president tends to "give guidance" to political and social organizations, rather than clearly articulating interests and policies. The president issues definitive and absolute decisions, which are known as Sabda Pandita Ratu. And the president gives his endorsement (*restu*, literally "blessing") to a person favoured by the government to be installed in a particular position (i.e., as head of a non-governmental organization), rather than leaving the organization to select its leader without influence from the government.

The third factor is the personal authority of the individual holding the office of president. Both Sukarno and Soeharto emerged as president — and retained their office for long periods of time — because of their unique personal qualifications and attributes. Sukarno dominated the government, in part because of his role as a founding father, co-proclaimer of Indonesian independence, and integrator of the Indonesian nation as well as holding the office of the president. Similarly, Soeharto was powerful because of his role as the founder of the New Order, slayer of the PKI (Communist) beast and saviour of the nation, and the "Father of Development". Although Sukarno held the constitutional power of the president as commander-in-chief of the armed forces (ABRI), President Soeharto had far more authority over the armed forces because Soeharto was a general who had actually commanded troops.

Fourth, the New Order's bureaucratic-authoritarian political system ensured that the president is the ultimate authority in virtually all economic and political fields, with no significant checks and balances provided by other formal political institutions. For example, more than half of the members of Parliament, and of the larger People's Consultative Assembly (MPR) which meets every five years to elect the president and approve broad national policy guidelines, are appointed by the president. So are virtually all heads of government departments, agencies, and boards (such as the State Audit Body, the Supreme Advisory Council, and the Supreme Court).

The president's pervasive influence is felt throughout the polity. The electoral system, the political parties, the system of interest group representation, and local government ultimately give the president and other senior members of the executive branch the power to intervene in almost all matters. For example, the civil and military bureaucracy's screening (*penelitian khusus*) of all candidates for national and local elective office as well as all candidates for party leadership shows the degree to which electoral institutions and parties are directly within reach of presidential intervention. An additional example is the role of the armed forces' Bakrotanasda (the military internal security agency, the head of which is directly appointed by the president) in deciding which news can be published and which persons can be allowed to speak publicly.

Fifth and finally, the good economic performance of the New Order provided for improved general levels of prosperity, such as increases in rice production, literacy, health services, education, transportation and communication, and employment opportunities in industry. As the "Father of Development" (an official title bestowed on Soeharto by the Parliament) the president was accorded personal recognition and credit for his central role in these accomplishments.

President Soeharto also exercised direct control over huge financial and economic resources. These resources grew as a result of successful economic development, and he skilfully used these resources to effect particular political and economic outcomes. The president's control and distribution of economic resources have directly or indirectly brought about compliance from people and organizations who seek access to the resources over which the president has authority. The following is a brief overview of the financial resources controlled by the president and his family.

The president has final approval over budgets for all government departments and agencies and state-owned companies (BUMN). Additionally, President Soeharto personally was head of six rich and influential foundations (yayasan).[1]

An additional economic resource for President Soeharto was his ability to ask financial favours from many indigenous and Indonesian Chinese businessmen who had close personal and financial relationships with the president or who had received official patronage for their companies. These included such figures as Sudwikatmono, Prajogo Pangestu, Bob Hasan, Liem Sioe Liong, Baramuli, Eka Cipta, and Burhan Uray.

Finally, as noted in Chapter 1, the Soeharto family had direct control of substantial financial resources through the family business interests. These included very large business groups run by the four most prominent children. As of 1993, these four children were estimated to control assets worth nearly US$700 million, and the president's two other children and at least one grandchild had other business ventures as well (Vriens 1995).

Of course, these five factors are intricately interwoven. For example, the president's constitutional power was supported by his economic power. Culturally derived justifications for particular policies or political structures are maintained and strengthened by a strong economic performance. The president's authority as commander-in-chief of the armed forces was both constitutionally mandated and reinforced by his control over licensing and protection of a variety of companies belonging to the armed forces and through his patronage of ABRI foundations (discussed further in Chapter 5 below).

Vastly expanded economic resources assist the government, and indirectly the president, in obtaining people's obedience and loyalty without physical coercion. That is, economic growth has given government (and therefore the president) financial and economic instruments to accomplish both political and economic objectives. These instruments include both rewards and punishments. In some cases, political enemies have been weakened by restricting their economic activities in both the public and private sectors.[2]

As already noted, Indonesia's founding fathers envisioned — and crafted — a constitution that provided for a very strong executive. So it is fair to conclude that the institutional powers of the Indonesian presidency provided President Soeharto a foundation upon which he built up his personal power and authority, including economic power.

So far-reaching was the influence of the presidency that the question of succession became the central contemporary political issue in Indonesia. A great deal is at stake in the presidential succession, not only control over the New Order's political system but also control of huge economic resources. However, it is not clear that the office of the presidency itself was strengthened by Soeharto and whether his expansive authority would easily transfer to the next incumbent.

THE SUBORDINATE CABINET

The structure of the cabinet and the decision-making process at the cabinet level were modified in some notable ways during the course of the New Order, in part due to the increasingly complex nature of Indonesia's political economy. At least four changes took place in the structure of the cabinet. First, it grew from thirty departments in the First Development Cabinet to forty-one in the Fifth and Sixth Development Cabinets. The size and composition of the cabinet is determined, in part, by political considerations (i.e., the distribution of power among various factions in the bureaucracy). But many of the new departments were created in order to deal with a more developed and complex economy — i.e., Investment, Tourism and Telecommunications, Research and Technology, and the Co-ordinating Minister for Industry and Trade.

Another major change in the cabinet was the delegation of decision-making authority. Decision making was delegated to a variety of levels, including subgroups of the cabinet (on development supervision led by the president or by the vice president, on economic departments led by the president, and groups of related departments led by the co-ordinating ministers), individual departments, and the planning boards. In the past, there were only four major levels for cabinet decision-making, namely the full Cabinet Session, the Economic Session, the individual departments, and the National Development Planning Board (Bappenas).

Third, the number of co-ordinating ministers supervising groups of departments and agencies (Menteri Koordinator, or "Menko") was increased from three to four. There are now Menko positions for: Politics and Security Affairs; Peoples' Welfare; Economic, Finance and Development Supervision; and the new Menko for Industry and Trade created in 1993. Finally, in the development field, in addition to the National Development Planning Board a new agency was created to deal with technological planning, the Agency for the Study and Application of Technology (BPPT).

In addition to these structural changes, it is also relevant to consider whether the cabinet, like the presidency, became more or less influential as an institution, or was altered in other ways, by high economic growth. Two cabinet decisions illustrate the power and authority of the cabinet — and the impact of cabinet factionalism — in dealing with economic issues *vis-à-vis* the power of other formal government institutions, particularly the presidency.

The first case involved the Chandra Asri petrochemical complex. Alarmed by Indonesia's burgeoning foreign debt in 1991 and 1992, some of the senior "technocrat" economic ministers, particularly then Co-ordinating Minister for Economy, Finance, Industry and Development Supervision Radius Prawiro, urged tighter control on offshore borrowing and developed a schedule listing eligible projects approved for foreign borrowing. The Chandra Asri complex was a massive (US$1.6 billion) proposed petrochemical project. Partners involved in Chandra Asri included members of the president's family and some of the most well-connected business tycoons. A problem developed when the team of economic ministers did not approve Chandra Asri for foreign borrowing. This generated intense lobbying on behalf of Chandra Asri by senior officials associated with the project, Soeharto family associates, and some cabinet ministers led by the Minister for Investment and Minister of Technology. When the Minister for Finance, who chaired the commercial offshore loan team and opposed the Chandra Asri project on the grounds that it was inefficient, refused to approve an exemption, the president dissolved the loan team and established a new one. The new team was chaired by the Co-ordinating Minister for Industry and Trade, a non-technocrat who supported Chandra Asri. The Minister for Finance was demoted to vice chairman. The new team granted an exemption to Chandra Asri after the president (in a speech before the DPR) sent a clear signal that he preferred this course of action (Schwarz 1994, pp. 141, 151–53).

The second case concerned the officially regulated price of cement (Harga Patokan Setempat, or HPS). The setting of the price for this key commodity involved intense pressure on the responsible cabinet ministers from individuals and organizations with financial interests in the Association of Indonesian Cement producers (Asosiasi Semen Indonesia, ASI). Particularly noteworthy in this connection was the fact that two-thirds of total Indonesian cement production comes from PT Cement Nusantara, which is owned by a group of businessmen personally and financially close to the president.

In early 1995, the ASI asked for an increase in the HPS of at least 20 per cent. The departments of trade and industry opposed any price increase, on the grounds that the producers of cement gained enough profit from the existing HPS. However, the pressure was so strong that the trade minister eventually issued a decision which raised the HPS by 40 per cent in Java and 52 per cent in areas outside Java. The stated explanation for the increase was that it was necessary to provide incentive to the private sector to produce more cement, since the annual national demand for approximately 27 million tons outstripped the supply capacity of about 25 million tons.

After the 40 per cent increase was announced, the public protested the new prices as unwarranted. Spokesmen for the government political organization Golkar stated that they also regarded the increase as too high, and proposed 30 per cent as a reasonable increase. The president then entered the controversy and instructed the Minister for Trade to reduce the increase by 10 per cent, so that the new price was "only" increased by 30 per cent. Thus, Golkar and the government could claim political credit for being responsive to the public (particularly useful with an election on the horizon), while the producers enjoyed a 30 per cent increase in their profit.

In both of these examples, big companies or conglomerates seemed to have more influence over government decisions than the responsible ministers. Since the owners of the companies involved in both cases had strong financial and family ties with President Soeharto, it is fair to assume that their efforts to counter the ministers' initial positions in both cases were directly or indirectly known by the president himself. It also seems clear that differences of orientation among members of the cabinet and other high-level officials facilitated the process of obtaining changes in the initial decisions. What is incontrovertible is that, in the cases of Chandra Asri and the HPS, the responsible cabinet ministers were prevented or dissuaded from taking otherwise sound decisions (denying Chandra Asri loan guarantees and preventing a cement price increase) by extra-governmental pressures from individuals with close ties to the president.

Therefore the changes in the structure of the cabinet — the increases in size and complexity — may be more cosmetic than substantive. In reality presidential influence dominates decision making even on relatively small matters such as choosing the winner of a bidding process, credit allocation (Chandra Asri), commodity prices (cement), and domestic trade orders for strategic commodities.

THE POWERLESS PARLIAMENT?

Has sustained high economic growth strengthened the Parliament (DPR)? Throughout the New Order period, the Parliament had very little input in the formulation and implementation of state policy. Nor did the DPR exercise vigorous oversight of the executive branch. In fact, the DPRs elected under the New Order never proposed a draft law (see Table 3.1) and never amended any allocations in the national budget, which was submitted by the president.

Constitutionally, the DPR has more power concerning the national budget than do the president and executive branch. In practice, however, the DPR has not exercised any substantive authority over the budget. Members of Parliament do make general suggestions before the government proposes the draft of the annual budget, and make suggestions regarding the allocation of funds when the parliamentary factions formally approve the proposed budget. Nevertheless, the president and the bureaucracy have completely dominated in the decision making on both the revenue and expenditure sides of the annual budget. The DPR also tends to have no influence over legislation on the political structure, such as the 1995 revision of the law regarding the composition of the DPR in which the military representation was reduced from 100 seats to 75 seats.

TABLE 3.1
Laws Passed by the Indonesian Parliament (DPR),
by Period, 1966–95

DPR Period	Laws Proposed		Laws Passed	
	By Government	By Parliament	Government-initiated	Parliament-initiated
1966–1971	98	25	81	7
1971–1977	43	–	43	–
1977–1982	59	–	55	–
1982–1987	46	–	46	–
1987–1992	55	–	55	–
1992–1997 (92–95)	60	–	60	–
Total	361	25	340	7

Note: Table compiled by M. Djadijono.
Sources: Data from the period 1966–87: Setyabudi 1992.
         Data from the period 1987–92: General Secretariat of the DPR-RI 1992, pp. 90–157.
         Data from the period 1992–93: *Himpunan Peraturan Perundang-undangan Republik Indonesia* (Collection of Legislative Regulations of the Republic of Indonesia) 1993 and 1994.
         Data from the period 1994–1995: *Business News* (Jakarta), 29 December 1995.

However, the Parliament has frequently amended drafts of legislation in other areas such as criminal law, taxes, and social and education laws.

Nor are the laws passed by the Parliament necessarily the most relevant factor in governing and state policy. For example, detailed regulations dictating policy implementation and budget allocation generally emanate from the executive branch, in the form of government regulations, presidential decrees, and presidential instructions. Additionally, ministerial decrees are also generally more policy-relevant and detailed than laws promulgated by the DPR. Therefore, in practice it is the executive branch and the bureaucracy that exercise real legislative power. Except for crime and some other areas such as education, the lives of ordinary Indonesians are not regulated so much by laws made or consented to by the Parliament, but rather by decisions issued by the president, ministers, director generals of departments, provincial governors, and district heads (Bupati).

The reasons for the inability of the Parliament to initiate legislation and its failure to exercise its constitutional authority in the budget process are more structural than a question of the qualifications of members. Parliament has been regarded by the executive and the bureaucracy as a symbolic institution whose duty is to follow the executive's initiative. The executive has not recognized the DPR's right to initiate its own programmes or legislation.

The New Order government's justification for its dominance of the legislative process was based on an ideology that regards development (*pembangunan*) as a technical rather than political matter. Therefore, development should properly be a subject for decisions by the "experts" in the executive branch and the bureaucracy, not politicians in the Parliament. Additionally, given the importance of development to its own performance and legitimacy, the government viewed the involvement of politicians in the decision-making process as inefficient and wasteful of government time and energy.

At least two structural factors can be identified as the primary mechanisms for ensuring a compliant and ineffective DPR. First, a series of laws that regulate political parties, the electoral system, the system of popular representation, and the working procedures of the DPR all function to severely limit the autonomy of the DPR. Laws regulating the political parties and the electoral and representative systems delegate authority to the bureaucracy to intervene in the internal affairs of these ostensibly democratic institutions. Further, the DPR's Rules of Order (Peraturan Tata Tertib) give more powers to parliamentary groups (Fraksi) representing political parties than to individual members. This ensures tight party, or faction, control of members who may be inclined to oppose particular government initiatives or laws. The rules make it extremely difficult for individual members to speak out or introduce legislation.

In recent years, some individual members of Parliament were outspokenly critical of government policies and actions on a variety of economic matters. These included credit allocation from the state banks, domestic trade orders for agriculture and industry, price levels of some public goods (such as public transportation and electricity fees), the role of monopolies, and the poor performance of some public enterprises (BUMN). However, the expulsion of two of the most vocally critical parliament members (Bambang Warih Kusuma from Golkar and Sri Bintang Pamungkas from PPP) in 1995 — by their own factional leadership but clearly at government instigation[3] — may well have detered other members from so openly questioning government policy and performance.

The second structural reason for the inability of the DPR to play a significant national role is that the budget, support facilities, and staff of the Parliament are all controlled by a presidential office, the State Secretariat (Sekretariat Negara). It is ironic that the Parliament, which is supposed to have power over the state budget, is in fact wholly dependent upon the executive for its own operating funds. All parliamentary staff members are also members of the civil service, and are appointed, promoted, paid, and supervised by the State Secretariat, not the DPR itself. At one point the DPR attempted to directly hire experts to provide specialized advice for the various factions and committees, but this effort failed due to the inability to secure necessary funds from the State Secretariat.

It appears that the vastly expanded national development budget has had no significant impact on the Parliament's budget. Members received an increase in salary, from about one million rupiahs to four million rupiahs (about US$2000) per month, though the increase was partially offset by inflation that had eroded the real value of the previous salary level. However, the DPR itself has no real power (despite its constitutional authority) to influence the allocation of the budget, and (for the ideological and political reasons noted above) there is no political will on the part of the executive to strengthen the DPR. (As discussed further in Chapter 6, the political parties are even financially incapable of holding their national congresses without support from the government.) Clearly, a situation where parties and parliamentary factions are financially dependent on the executive creates strong pressures on the parties to avoid antagonizing the government.

THE DEPENDENT COURTS

The Indonesian judicial system, including the Supreme Court, was affected in several ways by the nation's rapid economic growth. First, in terms of its substantive caseload, a significant number of the appeal cases heard by the Supreme Court concerned conflicts over land and appropriation of land for various development purposes. Second, expanded state revenues have no doubt made possible an increase in the salaries of court officers (on the order of one hundred per cent for judges). Third, the government provided for the establishment of eight State Administrative Courts (including building infrastructure, judges and staff, and other support facilities) all over Indonesia.

All Supreme Court judges, including the Chief Justice and his deputies, have in the past been appointed by the president from a list of candidates proposed by the DPR. However, the constitutional authority of the Indonesian Supreme Court diverges sharply from, for example, that of the United

States Supreme Court. The Indonesian Constitution does not give the court the power of judicial review — the power to decide whether government policies or actions are consistent with the Constitution.

Further, all judges in Indonesia (both at the district and high court levels) are members of the civil service, and are therefore appointed, promoted, paid, and supervised by the Department of Justice. Court budgets, staffing and facilities are also determined by the State Secretariat. In matters of law and the professional execution of their duties, Indonesian judges are under Supreme Court supervision. However, in their capacity as members of the civil service (which is the source of their salaries), judges are under the Department of Justice. Thus judges can easily be torn between their professional responsibilities as officers of the court and their perceived political loyalties as civil servants and members of the government.

So the Indonesian courts, including the Supreme Court, are clearly constituted as part of the government rather than as a check on it (much as in the case of the DPR). However, in two recent high-profile cases courts at least initially acted in a rather independent fashion. These cases warrant some further examination.

The first case concerned the Kedung Ombo Dam in Central Java. A number of landowners whose land was appropriated by the state and destined to be inundated by the dam sued for better monetary compensation for their confiscated land. Contrary to expectations, the Supreme Court found in favour of the landowners, who were mostly poor farmers, and ordered that higher compensation be given. However, after intense pressure on the court from the government, the Supreme Court decided to annul its own previous decision in favour of the farmers and instead backed the government, rejecting the farmers' claims. Thus the judges were initially prepared to decide the case as a matter of law, without regard to political issues — deciding that the landowners were illegally deprived of their land and not given appropriate compensation for it. However, in its later decision the court gave in to the executive branch. In arguing for a reversal, the government asserted that the first decision favouring the plaintiffs was detrimental to economic development by prioritizing individual needs over the interests of *pembangunan*.

An even more striking example of judicial independence was the May 1995 ruling by the Jakarta State Administrative Court that an action by the information minister revoking the publication permit of *Tempo* magazine in June 1994 had been illegal.[4] Further confounding expectations, in response to the minister's appeal, the first level appeal court in November 1995 reaffirmed the administrative court's ruling. The government then appealed to the Supreme Court, which in June 1996 overturned the lower courts' decisions and upheld the revocation of *Tempo*'s permit. Nonetheless, the initial decision by the Administrative Court to overturn the ban, and to order the information minister to grant *Tempo* a new publishing license, was regarded as a landmark development in Indonesian judicial and press freedom.

Given the subject of this study, it is perhaps also worth noting here that *Tempo* and its owners had themselves benefited greatly from the socio-economic changes wrought by rapid development. The increasingly well-educated population were the main readers of *Tempo*. Thus by contrast to the plaintiffs in the Kedung Ombo Dam case, who had been displaced by development, in the *Tempo* case the beneficiaries of development challenged the government over what they regarded as arbitrary and illegal decisions.

Although the changes in Indonesian society brought about by its changing political economy have brought a large number of new types of cases into the courts — i.e., land appropriation issues and press freedom — overall there has still been little movement towards the development of an independent court system. At bottom, most of the ruling élite continues to believe that "laws have to be used for the sake of development". And the government certainly does not view an independent Supreme Court or judicial system as a whole as being in the best interest of economic growth and development.

ECONOMIC GROWTH AND GOVERNMENTAL PROCESSES

The impact of high economic growth on governmental processes can be seen in changes in some development policies, the scope and procedures of bureaucracy, and some small, though primarily cosmetic, instances of democratization of decision-making processes. We will look briefly at examples in five specific policy areas: social justice issues, foreign investment, land disputes, economic deregulation, and democratization.

Social Justice

Throughout the course of the New Order and Indonesia's development success, economic growth prompted public demands for social justice.

High economic growth both sharply increased absolute differences in living standards between rich and poor, and increased consciousness of inequalities in Indonesian society. Income inequalities in turn resulted in demands that the government make changes in development policy.

The first significant instance of a change in development policy of this sort occurred after the student protests over inequalities in national development that led to the so-called "Malari" riots of January 1974. Following this event, changes were formally written into the 1978 Broad Outlines of State Policy (or GBHN 1978) passed by the People's Consultative Assembly (MPR) officially making equality (*pemerataan*) one of the guiding principles of development policy, alongside high economic growth and political stability. At least seven special redistributive programmes in the form of Presidential Instructions, known as Inpres, have subsequently been initiated as a means of fostering *pemerataan*. These redistributive programmes cover a wide range of areas including rural development, local government, markets, public health, education, reforestation, and public works.

In the 1993 Broad Outlines of State Policy, equality (*pemerataan*) was identified as the first of the three guiding principles of national development (known as the *trilogi pembangunan*). Two additional special redistributive programmes have since been launched, a programme of assistance to disadvantaged areas (known as Inpres Desa Tertinggal), and a programme under which five per cent of public enterprises' profits are to be allocated to small scale industries.

Foreign Investment

A hotly debated economic policy change was the 1994 Government Regulation on Foreign Investment. This regulation allowed foreign investment and ownership (including one hundred per cent foreign ownership) in nine economic areas that were among those which, according to Article 33 of the 1945 Constitution, must be controlled by the state. As discussed in Chapter 2, the government denied that the change in foreign ownership policy violates the Constitution, but its basic argument for the policy change was that it was required for the sake of continued rapid economic growth.

The government position was that maintaining a steadily increasing flow of foreign capital was essential to Indonesia's development plans. Specifically, foreign investment was considered critical in order to maintain an annual six per cent economic growth rate and to achieve the target of sixty trillion rupiahs in investment in the current five-year development plan period, because neither the public sector nor Indonesia's own private sector could sustain the necessary rates of capital investment alone. To achieve these development objectives, Indonesia had to remain attractive to foreign investors. Many of Indonesia's competitors for investment, particularly China and Vietnam, had previously promulgated foreign investment policies allowing one hundred per cent foreign ownership. Thus Indonesia had no choice but to further liberalize its own conditions for foreign investment.

Land Disputes

The third policy change prompted by sustained economic growth relates to the nation-wide proliferation of land disputes in recent years. The heightened demand for land for a variety of development purposes — industry, housing, highway construction, etc. — was accompanied by sharp disputes between developers (government or private) and landowners or tenants, usually relatively poor farmers. Land disputes became the most common complaints received by the DPR and the DPRDs (provincial level parliaments), as well as by the National Commission for Human Rights. Prominent examples of such land conflicts in rural areas are the previously-mentioned 1989 court case over the Kedung Ombo Dam in Central Java, and the 1993 Nipah Dam project in Madura, East Java.[5] The fundamental complaints were lack of appropriate compensation for land and lack of consultation between the government and the local residents. Similarly, local governments in urban areas forced poor people to vacate state land (where they may have been squatting illegally) without giving them any housing alternatives. Other common urban land problems involved transportation projects in which municipal governments failed to pay the market price for land appropriated for road widening and construction. If the owners/occupants refused low compensation for their land they were often forcibly evicted by the authorities.

The resistance of residents to involuntary resettlement and the forced release of their land without just compensation not only delayed the implementation of the development project in question, but also created an image that the government does not respect human rights. These two reasons compelled the government to change the procedures for appropriation of land. The previous policy on land confiscation, issued by the

Department of Home Affairs in 1969, was changed substantially in 1994 to allow for more equitable resolution of land disputes between owners/ occupants and government authorities or private developers.

The policy was no longer called "land release" but the "buying of land for public purposes". Moreover, the definition of "public purposes" was spelled out in some detail. Compensation for land was to be not only determined by the type of ownership but also based on agreement between the parties concerned. The price of land for public purposes, according to Presidential Decree No. 55/1994, is to be negotiated by both parties with the stipulation that the final price will be between the sale price of taxable property (known as Nilai Jual Objek Pajak) that is annually set by the government, and the current market value. Through this price-setting process it was hoped that land disputes will be more equitably resolved.

Deregulation

The impact of rapid economic growth can also be observed in the changes in the scope and procedures of the state bureaucracy, namely through the deregulation and debureaucratization of the economic sectors in recent years. This process of deregulation began in 1983. An example of deregulation of the bureaucracy — in an effort to make it more responsive to developmental demands — is the pilot project on local autonomy launched in 1995 (and discussed further in the next chapter). This project envisions devolving authority for the implementation (though not initiation) of development policies to provincial and district officials. Although this delegation of authority to the district level is quite limited, nevertheless it has been welcomed by many political observers as a step towards empowering local people in the political process.

Democratisation

High expectations on the part of a rising middle class for greater individual autonomy and increased participation in government have resulted in demands for democratization. Popular pressures have encouraged the government to debureaucratize political processes and to respect human rights. The government has responded to these demands, but often in ways that appear more cosmetic than substantive. For example, starting with the 1993 session of the MPR, the government no longer prepared the draft of the Broad Outlines of State Policy (GBHN) for consideration by the assembly. Rather, each parliamentary faction was allowed to prepare its own draft. In this way, theoretically the responsibility for creating broad state policy was devolved to the people's representatives in the MPR. However, since the government still thoroughly controls the decision-making process in the assembly, this change of procedure does not involve a real increase in public participation in the formulation of state policy or in the authority of the representative institutions.

In 1989, the president and other government leaders made a series of statements embracing the concept of "openness" (*keterbukaan*), particularly in the DPR and in the press. For about four years the press and the public enjoyed greater freedom to express opinions, including views critical of the government. However, in practice the openness policy allowed only marginally more public space for debate, without increasing access to or influence in decision making. Moreover, heightened freedom of speech was permitted as long as it did not touch the president or his family. Seminars on political topics continued to be cancelled or ended because authorities did not issue the proper permits. And the new openness policy was effectively ended with the closure of *Tempo* and two other journals in June 1994. Newspaper and magazine editors routinely received warning telephone calls from officials urging a particular slant to coverage of various issues.

Another response by the government to demands for democratization took the form of a presidential instruction to the Indonesian Institute of Sciences (LIPI) to conduct research on appropriate future election systems for Indonesia, including the specific question of the proper number of seats in Parliament that should be allocated to the armed forces. Before the LIPI study was completed, however, the government proposed the reduction of ABRI seats from 100 to 75. In any case, since the Parliament does not play a central or independent role in national decision making, this initiative seemed to be more a matter of symbolism and political positioning than a serious proposal for structural change.

The combination of rising external and internal demands for greater respect for human rights in Indonesia led the government to create, in 1993, the National Commission for Human Rights (Human Rights Watch/ Asia 1994, Ch. 9). The commission was initially greeted with scepticism by the public (who thought it would be only another powerless, rubber-stamp agency), but it has since demonstrated considerable independence by its effective handling of several cases of human rights abuse. As a result, ordinary people have begun to file their grievances with the Human Rights Commission rather than with the DPR or the political parties. The long-term responsiveness, effectiveness, and independence of the commission remain to be seen, but it has been a positive example of institutional change.

CONCLUSION

Three general conclusions can be drawn from this study of how formal political institutions may have been affected by rapid economic growth. The most apparent direct impact of changes in the Indonesian economy resulting from sustained high economic growth on formal institutions has been an increase in the power and resources of the presidency and the executive branch, while the impact of growth on the Parliament and courts is much less visible. However, it is difficult to conclude that even the presidency (or the executive branch as a whole) has been strengthened *as an institution*, because the distinctions between the president's personal and institutional authority remain blurred.

Government efforts to sustain economic growth, and government responses to new demands and pressures created by economic change, have produced a number of changes in government policies, structures and processes in recent years. These changes have tended to be incremental and *ad hoc* rather than comprehensive or part of any clear long-term political development strategy. And some of the most promising (e.g., the "openness" policy) have subsequently been reversed. But the process as a whole does indicate a degree of responsiveness by the political institutions to economic change.

These indications of political evolution notwithstanding, the governmental structures and processes of the New Order remained pervasively authoritarian and overwhelmingly under the control of a strong president. This authoritarian bureaucratic structure was ideologically justified on cultural and economic as well as political-security grounds. And despite some interest in greater autonomy within the courts, the DPR, and even the cabinet, there was no fundamental change in the executive-heavy political structure.

Notes

[1]   The six foundations are: Yayasan Trikora for orphans, Yayasan Dharmais for retired members of the armed forces, Yayasan Supersemar for scholarships, Yayasan Amal Bakti Muslim Pancasila for building mosques, Yayasan Dana Kemanusiaan dan Gotong Royong for the victims of natural disasters, and Yayasan Dana Abadi Karya Bhakti

(DAKAB) for development and to promote the victory of the government's political organization Golkar in general elections. For details, see Lay 1994*b*.

2   For example, members of the Petition of 50 (Petisi 50) dissident group formed in 1979-80 were cut off from access to bank credits and loans and necessary government permits and licenses to work in business.

3   It is important to note that political party leadership in Indonesia is *de facto* chosen by the government and that parties receive their operating funds from the bureaucracy. Therefore, there is immense pressure upon party and faction leaderships to restrain individual members. (These points are discussed further in Chapter 6 below.)

4   The closing of *Tempo* and two other publications are described in more detail in Chapter 9. See also Human Rights Watch/Asia 1994.

5   For an overview of the Nipah Dam dispute, see Human Rights Watch/ Asia 1994, Ch. 8.

4

The Bureaucracy and Reform

T. A. Legowo

This chapter assesses the development of the Indonesian bureaucracy during the New Order era, and how it may have been changing in response to economic growth over this period. The Indonesian Government played a central role in the country's rapid economic growth from 1965 to the crisis of 1997/98. State institutions largely monopolized the formulation and implementation of economic development policy during this period. The bureaucracy therefore must be considered as one of the important factors in Indonesia's successful development record.[1]

Yet the central position of the bureaucracy in the development process does not necessarily mean that the bureaucracy has always acted in a rational, impersonal, and efficient fashion. In fact, the bureaucracy may well have hindered the process of national development because of the pervasive corruption of some government departments, and the inefficiency and overlapping duties of various agencies. Furthermore, as Indonesia's society prospered and the economy became increasingly complex and sophisticated, the bureaucracy had difficulty responding to new demands arising from successful economic development and industrialization.

Throughout this period there were attempts to reform and adapt the bureaucracy to the country's changing political economy. Therefore, this chapter focuses particularly on the reform process, including the question of what further steps seem required.

THE MAKING OF THE NEW ORDER BUREAUCRACY

The New Order leadership believed that the bureaucracy could be an effective engine of economic growth only if it had a single, highly centralized hierarchical structure of command under the political direction of the regime (Mas'oed 1989, pp. 15–20). Such a centralized structure was deemed necessary to ensure the loyalty of civil servants, which in turn was deemed a prerequisite for both national political stability and an unhindered development process. The requirement of political "monoloyalty" was part of the New Order's reaction to the experience of the previous period, when the bureaucracy had been sharply polarized ideologically and politically. The New Order considered that this had been one of the main causes of the failure of Indonesia to develop prior to 1965 (Moertopo 1984, pp. 139–42).

In the first ten years of the New Order, three basic steps were taken to develop an effective bureaucracy capable of carrying out the development objectives. The first step, as noted above, was depoliticization. The government created a single civil servants organization, KORPRI (Korps Pegawai Negeri Republik Indonesia), membership in which was compulsory for all civil servants. The second step was stabilization. A major instrument to stabilize and control the bureaucracy was the appointment of high-ranking military officers to strategic bureaucratic positions, including as ministers and in other positions in the first echelon of government departments (Table 4.1).

The third step was legitimization. A key element in this process was the transformation of Golkar (for Golongan Karya, or Functional Groups), which had originally been established by the military prior to 1965 as an anti-communist grouping, into a political organization which could mobilize public support for the regime. Golkar was comprised of organizations representing the military (ABRI), the bureaucracy (KORPRI), and functionally based interest groups such as farmers (HKTI), fishermen (HNSI),

TABLE 4.1
Military Officers in Ministerial and
Governor Positions, 1968–93

Period	Ministerial Positions		Governor Positions	
	Total	Military	Total	Military
1968/1973	23	7	26	19
1973/1978	22	5	26	20
1978/1983	30	12	27	16
1983/1988	37	12	27	14
1988/1993	38	9	27	12
1993/	38	7	27	13

Sources: Winarno and Say 1993; Sudibjo 1994.

and labour (SPSI).[2] Golkar was given full rights to participate in general elections and became, in effect, the official government political party (see the fuller discussion of Golkar as a political party in Chapter 6). Because of the requirement that civil servants support Golkar, it has also helped ensure the loyalty of civil servants to the regime.

Thus reorganized, the bureaucracy was increasingly effective in implementing the government's programmes of administration and economic development. It addressed numerous economic and social problems, including responding to market failures (Effendi 1990, pp. 7–8), introducing new programmes such as family planning (Singarimbun 1988, pp. 10–11), promoting new agricultural techniques and crop varieties (Nasikun 1986, p. 33), etc. In politics, the bureaucracy successfully performed as a political machine in mobilizing societal support for the regime (Imawan 1990, pp. 5–8). Thus, as noted by many observers (among others, Pangestu 1993), the New Order bureaucracy has been an effective instrument in enabling the government to accelerate economic growth, increase the level of social welfare, and maintain national stability.

INSTITUTIONAL DEVELOPMENT

The organization of the bureaucracy, as well as its functional responsibilities, changed with the growth and increasing complexity of the country's political economy. The institutional development of the bureaucracy is reflected in the increasing number of departments at both the central and regional levels (see Table 4.2). Another trend has been the continuing

TABLE 4.2
Number of Central Government Offices, 1968–93

Period	Technical Departments	Non-Technical Departments*	Non-Department Institutions**	Total
1968/73	18	5	21	44
1973/78	17	5	21	43
1978/83	17	13	21	51
1983/88	21	16	24	61
1988/93	21	17	24	62
1993/	21	17	24	62

Notes: * Including co-ordinating ministers and junior ministers of state.
** Including the central bank, the attorney general, and ABRI.
Sources: Winarno and Say 1993; Department of Information.

growth in the number of civil servants (Table 4.3). However, the rate of increase has not been steady over time. From 1988 to 1992, the rate of growth declined significantly (perhaps due to the shortage of funds after the economic crisis of the mid-1980s). Also, as a percentage of total government expenditures, spending on the bureaucracy fell substantially over the New Order period, from 68.3 per cent in 1969/70 to 44.6 per cent in 1993/94 (Table 4.4).

Prior to the launching of the five-year development plans (Repelita) in 1969, the main activities of the bureaucracy focused on routine government administration and public service. The development programmes significantly widened the scope of bureaucratic activities, with the bureaucracy now also responsible for implementing a wide variety of development activities. But the widening scope of bureaucratic activities has also increased the bureaucratic presence in societal life and, to some extent, the bureaucratization of the society. One result is that some institutions that should be independent in their activities have been consciously or unconsciously incorporated into the government bureaucracy (Setiawan 1990, pp. 68–69).

TABLE 4.3
Number of Civil Servants, 1980–92

Year	Total	Increase	
		Number	%
1980	1,956,864	–	–
1981	2,047,080	90,216	4.6
1982	2,047,080*	*	*
1983	2,628,474	581,394	28.4
1984	2,785,646	157,172	6.0
1985	2,956,082	170,436	6.1
1986	3,159,652	203,570	6.9
1987	3,403,408	243,756	7.7
1988	3,529,640	126,232	3.7
1989	3,655,428	125,788	3.6
1990	3,771,285	115,857	3.2
1991	3,876,892	105,607	2.8
1992	3,950,126	73,234	1.9

Notes: Data before 1980 not systematically available.
        * 1982 data not recorded.
Sources: BPS (Central Bureau of Statistics) 1980–92.

TABLE 4.4
Expenditure on Civil Servants, 1969/70–1993/94
(Rp trillion)

Fiscal Year	Central Gov't. Civil Servants		Regional Gov't. Civil Servants		Total Civil Servants	Gov't. Routine Budget	
	Amount	%	Amount	%		Total Amount	Civil Servants as %
Repelita I							
1969/70	103.8	70.2	44.1	29.8	147.9	216.5	68.3
1970/71	131.4	70.0	56.2	30.3	186.6	288.2	65.1
1971/72	163.4	71.0	66.8	29.0	230.2	349.1	65.9
1972/73	200.4	70.5	83.9	29.5	284.3	438.1	64.9
1973/74	268.9	71.2	108.6	28.8	377.5	713.3	52.9
Repelita II							
1974/75	420.1	67.5	201.9	32.5	622.0	1,016.1	61.2
1975/76	593.9	67.7	284.5	32.4	878.4	1,332.6	65.9
1976/77	636.6	67.0	313.0	33.0	949.6	1,629.8	58.3
1977/78	893.2	65.1	478.4	34.9	1,371.6	2,148.9	63.8
1978/79	1,001.6	65.7	522.3	34.3	1,523.9	2,743.7	55.5
Repelita III							
1979/80	1,419.9	67.9	669.9	32.1	2,089.8	4,061.8	51.5
1980/81	2,023.3	67.5	976.1	32.5	2,999.4	5,800.0	51.7
1981/82	2,277.1	65.3	1,209.1	34.7	3,486.2	6,977.6	50.0
1982/83	2,418.1	64.8	1,315.4	35.2	3,733.5	6,996.3	53.4
1983/84	2,757.0	64.1	1,547.0	35.9	4,304.0	8,411.8	51.2
Repelita IV							
1984/85	3,046.8	64.5	1,680.1	35.5	4,726.9	9,429.0	50.1
1985/86	4,018.3	64.1	2,247.6	35.9	6,265.9	11,951.5	52.4
1986/87	4,310.6	64.1	2,410.2	35.9	6,720.8	13,559.3	49.6
1987/88	4,616.9	64.0	2,592.3	36.0	7,209.2	17,481.5	41.2
1988/89	4,998.2	64.3	2,778.6	35.7	7,776.8	20,739.0	37.5
Repelita V							
1989/90	6,201.5	65.0	3,338.1	35.0	9,539.6	24,331.1	39.2
1990/91	7,053.5	64.0	3,961.4	36.0	11,041.9	29,997.7	36.7
1991/92	8,102.5	64.2	4,519.8	35.8	12,622.3	30,227.6	41.8
1992/93	9,465.7	64.2	4,906.3	34.1	14,372.0	34,031.2	42.2
1993/94	10,849.5	64.4	5,651.3	34.2	16,545.8	37,094.9	44.6

Source: *Financial Notes and the 1994/1995 Draft State Budget* 1994, p. 63.

An example is the case of the LSD (Lembaga Sosial Desa, or Village Social Institution). The original objective of the LSDs was to enable rural communities to run independent social activities organized by the communities themselves. In 1980, however, under a presidential decision (KEPPRES No. 28/1980) the name of this institution was changed to LKMD (Lembaga Ketahanan Masyarakat Desa, or Village Society Resilience Institution). This had the effect of changing the role and structure of the institution to one aimed at mobilizing societal participation in implementing the government's development programme. The LKMD was absorbed structurally within the government administration (Figure 4.1).

Today, many such society-based organizations have been similarly bureaucratized.[3] In most of these cases, the only alternative has seemed to be extinction. This phenomenon has led some observers to apply to Indonesia such terms as "bureaucratic polity", "bureaucratic pluralism", or "bureaucratic authoritarianism".[4] Whatever the distinctions between them, all of these terms imply that the Indonesian bureaucracy has come to dominate the society.

THE NEED FOR REFORM

The success of a developing country in conducting economic development can never be separated from the quality of the country's administrative system. The administrative system can accelerate national development, but it can also be a constraint on the development process. In practice, both effects can take place at the same time. Therefore, it is reasonable to argue that in order to effectively promote development, a government needs to optimize the power of the bureaucracy for development while at the same time minimizing the development constraint imposed by bureaucratic malfunctions.

Further, even when the bureaucracy is significantly assisting the process of development, there is always a requirement for increasing efficiency and enhancing effectiveness (Tjokrowinoto 1989, p. 3) and for adaptation to the changing level of development and other changes in the environment. Moreover, there is a common tendency for a bureaucracy to expand, especially if it is playing a dominant role. The combination of expansion and domination may eventually produce conditions that are conducive for bureaucratic misconduct and unresponsiveness to the changing demands of society and the environment.

These phenomena produce a requirement for continuing bureaucratic reform. The reform process is a multiple effort, to develop bureaucratic

FIGURE 4.1
The Structure of Indonesia's State Administration

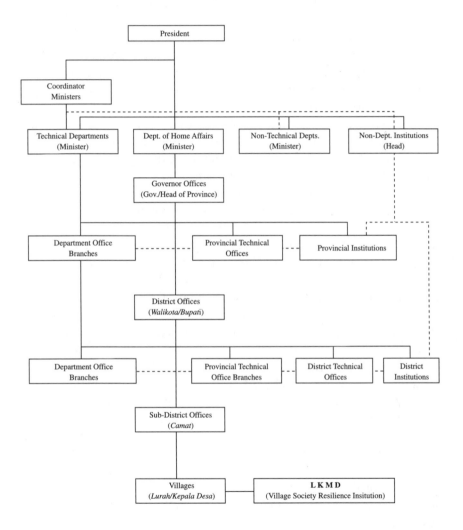

Note: Unbroken lines are command relationships; broken lines are functional/coordinating relationships.

efficiency and autonomy while simultaneously preventing the onset of rigidity and the blurring of objectives and also empowering the broader society as a check on bureaucratic misuse of authority and unresponsiveness to changing needs and conditions (King 1989, p. 23).

One can argue that, in the largest sense, reform of the Indonesian bureaucracy has been taking place ever since the birth of the New Order regime. But this has also been a highly pragmatic process, aimed at solving the challenges and demands of each phase of development. As one observer has commented, such efforts constitute "*ad hoc* treatments" (Tjokrowinoto 1987, p. 82).

There have been at least three major phases of the reform process in the New Order period, corresponding to the different kinds of problems confronted at each stage. As previously mentioned, during the first decade of the New Order, reform was generally aimed at improving bureaucratic efficiency, to make effective use of the bureaucracy for the maintenance of national stability and the pursuit of national development. Examples were the introduction of new laws regulating regional and village governments (Law No. 5/1974 and Law No. 5/1979), and the various programmes to increase internal quality controls within the government apparatus.

Up to the end of the 1970s, the government faced no real problems in financing a large bureaucracy. The oil boom of the 1970s and significant flows of foreign aid greatly eased the government's financial burdens. One may argue that this decade was a "golden age" for the bureaucracy, because there was no real challenge to bureaucratic deviations. Corruption, misuse of authority and the like, even though they resulted in bureaucratic inefficiency and a high cost economy, were not considered by the government as serious threats to the continuing process of development or to the government's credibility.

The oil shock of the early 1980s and the long-term world economic recession that followed changed economic conditions drastically. The growth rate declined sharply in 1981–82, and although it recovered somewhat in the immediately following years, it could not match the achievements of the 1970s (Tjokrowinoto 1989, p. 5). This affected the government's ability to finance both development projects and routine expenditures. In response, the government rescheduled numerous projects and embarked on concerted efforts to economize routine expenditures.

Despite government efforts to revive economic growth through a variety of means including tax reform, obtaining more foreign aid and increasing non-oil exports, these were not sufficient to overcome the revenue losses due to the drastic declines in the price of oil. This situation was made worse by, and highlighted, various problems in government administration. These included misconduct and inefficiency in the management of government credit programmes (e.g., in commodity stabilization and housing credit programmes), large-scale corruption in granting forestry concessions, etc. (Effendi 1989, p. 12).

These conditions provided the background for government efforts beginning in the mid-1980s at privatization, deregulation, and debureaucratization (Tjokrowinoto 1989, p. 5; Effendi 1989, pp. 13–14). These efforts were aimed primarily at increasing the role of the private sector in the development process, a process that had to this point been largely dominated by the government through the bureaucracy (Mas'oed 1990, p. 135). As discussed in Chapter 1, there was a particular focus on expanding participation of the private sector in finance. Other measures included tightening controls on the bureaucracy, and reconsideration of the role and structure of state enterprises (BUMN) as described in Chapter 2.

During the last years of the 1980s, the regime initiated a third round of efforts at bureaucratic reform. In this case, however, the objectives were more principled and comprehensive than those of the two earlier programmes. There was a growing recognition that the high-growth development process of the 1970s and early 1980s, while it had raised income and welfare levels, had also produced deterioration of the ecology, widening socio-economic disparities, and a lessening of creativity and initiative (Effendi 1991, p. 37). Correspondingly, it became apparent that long-term growth could only be sustained through increasing the quality of human resources. This in turn meant that development priorities needed to be changed. For this reason, starting with the fifth development plan period (Repelita V, 1989–94), the government adopted sustainable development as a guiding principle of national development.

Adoption of the principle of sustainable development required a basic and comprehensive reform of the development system that had been in place since the early years of the New Order period. One of the major targets of reform was a bureaucracy that remained very mechanistic, susceptible to corruption, lacking in effective controls and insulated from public scrutiny.

The other motivating force for the most recent reform effort has been an increase in public demands for accountability and responsiveness from government and the bureaucracy. Traditional Indonesian attitudes towards government officialdom (and other powerful figures) have emphasized respect and deference (Muhaimin 1990, pp. 24–27), and the New Order's use of government had consciously made use of and reinforced this cultural pattern. However, especially in urban society, attitudes towards government and the bureaucracy have been changing. Since then Vice President Sudharmono opened a special post-office box for complaints in 1988, and thousands of letters from all levels of the society have come in. Most demanded more serious government attention to instances of bureaucratic misconduct. The letters pages of newspapers and magazines have been filled with similar complaints. Still more openly, groups began to hold demonstrations at the Parliament protesting against arbitrary and unjust bureaucratic actions.

FORMS OF REFORM

Efforts at bureaucratic reform in the 1990s have included many specific programmes. Examples are: job analysis, functional position descriptions, upgrading bureaucratic leadership skills, simplifying recruitment and public service procedures, improving information systems, increasing the quality of bureaucratic controls, and granting greater regional autonomy (Kantor Menpan 1993, pp. 100–101).

None of these efforts, however, seems to have been able to bring about fundamental change in the bureaucratic culture. The bureaucracy continued to be considered the main source of inefficiencies, high economic costs, and constraints on national development. The negative image of the bureaucracy has been documented in studies of daily life (e.g., Sihbudi 1994, pp. 316–17; Tjokrowinoto 1987, p. 67). Others have commented on the continuing neo-traditional behaviour patterns of the bureaucracy — paternalism, status consciousness, high centralization and low initiative and autonomy (Santoso 1994, pp. 142–43; Effendi 1991, pp. 39–40; Santoso 1993, p. 20).

As examples of the problems encountered in the reform effort, the following sections describe and assess two specific programmes: increasing the quality of bureaucratic control and increasing regional autonomy.

Quality Control

From Repelita II to Repelita V (1974–94), the government issued eleven separate regulations aimed at increasing bureaucratic quality control through a variety of systems and structures of internal as well as external controls. Together, these measures comprised a complex and comprehensive network of controls aimed to significantly reduce opportunities for bureaucratic deviations.

During Repelitas II and III, the following internal controls were instituted: (a) a general inspectorate in each government department, (b) a government-wide general inspectorate of development, (c) a "rule and order" campaign (Opstib) at the central and regional levels, (d) the establishment of the State Ministry of Development Control and Environment (in the third cabinet), (e) the co-ordinating team for management and control of regional development projects, and (f) inspectorates in the provinces and districts (Tjokrowinoto 1989, p. 8).

During Repelita IV, the government initiated a co-ordinating system that integrated the various functional controls into a single line of command. The major elements of this system were: (a) assignment of the vice-president, assisted by the Co-ordinating Ministry of Economic, Monetary, Industry and Development Control, to co-ordinate all apparatuses of bureaucratic control at the central and regional levels; (b) formation of the Control Institution for Finance and Development; (c) imposition of general controls on the authority and the use of state financial resources; and (d) creation of a working mechanism for integrating functional controls (Tjokrowinoto 1989, p. 8).

Finally, under Repelita V, the government introduced a programme intended to reform administrative behaviour and culture. This was to be achieved through linked training, from the top to the lowest echelons.

However, these efforts do not seem to have been very successful, in the sense that they did not qualitatively alter the performance of the bureaucracy. It is of course impossible to know how much misconduct there has been in the bureaucracy and therefore how much may have been deterred by the new mechanisms. What is known is that the control programme has only taken action on 902 cases of misconduct, which amounts to only two to three per government institution, and that only 1,045 civil servants have been found guilty of misconduct and punished.

The case record provides very little information about the effectiveness of the various programmes in increasing bureaucratic quality, so this cannot be used as the measure of success of the programmes. However, one research report confirmed a variety of weaknesses in the programmes reviewed (Kantor Menpan 1993, pp. 135–37). Thus it can be argued that the new control mechanism has not brought about significant increases in "administrative efficacy", i.e. in the capacity to create desired effects. But because these programmes have attempted to deal with dysfunctions in the bureaucracy not by restructuring but by creating new structures, one certain outcome is that the bureaucratic control process has become much more expensive (Tjokrowinoto 1989, p. 9).

Regional Autonomy

Another major element in the effort at bureaucratic reform is the regional autonomy programme. This programme was set up through Law No. 5/1974 on the Principles of Regional Government, which stipulated among other things that regional governance was to be implemented on the basis of the principle of decentralization. Under this principle, regional policies, development plans and their completion, and the operational cost of regional governance should all have become the responsibility of regional governments.

Since the enactment of Law No. 5/1974, some elements of autonomy have been transferred to regional governments, as illustrated in the establishment of offices of various government services in the provinces as well as districts (see Figure 4.1 above). Seventeen areas of governance are to be handed over to regional governments; these are shown in Table 4.5. (This does not include the four basic areas that are the prerogative of the central government: foreign affairs, defence and security, the judiciary, and monetary policy.)

However, implementation of the regional autonomy programme was not going according to the original plan or principle. Minister of State for Administrative Reform T.B. Silalahi (1994), acknowledged that:

> This type of conflict has led to complex difficulties in the state administration such as duplication or overlapping of functions, and problems of allocating and distributing state funds. This also explains why some development projects have failed despite the involvement of many institutions and government apparatuses in the projects. For example, an agricultural project in a district usually involves at least the regional office of the Department of Agriculture, the provincial agricultural service office, and the district agricultural service office. Such complexity is not only confusing for the consumers of government services but also very inefficient.

The reluctance of the central government to give up real authority to regional governments may be influenced by negative experiences in the past, such as regional upheavals and separatist movements. The New Order regime placed highest priority on creating and maintaining national stability. There remains a fear that regional autonomy might stimulate regionalist sentiments that in turn could endanger national stability.

TABLE 4.5
Transfer of Government Functions to Regions

Area	Functions to be Transferred	
	1994	Future Years
Trading	–	7
Cooperatives &		
Small Business	–	3
Information	–	6
Transmigration	–	7
Religion	–	4
Industry	–	10
Education & Culture	14	–
Labour	6	12
Health	19	23
Agriculture		
a. Food Farming	6	12
b. Veterinary	4	4
c. Fisheries	5	12
d. Plantations	3	8
Public Works		
a. Roads	3	4
b. Irrigation	1	2
c. Public Buildings	13	13
Tourism, Post &		
Telecommunications	7	17
Communication	8	13
Forestry	5	9
Social Affairs	3	7
Mining & Energy	4	7
Land & Building Tax	–	5
Total	96	199

Source: *Republika*, 13 December 1994.

This fear of regionalism is reflected in the actual control of the central government over regional politics. For example, in elections for regional (province or district) leaders, not only must all candidates obtain prior approval from the central government, but after the vote on the candidates in the regional legislature, the final decision is still made by the central government. It is quite possible that a candidate with a minority vote may be appointed as the regional head.

Another fundamental constraint on the regional autonomy programme is the lack of human and financial resources at the regional level. Less than fifteen per cent of total government employees are regional civil servants, which is even less than the number of central civil servants seconded to regional governments (around thirty-five per cent of total government employees). The central government has to bear the largest share of the financial cost of routine as well as development expenditures by regional governments. At the district level, more than fifty per cent of district governments' income comes from contributions and assistance from the central as well as provincial governments (Table 4.6).[5]

FURTHER STEPS IN BUREAUCRATIC REFORM

It is not difficult to identify the characteristics of a bureaucracy that would be suitable to the needs of Indonesian society in the context of sustained rapid economic growth and the accompanying social transformations. This bureaucracy should be, at a minimum: adaptive, efficient and respon-sive, and responsible and accountable. Adaptive means open to innovative ideas, and alert to the changing environment and the growing demands of the society (Saxena 1986, p. 52). Efficient and responsive mean able to increase the productivity and quality of public services provided (Santoso

TABLE 4.6
Sources of Income of District Governments,
1988/1989 and 1991/1992
(Rp trillion and per cent)

Source	1988/1989	%	1991/1992	%
Districts' Direct Income	403.93	16	705.28	13
Districts' Share of Tax & Non-Tax Revenue	266.69	10	677.37	12
Contributions from Central and Regional Gov'ts.	1,790.94	70	3,833.37	70
Borrowing	31.53	1	79.68	2
Residue from Past Year	74.93	3	155.66	3
Total	2,568.02	100	5,451.36	100

Source: Financial Notes (Nota Keuangan) 1994/95.

1994, p. 144). Responsible means having high integrity, and accountable means being subject to continuous public oversight.

The more important and difficult question, however, is how this objective (or anything close to this ideal) could be achieved in practice, in the real world conditions of the contemporary Indonesian Government. There clearly are no simple answers or magic formulas for this, but some initial suggestions do emerge out of the reform efforts that have been attempted so far. Three steps in particular seem to hold promise of increasing administrative efficiency, streamlining bureaucratic organization and procedures, and building a more professional civil service.

Decentralization

The first step would be to carry through a genuine programme of enhancing regional autonomy. This should not only reduce the financial cost of government and increase the efficiency of delivering government services, but by empowering regional governments and societies should stimulate local initiative and genuine participation in national development. Also, the increased burdens involved should force the district governments to find ways of financing themselves and the region's development projects, making the district governments both more independent and ultimately more responsible.

The pilot regional autonomy programme launched in twenty-six selected districts in 1995/96 could show the way and lead to such a national programme. If this project is carried through according to its original plan, fundamental changes could occur not only in streamlining the structure of the bureaucracy but also in its performance as a modern public service organization. However, it still remains to be seen whether the pilot project will involve real transfers of financial and human resources, and decision-making authority, from the central to the regional and district levels — in other words, a genuine transfer of greater autonomy. Responses from some government departments to date are not encouraging on this score (though in fairness it is still too early to offer any firm judgements on this project).

Structure and Procedures

The second step would be to institute genuine structural change in the bureaucracy. Success in the decentralization programme in fact requires new structures and procedures to provide wider space and more opportunities for autonomous decision making at lower levels.

One model for relaxing structural constraints and stimulating initiative within the bureaucracy is already available in the programmes of deregulation and privatization in the economic field that have been undertaken since the mid-1980s. Of course, a thoroughgoing effort of this sort would involve many more elements as well, including revisions of the methods and curricula of virtually all civil servant training programmes.

The Civil Service System

The third step is reform of the bureaucratic personnel system, a logical consequence of the two other reforms just discussed. The personnel system is such a vast area — including at least recruitment, rank structure, promotion and payment systems — that the full subject is beyond the scope of this paper. However, a brief discussion is warranted.

One obvious means of increasing civil service performance and quality would be to introduce a merit-based system of promotion and pay. In many areas of government, quantitative measures of performance are even feasible, creating the possibility of productivity-related bonuses and other incentives. Such a system might help recruit and retain abler individuals, who now have increasing incentive to move to private companies that provide both opportunities for self-development and significantly greater financial rewards than the civil service.

It is worth noting in this connection that a survey done by *Tempo* (6 February 1993) among university students showed that seventy-five per cent of the respondents intended to apply for private companies, while only twenty-five per cent wanted to work in the civil service. Then Minister of State for Administrative Reform Sarwono Kusumaatmadja stated rightly that "it is not impossible that the Indonesian bureaucracy will be filled by a 'second class' type of employee" (*Tempo*, 6 February 1993, p. 14). This points to a key problem with the Indonesian civil service, which is that it is poorly paid, badly trained, and not given the kind of performance incentives which would promote efficiency.

In part, this discussion only serves to underline the problems of the present bureaucratic structure and the obstacles in the way of bureaucratic adaptation to the changes that are taking place in the wider society and environment. However, it also suggests that, if public pressure for change continues to grow, and if the government leadership continues to be interested in undertaking reforms of the bureaucracy, avenues for constructive, practical change are available.

CONCLUSION

The most influential factor in stimulating reform of the Indonesian bureaucracy in the New Order era has been the vast changes in the internal and external environment, especially in the economic field. The desirable directions of reform are clear, and there has been clear political will on the part of the government to reform the bureaucracy. However, reform efforts to date have been largely pragmatic and incremental, and the programmes have not been effective in meeting the demands of the society or the needs of the changing environment. Consideration needs to be given to more comprehensive and holistic approaches to reform.

Nevertheless, to carry out such reforms ultimately requires more than just political will on the part of the regime, but real political courage. A first and fundamental requirement would be an initiative to "neutralize" the bureaucracy from pressures to give preferential treatment to politically connected vested interests. However, a full discussion of this issue would require a forum of its own.

Notes

1   As used here, the "bureaucracy" refers to the whole government organization that carries out public administration, provides public services, and devises and implements national development. The term includes the central as well as regional, provincial, district, and village governments. The bureaucracy is also referred to as the state administration, or the civil service system — terms that are used interchangeably in this chapter. The apparatus of the bureaucracy is the civil service, which includes all government employees, at the central and regional levels.

2   ABRI is the acronym for Angkatan Bersenjata Republik Indonesia (Armed Forces of the Republic of Indonesia). KORPRI stands for Korps Pegawai Negeri Indonesia, Indonesian Civil Servant Corps. HKTI is Himpunan Keluarga Tani Indonesia, Assembly of Indonesian Farmer Families. HNSI is Himpunan Nelayan Seluruh Indonesia, or All-Indonesia Assembly of Fishermen. SPSI is Serikat Pekerja Seluruh Indonesia, All-Indonesia Workers' Union.

3   Other societal institutions that have been subsumed under the government's development programmes include: (a) in the field of social

welfare, Gerakan Pendidikan Masyarakat (Public Education Movement), Gerakan Pembangunan Masyarakat Desa (Village Society Development Movement) and Gerakan Pendidikan Kesejahteraan Masyarakat (Social Welfare Education Movement); (b) in the field of economic enterprises, Koperasi Unit Desa (Village Cooperatives), Kredit Industri Kecil (Small-Scale Industry Credit), and others; (c) in the field of production, Gerakan Padat Karya (Labour Intensive Movement), Gerakan Penghijauan (Reforestation Movement), Gerakan Bimas dan Inmas (agricultural intensification programmes), and others; and (d) in the field of socio-demography, Gerakan Keluarga Berencana (Family Planning Movement), Gerakan Kesehatan Masyarakat (Public Health Movement), Gerakan Kesehatan Mental (Mental Health Movement), and others.

[4] See, among others, Emmerson 1978 and 1983, and King 1982. For a comprehensive review of the scholarly debate about Indonesia's bureaucratic polity, see Macintyre 1992, pp. 6–18.

[5] For a more detailed discussion of this problem see, among others, Ranis and Stewart 1994, pp. 41–72.

5

The Armed Forces

J. Kristiadi

The Indonesian Armed Forces (Angkatan Bersenjata Republik Indonesia, or ABRI) have not been exempt from the new pressures and challenges that have arisen from social changes caused by rapid economic growth. The purpose of this chapter is to assess the ways in which ABRI may be adapting to social change by modifying its institutional structure and/or shifting its role in Indonesian national life.

Four phenomena that have accompanied rapid economic growth over the past several decades have significantly impacted ABRI as an institution. These are: vastly expanded economic opportunities, a growing middle class, higher levels of education, and the emergence and articulation of new demands for democratization and wider political participation. These developments have impacted in different ways on ABRI's financial condition, its conception of its proper role in society, and the makeup of its personnel.

Before exploring these various impacts, however, it is useful to briefly review the origins of the Indonesian armed forces as a basis for understanding the ways in which ABRI is reacting to the challenges it faces.

ABRI'S PERCEPTION OF ITS MISSION, FUNCTION, AND ROLE

The Indonesian army was established prior to the creation of the Republic of Indonesia. In global military history there are very few examples of the establishment of a national military organization prior to the creation of the state itself (see Soebijono 1991, p. 11; Nugroho 1979, p. 17). Noted Indonesian military analyst Salim Said illustrates the unique characteristics of the army in the following way:

> The Indonesian Army was a self-created army in the sense that
> it was established neither by the government nor by a political

party. Instead, the military created, armed and organized itself out of the shambles of the Japanese-trained Indonesian militia following the surrender of the Japanese and the proclamation of independence (1945), when the newly organized government was reluctant to raise an army. The central government under Sukarno, which was afraid of antagonizing the Allies, wanted to achieve independence peacefully. The youth then took the initiative to arm themselves and defend the country. (Said 1987, p. 16)[1]

One of the defining characteristics of the Indonesian armed forces was that it was not initially a conventional army. It fought as a guerrilla force which relied deeply on the goodwill and co-operation of the local citizenry. Additionally, from the initial days of the revolution the military interacted with the politicians who fought for independence through diplomacy and negotiations. Yet the army has always perceived that the independence struggle through diplomacy and negotiations was too weak and compromising *vis-à-vis* the Dutch.

An early event set the tone for a half century of military scepticism towards the civilian political leadership — the surrender of Sukarno and Hatta during the Second Dutch "Police Action" in December 1948. The surrender of the civilian revolutionary government was not followed by the guerrilla units. Instead, Sudirman, the head of the Indonesian Armed Forces, ordered the armed struggle to continue with or without the government's order.

These revolution-era events instilled in ABRI a very strong perception that it was uniquely qualified to protect and save the nation. Moreover, ABRI strongly views itself not as a government-formed instrument for use against external threats, but as an institution which helped create the Indonesian nation. As a consequence of its perception that it helped create the nation, ABRI firmly believes that it is not limited to merely military security functions, but has the duty to ensure national unity and guard the national ideology in all fields. Therefore, ABRI considers its participation in other areas, especially in politics, to be as important as traditional defence and security functions (Said 1991).

The armed forces' perception of its rightful place in Indonesian politics and national life was formulated into doctrine during the mid-1950s and 1960s. There are three key developments in the formation of ABRI's political doctrines. First, General A.H. Nasution enunciated the concept of the "Middle Way" in which ABRI declared that it would neither abstain wholly from politics, nor completely take over government. Second, under Sukarno's Guided Democracy the army took on an even greater political role as the main countervailing force against the Indonesian Communist Party (PKI). Third, the military became deeply entrenched in governing after the establishment of the New Order in 1965–66. The attempted Communist coup of 1965, which was defeated by the army, dramatically strengthened ABRI's role in politics. The supporting doctrine is commonly known as the "dual function" (*dwifungsi*). ABRI's social and political role was codified in MPR decisions of the 1960s and subsequently in law (Act No. 2/1982).

GROWTH AND THE MILITARY BUDGET

It is perhaps ironic that, in a period in which Indonesia's economy has been growing rapidly and the national development budget has been similarly expanding, the armed forces have remained in many ways starved for basic operating funds. However, ever since the 1950s, budget shortfalls have been the norm for the Indonesian military. Tasked with defence of a vast geographic area against a multiplicity of enemies, both internal and external, the army has never received an adequate "official" budget allocation from the national government to perform these functions. To meet their responsibilities for national security, *and* to keep the loyalty of their troops, most officers in all ranks and services became very adept at creatively supplementing their official allocations. This financial creativity has had consequences for ABRI's role in the New Order's political economy.

In the 1950s the Indonesian army was too weak politically to force the government to allocate sufficient funds. However, when ABRI became the central political institution in the New Order, it did not use its newly powerful political position to rectify the long-standing budget shortfalls. Since 1969–70, the proportion of the national budget allocated to defence and security has continually declined, from twenty-seven per cent to seven per cent in the 1990s (Table 5.1). Thus it is clear that ABRI's dominant institutional position in the New Order's political life has not been matched by its share of the budgetary benefits of the relatively high and constant economic growth that Indonesia has enjoyed for nearly three decades. Although what is actually deemed a sufficient amount for ABRI to function effectively is highly subjective, it is clear that the military budgets remain very small (both in absolute terms and as a percentage of the national budget outlays).

TABLE 5.1
Military and National Budgets, 1969/70-1993/94
(Rp billion and per cent)

Fiscal Year	Military Budget			National Budget	
	Routine Spending	Development Budget	Total Military* Spending	Total Budget	Military Share (%)
1969/70	88,027	4,541	92,568	323,003	29
1970/71	108,100	4,459	112,559	421,053	27
1971/72	124,347	7,435	131,782	508,795	26
1972/73	155,283	4,864	160,147	691,671	23
1973/74	196,299	6,577	202,876	1,106,074	18
1974/75	285,643	12,455	298,098	1,977,635	15
1975/76	438,045	35,995	474,040	2,675,652	18
1976/77	496,985	59,462	556,447	3,176,267	18
1977/78	564,470	56,308	620,778	3,620,411	17
1978/79	610,852	123,635	734,487	4,618,492	16
1979/80	738,900	179,900	918,800	7,478,900	12
1980/81	974,800	339,200	1,314,000	11,000,000	12
1981/82	1,237,200	544,000	1,781,200	13,769,200	13
1982/83	1,296,800	520,200	1,817,000	14,407,700	13
1983/84	1,397,700	573,457	1,971,157	18,311,000	11
1984/85	1,467,000	697,000	2,164,000	19,380,900	11
1985/86	1,695,600	714,100	2,409,700	22,824,600	11
1986/87	1,746,300	554,000	2,300,000	21,421,600	11
1987/88	1,678,300	634,000	2,312,300	22,783,100	10
1988/89	1,860,600	555,600	2,416,200	37,861,200	6
1989/90	1,982,700	812,600	2,795,300	36,574,900	8
1990/91	2,032,000	981,600	3,013,600	42,873,100	7
1991/92	2,293,500	1,085,300	3,378,800	50,555,500	7
1992/93	2,621,800	778,000	3,399,800	56,108,600	6
1993/94	3,258,600	1,147,000	4,405,600	62,322,100	7

Note: *Includes Police budget, approximately 20 percent of the total military budget.
Sources: Department of Defence and Security; Kuntjoro-Jakti and Simatupang 1987, p. 120.

ABRI's reluctance to press for a larger share of the government budget was partly due to the ideological commitment of the military-backed New Order to economic recovery and development, which from the first gave priority to improving national welfare and increasing the people's prosperity over meeting the military's financial needs. However, it was also in part due to the fact that by the mid-1960s the military had a

well-developed system of extra-official ways to finance military operations, provide for soldiers' welfare, and help meet procurement needs.

Military Self-Financing

The key to the military's ability to meet much of its own financial needs
is a long-standing pattern of direct military involvement in business and
the economy. In the 1950s, provincial and district military commanders
were not only responsible for their soldiers' welfare, but were also responsible for routine military expenditures. To meet these needs, they began to
develop relationships with local businessmen.

Ruth McVey argues that the military financing patterns that developed
in the 1950s have permanently influenced the overall relationship between
military and civilian personnel and have determined the ways in which the
army has operated in the national political economy:

> The military's local financial dealings not only served to keep
> troops well-fed and loyal, but padded the pockets of the com-
> mander and those who assisted him in his dealings. The fact
> that many of the most lucrative arrangements involved smug-
> gling from the export-producing border areas only increased
> the tendency of military men to draw the conclusion that
> soldiers need not take the law too seriously and did not provide
> a particular example of honesty. There thus began, at quite an
> early stage, the process of personal corruption and entanglement
> with civilian concerns that has plagued the military ever since.
> (McVey 1971, pp. 152–53)

Harold Crouch further argues that the military's financial practices of
the 1950s created a vast system of military-affiliated businesses that were
later to significantly benefit during the sustained economic growth of the
New Order:

> The involvement of the military in economic affairs suddenly
> expanded after the introduction of martial law in 1957. Martial
> law put military men in positions of considerable power, espe-
> cially in the outer islands where countervailing civilian forces
> were relatively weak. Although regional commanders did not
> always exercise their emergency power to the full, they often
> took a direct interest in the administration of economic matters

such as tax collection, the issuing of licenses and the granting of other facilities. ... [At] the end of 1957, when nationalist demonstrators began to take over the Dutch enterprises [following an adverse vote on West Irian in the United Nations]... [t]he army immediately responded by using its martial law powers to place all Dutch enterprises under military supervision. (Crouch 1975, pp. 520–21)[2]

Over time the military came to control particular sectors of the national economy through the domination of important national economic planning and allocation bodies. As early as 1958, for example, Col. Suprayogi became state minister of economic stabilization, Col. Suhardiman was assigned to control the nationalization of Dutch enterprises through the state Nationalization Board, and the nationalized local Dutch firms were administered by the Local Enterprise Administration Board led by General Baramuli (Muhaimin 1991, p. 238). In the 1960s, the military's role in the national economy grew still further through the expropriation of British firms in 1964 and some American enterprises in 1965.

A second feature of the military's economic activities was the development of an intricate pattern of mutually co-operative business relationships between Indonesian Chinese businessmen (called *cukong*) and key military officers. These relationships became much more deeply entrenched in the New Order.

In the early 1960s ABRI officers began a pattern of establishing nonprofit (tax-free) foundations (*yayasan*) in order to raise other sources of funding. The use of *yayasan* intensified in the New Order. For example, one large ABRI foundation is Yayasan Kartika Eka Paksi. This foundation, owned by the army and established in 1972 with President Soeharto's endorsement, controls twenty-six firms of which twenty-two are run by Tri Ubaya Bhakti (Truba) and the rest are individually managed (*Editor*, 4 July 1992). According to its treasurer, Yayasan Kartika Eka Paksi is used primarily for soldiers' welfare, especially for housing. It also subsidises ABRI University Ahmad Yani (in Bandung), and provides Lebaran (Muslim new year) and Christmas bonuses. The other armed services (Navy, Air Force, and Police) have similar arrangements (*Jakarta Post*, 1 October 1995).

Over time, as ABRI firms and foundations became more entrenched and successful, they became involved with other projects unrelated to military needs. The deepening involvement of military enterprises in nonmilitary businesses for pure profit was accomplished, in part, by the ability of high-ranking officers to use their positions as heads of civilian governmental bodies to facilitate their business activities by ensuring that their companies received the proper licenses, permits and bank loans. (However, it should be noted that the most reliable and explicit information on the use of ABRI *yayasan* funds is limited to soldiers' social welfare projects; there is no reliable information on the use of profits generated by the foundations for procurement of military hardware.)

During the 1960s and 1970s the military was also able to use its control of state firms such as the state oil company Pertamina and Bulog, the national logistics board which controlled rice and other commodities, to generate funding. However, since Pertamina's embarrassing financial collapse in the mid-1970s, ABRI's opportunity to raise funds through these high-profile state companies has been limited. Nevertheless, the *yayasan* continue to be an effective way to raise extra-budgetary revenue.

In addition to military control of key economic boards and the establishment of *yayasan*, high-ranking officers are routinely appointed as directors of both private firms and public enterprises. For example, in early 1995, army Major General Arie Sudewo, retired chief of strategic intelligence, became the president commissioner of PERURI (National Currency Company); army Major General Kuntara, retired chief of the army Strategic Commandos, became the chief commissioner of a cement factory, Indosemen Tunggal Prakarsa; army Major General Umar Said, retired commander of ABRI's expert staff, became the chief commissioner of Bank Bumi Daya; and army Major General Sugito, retired head of the army Strategic Command, was named as one of the commissioners of the major conglomerate Astra.

This situation eventually created a strong commercial orientation among the officer corps throughout all ranks (Muhaimin 1991, p. 238). Harold Crouch observes that officers swiftly developed an affinity for business:

> If, at the beginning, the officers were cornered to do some commercial work, then they adjusted themselves very quickly to the tasks... [M]any of them [came to] feel more comfortable in dealing with Chinese or foreign businessmen than leading the soldiers in the field. The commercial ethos spreads out very quickly among officers who are directly assigned to manage the Armed Forces' firms (Crouch 1986).

President Soeharto had personal experience in raising funds outside the official budget while he was chief of the Diponegoro territorial command in Central Java in the 1950s. Soeharto reviews this activity in his auto-biography, *Pikiran, Ucapan dan Tindakan Saya* [My Thoughts, Words, and Actions] (1989). One and a half decades later, when General Soeharto became the leader of the New Order, he faced the same problem — that is, the budget allocation for defence and security was too small. However, as president, Soeharto did not initiate a permanent increase in the military budget; rather, he continued to rely on the previous pattern of military finance.

The Debate over Self-Financing

Some ABRI leaders openly justify and advocate the military's involve-ment in the business economy. Lt. General Suyono, ABRI's chief of the general staff, declared that to do business is an urgent matter for the armed forces. He stated:

> As part of the nation, we (the armed forces) have the same opportunity to do business [as others]. Why should not ABRI be allowed to do business? We will be narrow-minded in the sense that we will not have an appropriate economic perspec-tive, if we do not do business. Moreover, in the future eco-nomics will dominate the world. We do not want to be small-minded. We have to move forward.... If we are not pre-pared, we will be left behind.... We must have a better eco-nomic perspective. A strong state must have a strong economy. A strong ABRI [alone] does not guarantee a strong state. (*Forum* 4, no. 14, [23 October 1995])

However, other senior members of the armed forces have severely criti-cized ABRI's economic activities. For example, retired General Hasnan Habib argues that individuals inappropriately use the military as a means of personal enrichment and for political power. This in turn, he believes, perpetuates feudalistic practices and retards the development of a profes-sional military (Habib 1990, p. xxvi).

The underlying question is whether ABRI can maintain its military doctrines, fighting readiness, and other defence and security functions when many of its officers are more comfortable leading a company than commanding troops. Retired Major General Subiyakto, former governor of the National Defence Institute (Lemhanas), noted sardonically that ABRI is now capable of any tasks *except* arranging a defence and security concept. In this view, for ABRI to function as an effective, modern, and professional military force it must concentrate more fully on its security functions and less on politics (*Simponi* 4, 10 October 1994).

In addition to the potential damage to officers' *esprit de corps* and the negative impact on military readiness and professionalism, a more immediate and direct consequence of the budget shortage is that most of ABRI's weapons are out of date. Based on data published by the International Institute for Strategic Studies (1995) in *The Military Balance 1994/1995*, much Indonesian military equipment dates from the 1940s, 1950s, or the 1960s. Nevertheless, the Indonesian military continues to give higher priority to the development requirements of the nation as a whole than to its own hardware needs. ABRI leaders consistently argue that national defence and security are best served by maintaining and increasing the prosperity of the entire nation.

CHANGING SOCIAL DYNAMICS AND ABRI'S ROLE AND MISSION

In recent years, criticisms have begun to be heard, particularly from the middle class,[3] directed at ABRI's institutionalized political and socio-economic roles. The major question raised in these criticisms is whether ABRI's "dual function" (*dwifungsi*), which has been the hallmark of ABRI's role in the New Order, is still relevant, or whether it should be adapted to a changing society.

The military's pervasive involvement in the nation's political and social affairs has its origins in ABRI's broad perception of its role and mission discussed at the beginning of this chapter. As a result, military officers hold positions as ministers, director generals of important departments, general secretaries, ambassadors, governors, mayors, subdistrict and village heads, as well as senior positions in public firms, state enterprises and private companies. Additionally, ABRI also dominates ostensibly civilian political and social organizations through military organizations such as FPPKI (Forum for Children of ABRI Members), Pemuda Pancamarga, and others. Although Golkar was led by a civilian (as of 1998), Minister of Information Harmoko, many of its regional functionaries were retired officers. For example, eighty per cent of district Golkar chiefs were retired officers, and out of the twenty-seven provincial Golkar heads, only two were not retired or active ABRI officers. Through numerous Golkar-affiliated organizations, such as KNPI (National Committee of Indonesian Youth), ABRI extends its reach deep into civil society.

This pervasive military presence, even in ostensibly civilian organizations, is increasingly being challenged, not only by members of the increasingly prosperous and numerous middle class but also from within ABRI itself. Prominent retired military leaders such as General Soemitro (former chief of the security command), Lt. General Sajidiman Surjohadoprodjo, Lt. General Ali Sadikin (former mayor of Jakarta), Lt. General Kharis Suhud (former Speaker of Parliament), and Lt. General Sembiring Meliala have all suggested that ABRI has become too deeply involved in the political process. Indirectly, President Soeharto himself suggested that ABRI should lessen its domination of civilian government positions, and he stated that it is time for ABRI to practice the attitude of *"tut wuri handayani"* ("to give guidance from behind").

The pressure on ABRI to reevaluate its dual function role is prompted by the convergence of two phenomena. One, already noted, is the growing assertiveness of Indonesia's middle class, particularly the intellectuals. This group demands that it should have a more prominent role in the political decision making process.

Second, there is a noticeable difference in public perceptions of the (now-retired) officers of the so-called "1945 Generation" who fought in the revolution, and the post-independence, academy-trained officers who now lead ABRI. National leadership by the 1945 Generation was accorded legitimacy by both civilian and military actors because of the key role of the armed forces in the revolution and subsequent national crises. But leadership by post-independence officers is increasingly seen as less valid because they lack direct links to the legitimizing experiences of the earlier period.

Additionally, the post-1945 officers have different professional orientations than their predecessors. This change in the values of the armed forces is captured in the following analysis by the prominent military historian Nugroho Notosusanto:

> From either formal or informal sources, we can conclude that there is a changing value system [in ABRI]... [T]hose who were born after the Independence War and brought up in relatively better conditions than the generation before... are more political, pragmatic and realistic. They are less idealistic and ideological. They tend to prefer *education fields* or other positions that will give more profit. (Nugroho 1991, p. 325)

Thus, while ABRI argues that its institutional duty is to guard the national ideology, many civilians now contend that they are as committed and patriotic as ABRI.

ABRI AND DEMOCRATIZATION

Will ABRI be able to accommodate the demands for greater democratization of Indonesian society that seem to be accompanying the development process, or will it come to be increasingly perceived simply as an authoritarian vested interest group? Internally, ABRI has embraced egalitarian principles that indicate a predisposition towards some aspects of political democracy. For example, ABRI does not differentiate between its members' regional origins, social status, race, religion, and other "exclusive" or "primordial" characteristics. Thus ABRI does harbour and cultivate some of the most fundamental values of a modern, open society — social tolerance and respect for diversity.

Additionally, ABRI officers and analysts point to two historical events in which ABRI declined opportunities to seize political power for itself. Following the independence struggle, the military had the power and opportunity to take over the government. Instead, ABRI left politics to the civilian politicians and a system of parliamentary democracy. Unfortunately, as the liberal democratic period of the early-to-mid 1950s was increasingly plagued by chaos and political turmoil, ABRI eventually concluded that the civilians had not exercised political authority well. Then, after the defeat of the attempted coup in 1965, ABRI could have retained power for itself alone (Soedjati 1980, p. 79). But it did not. Instead, ABRI initiated a dialogue which basically tried to develop a political format which would not threaten the nation's unity but was also democratic. What emerged from this process was agreement to maintain a constitutional and parliamentary framework but that ABRI would retain special political rights as a guarantor of national stability and that "primordial" politics would be prohibited.

For a variety of reasons, military representation in the cabinet has steadily declined over the years of the New Order, and the proportion of governorships filled by ABRI officers has also decreased significantly (see Chapter 4, Table 4.1). There were other indications of a restructuring of ABRI's role in national life. For example, in 1989 the former internal security agency KOPKAMTIB was replaced with the considerably less powerful Agency for Co-ordination of National Development Strategy

(Bakorstranas). The move in late 1995 to lower the number of armed forces members of the DPR from one hundred to seventy-five reduces ABRI's direct influence in the national legislature.

The real reasons for and significance of the changes up to 1998 are subject to some question. For example, ABRI argues that the precise number of ABRI representatives in Parliament is not crucial to ensure a stable political system. And of course ABRI continued to exercise major political influence both at the national and provincial levels, such as through control of the directorates for social and political affairs. But the changes that have taken place at least indicate that ABRI's position is not immutable and that there is a possibility of further evolution in its political role towards a more abstract position as guardian of the national ideology rather than pervasive involvement in day-to-day politics and governance.

PERSONNEL RECRUITMENT

For the long run, perhaps the most significant change in ABRI as an institution is in its personnel makeup and recruitment strategies. In the first two decades after independence, a career in ABRI was generally considered by young Indonesians as among the best channels through which to achieve professional and personal success. This is entirely understandable, as the range of professional options was extremely limited prior to the New Order. Becoming a military (or civilian) bureaucrat offered both status and reasonable economic benefits.

The perception of the armed forces as a desirable profession has changed since the 1950s. Economic growth has given society's youth vastly expanded professional and educational opportunities. Private enterprise increasingly offers prospects for interesting and well-paying careers. But did the explosion in career opportunities under the New Order actually reduce interest in military careers? The picture is not as clear-cut as one might expect. For one measure, we can look at the national military academy (AKABRI).

AKABRI was established in the late 1950s and became the major channel for recruiting and training the military's élite cadres. In the 1960s and 1970s, applicants to the academy included many of the best students in the country, and the competition for admission was quite stiff. Those who were accepted were young people with the highest intellectual achievements and in first-rate physical condition.

The sheer number of applicants for positions at remains quite large. However, in the 1980s and 1990s the relative quality of the AKABRI cadet candidates has not been sustained. Table 5.2 illustrates the quality of students who apply to AKABRI. It shows that, in two recent academic years, AKABRI applicants were generally those with middle to lower scores on the national standard academic measurement (NEM). While a standardized score does not give a full picture of the quality of individual applicants, it does provide an overall sense of the applicant pool and general trends. The data indicate that those with excellent NEM scores (higher than 50) in these two acceptance periods were about 200–300 out of 2,500 applicants. In other words, only approximately twelve per cent of the applicants scored in the highest possible range.

In addition to the increased attractiveness of civilian careers already mentioned, another factor which has influenced the decline in the number of top applicants for AKABRI is the dramatic improvement in the civilian universities and increasingly aggressive competition for good students. University recruitment strategies include identifying promising students while they are still in high school.

To increase the quality of AKABRI entrants, ABRI has recently established SMA Taruna Nusantara, an élite high school specifically designed

TABLE 5.2
Academic Qualifications of Candidates for the Indonesian Armed Forces Academy, Academic Years 1993/94 and 1994/95

Academic Year 1993/94			Academic Year 1994/95		
NEM*	Total	%	NEM	Total	%
25–29.99	19	1			
30–34.99	32	1			
35–39.99	1,049	43	35–37.99	48	2
			38–41.99	1,024	40
40–44.99	717	29	42–45.99	808	31
45–49.99	391	16	46–49.99	412	16
50–54.99	200	8	50–53.99	199	8
			54–57.99	73	3
55–67.99	58	2	58–59.99	9	0
			60–63.99	1	0
Total	2,458	100		2,574	100

Notes: *National Standard Academic Score.
Source: Armed Forces Academy Command Office (*Markas Komando AKABRI*).

to funnel exceptional candidates into the military academy. Also, for the academic year 1993/94, for the first time a minimum NEM score (of 35) was set as a requirement for applying to AKABRI. For 1994/95, the minimum score was increased to 38, and for 1995/96 to 42. The higher minimums will necessarily increase the overall quality of the applicant pool.

The family background of AKABRI applicants is also of interest. According to AKABRI data, between academic years 1990/91 and 1994/95, applicants from ABRI families made up 30–50 per cent of the total, while those from civil servant families were 22–28 per cent. (The ABRI percentage fell, while the civil servant number grew over the period.) Clearly, AKABRI admissions are dominated by children of military and civilian officials — nearly 70 per cent of the total throughout. Children of businessmen/private firm employees have been averaging only 5 to 18 per cent of total admissions, while those of farmers are running from 4 to 8 per cent.

Interestingly, in interviews, most senior officers assert that their children are not interested in applying to AKABRI. This is not inconsistent with the declining percentage of ABRI-background applicants, but it may also be that more of the current applicants are the children of middle to lower ranking members of the military rather than the highest ranking officers. This is somewhat speculative, however, and fuller studies are needed for a more thorough explanation.

ABRI has made efforts to meet the need for increasingly well-educated officers. AKABRI has established a policy that all graduates should earn at least a Bachelor's degree (Sarjana 1, or S1). To realize this plan, a co-operative agreement with Gadjah Mada University was established in June 1979. More recently General Wismoyo, chief of staff of the army from 1993 to 1995, instituted a requirement that in order to study at the Army Command and Staff College (SESKOAD) an officer must hold the S1 degree. This policy, however, prompted controversy within the army. Some officers considered it an effective way to increase the qualifications and technical skills of ABRI officers. Others argued that the new requirements would distract officers from their primary duties. In response to the controversy, Wismoyo's successor, General R. Hartono, cancelled the plan (*Kompas*, 6 April 1995).

CONCLUSION

ABRI has not benefited from economic growth in the most direct sense of increased military budgets, hardware, and improved soldier welfare. Rather, ABRI's budget has steadily decreased as a proportion of the national budget. However, ABRI leaders at all ranks and in all services have been able to cover much of the perceived revenue shortfall through various well-established means of non-official fund raising.

Five basic consequences arise from both the permanent "solution" to persistent budget shortfalls and from societal changes that are pressuring ABRI to reduce its political role. First, both troop commanders and ABRI's senior leaders have created networks of personal relations with business-men. These relationships have created economic and political patronage networks which, in the long term, contribute to skewed and unhealthy national economic development, including pure profit seeking activities by military entrepreneurs. These business activities have also firmly em-bedded officers in civilian political and economic structures, boards, and agencies, which in turn deepen ABRI's non security-related involvements in national life.

Second, the business involvement of ABRI's leaders and troop com-manders in the rapidly growing civilian economy may undermine ABRI's ability to serve as the guardian of national unity and the national ideology. ABRI may become just another interest group which is satisfied only by sharing power with the government, rather than remaining above the fray and guaranteeing general political stability, as was the original intention of General A.H. Nasution's concept of the Middle Way. ABRI may well retain its institutional cohesiveness solely in order to maintain a strong bargaining position against other players in national politics and entrepre-neurial activities.

Third, the procurement, maintenance, and knowledgeable use of mod-ern weapons, which is a requirement for all professional militaries, is severely hampered under current conditions. Most ABRI equipment, par-ticularly in the Army, is World War II, Korean War, and Vietnam War vintage hardware. The Navy's condition is similar, despite recent ship purchases. Only the Air Force has been able to maintain a relatively modern inventory of equipment.

Fourth, the rising assertiveness of groups which can be loosely catego-rized as part of Indonesia's growing middle class has triggered demands for more democracy and political openness. Specifically, ABRI is increas-ingly faced with demands that it withdraw from day-to-day political activity and end its practice of dominating ostensibly civilian institutions. Some changes have been made in ABRI's structures and political involvement, including the agreement to reduce the number of ABRI seats in the DPR and declining numbers of military appointees to high positions in the civil government. However, there is no indication that ABRI's political domination has been significantly weakened by the changes that have taken place to date (1998).

Fifth, ABRI's recruitment of new personnel has been affected by the nation's economic growth which creates more promising and lucrative professional and occupational choices for young Indonesians. Although it is difficult to prove a direct causal link, it appears that the ability of AKABRI to recruit the best and brightest of Indonesian society has declined over the past decade. At the same time, the skill requirements for a modern military are constantly increasing; ABRI has made some efforts to respond to this need by raising academic standards, but the results thus far are inconclusive.

Notes

[1] On ABRI's perceptions of its role in national life, see also Said 1987 and Nugroho 1991.

[2] On military involvement in business, see also Robison 1986, especially pp. 250–70.

[3] "Middle class" is used here to refer in general to the growing numbers of people who, because of their educational levels, professional occupations, or income, are increasingly distinguishable from the rest of society (see Heryanto 1993).

6

Economic Growth and the Performance of Political Parties

M. Djadijono

This chapter examines the influence on political parties in Indonesia of the economic growth that has occurred during the New Order period. The principal question is whether the results of this rapid economic development have improved the performance of the political parties in developing democracy and in carrying out their political functions.[1]

The political parties in question are the Development Unity Party (Partai Persatuan Pambangunan — PPP), the Indonesian Democratic Party (Partai Demokrasi Indonesia — PDI), and the government-sponsored political organization, Golongan Karya (or Golkar, meaning "Functional Groups").[2] The PPP and the PDI are the products of the government-instigated amalgamation in 1973, which merged four former Islamic parties into the PPP and three nationalist and two Christian parties into the PDI.

To attempt to answer the principal question we look at four specific factors. The first is the process of leadership selection and internal management of the parties — the degree to which this process reflects the desires of the party membership. Second is the characteristics of the programmes that the parties put forward, looked at from the perspective of whether and how these programmes respond to the growing demands and political awareness of the public that result from economic development. The third factor is the degree to which the parties' activities in the Parliament (People's Representative Assembly or DPR) reflect the aspirations and demands of the society. And the fourth is the level of financial autonomy of the respective political parties in carrying out their political functions, rights and responsibilities. Finally, to the extent that economic growth has not yet had a significant influence on the political parties, we need to consider what might be the causal factors involved and what are the prospects for the future.

LEADERSHIP SELECTION AND INTERNAL PARTY MANAGEMENT

By Indonesian law and regulation, the leadership of a political party is completely determined by, and is under the authority of the organization involved.[3] The regulation on parties states that, "The leadership of political parties and Golkar will be determined by the respective organizations in accordance with their constitutions and bylaws."[4] Nevertheless, in fact the process of leadership selection for political parties is heavily influenced by the government.

The underlying motivation for this government involvement is the rationale that economic development can be more successfully achieved under conditions of limited political participation by the public. According to this logic, if the recruitment of political party leadership was left totally to the wishes of the members of the organizations, then leadership might well emerge which was not in accord with the course and interests of the government. There would also be more of an opening for critics of the government to disturb its economic programme, and the result would only be to create continual confusion. As a result, the leadership of the New Order government has preferred to ensure that the reins of the political system are in its hands, and that the political party leaders are of the same mind and can be persuaded to compromise and form a coalition oriented towards economic development (Mas'oed 1990, pp. 124, 126–28).

This has been the pattern from very early in the New Order period. As William Liddle (1992, pp. 197–98) has observed, the government was deeply involved in choosing the principal party leaders prior to the first general election under the New Order in 1971, and then defeated the parties decisively in that election. It then forced the parties to merge into the two new parties, the PPP and the PDI. (The government simultaneously took other steps to ensure that partisan activities were minimised between elections. These included a prohibition on party offices or activities below the district capital [kabupaten] and municipality [kota madya] level.)

Government intervention in the selection of political party leadership continued. The following cases are illustrative.

Indonesian Democratic Party (PDI)

The government opposed and rejected the action of the PDI's Fourth Congress in Medan in July 1993 to re-elect (by acclamation) Drs Soerjadi as the general chairman of the PDI's Central Leadership Council (Dewan

Pimpinan Pusat — DPP) for the period 1993–98. Minister of Internal Affairs Yogie Suardi Memed, after a meeting with the president, stated that because the term of the DPP for 1986–93 had ended in May 1993 and the party had not chosen a new DPP before that time, the leadership of the DPP was vacant (*Kompas*, 4 August 1993). The minister declared that there was a need to form a caretaker DPP for the PDI pending the selection of a DPP through an Extraordinary Congress, whose organization, including financing, would be fully supported by the government (*Merdeka*, 2 August 1993; *Suara Karya*, 27 August 1993; *Media Indonesia*, 4 September 1993).

At the subsequent Extraordinary Congress, held in Surabaya 2–6 December 1993, there were also clear indications of government intervention in the formation of the new leadership council, especially in the selection of the new general chairman. Several delegates publicly stated that their groups had been asked by the government apparatus in their regions to vote for the candidate for general chairman preferred by the government. They had agreed to the request, but then at the congress they withdrew their agreement, on the grounds that only the congress had the authority to determine the leadership. In the voting, Megawati Sukarnoputri (daughter of Indonesia's first president) received a majority, but the Congress ended in a stalemate. This was because the meeting rooms were closed and locked, preventing further sessions. Ultimately the Surabaya police chief announced that the permit to conduct the congress had expired.[5]

Subsequently, a National Conference (Munas) was scheduled to resolve the leadership crisis. The Department of Home Affairs announced that the conference would be held in Bogor, on 22–23 December. However, the Regional Leadership Councils (DPD) of the party threatened not to attend this conference if it was not held in Jakarta (*Merdeka* and *Republika*, 21 December 1993). Following a meeting between the commander of the Jakarta Military District, Major General Hendropriyono, and the Home Affairs Minister, the government agreed that the conference could be held in Jakarta (*Republika*, 22 December 1993)

Nevertheless, there was again pervasive government intervention in the Jakarta conference. A director of the armed forces intelligence organization BAIS, Brigadier General Agum Gumelar, and the Jakarta Military District's intelligence chief, Colonel Zacky Anwar, as well as Jakarta commander Hendropriyono were directly involved (*Republika* and *Merdeka*, 22 December 1993). The daily newspaper *Media Indonesia* (23 December 1993) reported that the leadership selection process was further complicated by a dispute between Megawati and the armed forces facilitators over the inclusion of members of the caretaker council among the formateurs of the conference. The armed forces facilitators ultimately convinced Megawati that the inclusion of a caretaker would not endanger her, and she was confirmed as the new party leader.

Government intervention in PDI leadership matters continued after the conference. A struggle over the formation of the Regional Leadership Council (DPD) for East Java occupied the party from July 1994 to December 1995. The provincial government refused to accept the DPD chairman designated by the party's Central Leadership Council (DPP), a rival provincial committee emerged, and East Java Governor Basofi Sudirman issued a call for a meeting of provincial party officials to resolve the dispute. The governor's involvement was supported by the Department of Home Affairs (*Republika*, *Media Indonesia*, and *Suara Karya*, 25 October 1994).

The prolonged conflict over selection of provincial party leadership in East Java and elsewhere eventually provided the rationale for holding a special party conference in June 1996, convened by opponents of Megawati with the clear support of the central government. Megawati was removed as general chairman, and the former chairman, Drs Soerjadi, was installed in her place. Megawati's supporters refused to accept this action, or to turn over the national party headquarters in Jakarta to the Soerjadi group. The forcible takeover of the headquarters building by pro-Soerjadi elements on 27 July, as government security forces stood by, precipitated a short-lived but destructive riot and a subsequent government crackdown on a variety of political opposition elements.

Development Unity Party (PPP)

The PPP also has not escaped government interference. One example was the removal of Dr H.J. Naro as general chairman of the PPP Central Leadership Council (DPP) at the party's Second Conference in 1989. Among other things, the cause was Naro's indication of his willingness to be nominated as vice president of the country during the 1988 session of the People's Consultative Assembly. Even though he withdrew his name before the voting was conducted, this break with the tradition of leaving the choice of vice presidential candidates to the president damaged Naro's standing with the government. The new general chairman elected at the 1989 conference was H. Ismail Hasan Metareum SH, identified with the "moderate conservative" group in the party. At the party's Third Conference, in 1994, the moderate conservative group appeared to further consolidate its position, at the expense of the other two factions, the traditional reformists led by Matori Abdul Djalil, and the radical reformers led by Ir. Sri Bintang Pamungkas. The latter were vocally critical of the government and the current political pattern (Ali 1994). (As noted in Chapter 3, Pamungkas was subsequently expelled from Parliament by the PPP parliamentary leadership, clearly at the behest of the government.)

Another example of government intervention in PPP affairs occurred during the party's Third Regional Conferences (Muswil) in 1995. In North Sumatra the regional government and security authorities denied permission for the holding of the regional conference, due to competition between two leadership groups within the party each of whom wanted to hold their own conference (*Republika*, 12 May 1995; *Media Indonesia*, 1 July 1995). The head of the provincial social and political directorate considered that the split had occurred because of budgetary irregularities. Party General Chairman Metareum reacted to this statement as a deeper intervention in the PPP, since budgetary matters are supposed to be a purely internal affair of the party (*Suara Pembaruan*, 5 July 1995).

Golkar

As for Golkar, government control of its political vehicle is almost self-evident. Selection of Golkar's Central Leadership Council (DPP) is controlled via the Council of Founders (Dewan Pembina). The president is the head of the Dewan Pembina, and every cabinet minister is automatically a member even if their knowledge and understanding of Golkar may be very limited.

The role of the Dewan Pembina in the selection of the leadership of Golkar's DPP was clearly demonstrated at Golkar's Fifth National Conference (Munas V), held in Jakarta on 20–25 October 1993. The nomination of H. Harmoko as general chairman and Ary Mardjono as secretary general for 1993–98 was announced by H. Munawir Sjadzali M.A., the daily leadership co-ordinator of the Dewan Pembina's presidium, in the third plenary session on 22 October. As of that time, most of the representatives of the Regional Leadership Councils (DPD) who had spoken had only mentioned general criteria for candidates for general chairman (*Pelita* and *Suara Karya*, 22 October 1993; *Kompas*, 23 October 1993; *Suara Pembaruan*, 24 October 1993). Many participants were critical of the Dewan Pembina's pre-emption of the normal process, and some characterized it as hampering democracy (*Kompas*, 23 and 24 October 1993; *Suara Pembaruan* 23 October 1993). A former head of the armed forces' social and political section (*Kassospol*), Lt. General Sugiarto, commented that if democracy within organizations was conducted in this manner, then it would be best in Indonesia not to talk too much about democracy (*Kompas*, 24 October 1993).

Rationale and Reactions

Retired General Sumitro, the former head of the security command (KOPKAMTIB), offered the following comment on this phenomenon of government selection of political party leadership:

> The socio-political and security obstacles resulting from the failed PKI coup and the process of de-*Nasakomization*,[6] together with concern for stability, led to a process whereby the socio-political growth and life of society were guided from above (by government). ... [C]ontinuous direction from above eliminates the autonomy of socio-political organizations that constitutes the soul of the practice and life of democracy. Ultimately there occurs a process of bureaucratization of socio-political forces. Indeed this process affects all social organizations including professional organizations. (Soemitro 1991, p. 58)

Similarly, the former vice chairman of the DPR/MPR, Major General Saiful Sulun, in a discussion at the Institute for Strategic Studies of Indonesia (Lembaga Pengkajian Strategis Indonesia — LPSI) in Jakarta on 18 September 1995, remarked that: "... each time there is a congress/conference/discussion meeting, there is always intervention in determining the management. The effort is made to ensure that the leadership of the political parties and Golkar consists of 'sweet children.' If 'naughty children' emerge, continuous problems are created" (*Kompas*, 19 September 1995).

Thus it can be said that government involvement in the life of political parties has been ubiquitous. The rationale has been to maintain stability in order to ensure the continuation of economic development. On the other hand, the public and party membership, whose standard of living, educational level, and political awareness have risen, are showing signs of disagreement with the pattern of government intervention in political recruitment.

One illustration of this can be seen in the case of the PDI. At its Third Congress in Jakarta in 1986, the delegates simply agreed to turn over the arrangement of the composition and management of the party's Central Leadership Council to the government. By contrast, at the Fourth Congress in Medan and the Extraordinary Congress in Surabaya in 1993, the delegates wanted to determine the leadership of their party themselves. A more nuanced disagreement with the system of government-determined leadership selection was apparent during the preparations for Golkar's Fifth National Conference in Jakarta in October 1993, when the armed forces mounted a concerted (albeit ultimately unsuccessful) effort to oppose the selection of a civilian as the new leader of Golkar. Thus a gap has occurred: on the one hand the society is increasingly aware of its political rights and interests, but on the other hand the government still desires to apply the old methods of forming party leadership.

The objectives of the government leadership are probably still the same, that is to ensure government control of the parties and party support for the government's policies. However, the danger in this approach is that the party leaders, and the political parties themselves, whose role should be to help form and oversee the government on behalf of society, just become instruments of the government, and the rest of society is left without a voice.

CHARACTERISTICS OF PARTY PROGRAMMES

One means of comparing the programmes of the political parties is to look at the themes of their election campaigns, in which the parties directly compete with each other to gain the support of the voters (Huckshorn 1984, p. 130; Kayden 1978, p. 6). This function of election campaigns is explicitly incorporated and endorsed in the Indonesian election law. Further, government regulations also stipulate the equality and comparability of the three parties in election campaigning.[7]

This section considers the characteristics of the themes and campaign programmes of the three contesting parties in the general election of 1992. Among other things, the 1992 general election was conducted at a time of increasing demands for more genuine democratization. Indicators included optimism over democratization in global politics, greater awareness of issues of basic human rights within Indonesian society, the growth of an attitude of constructive criticism within the society, and promises of greater openness from the government (Karim 1991, p. 38). Given these social dynamics, it was not surprising that the 1992 election was seen as a possible turning point for political change in Indonesia. The political parties were expected to be major actors in this process of change.

The question for consideration here is to what extent the political parties seized on these political dynamics and the desires of the society for change, as reflected in the themes of their 1992 election campaigns. We will examine the impressions of observers as well as the special characteristics of each party's programme and approach. Against this background we will then briefly assess the outcome of the election, in terms of the numbers of seats in the national parliament won by each party.

1992 Election Programmes — General Impressions

A number of observers have stated that the party programmes put forward in the 1992 campaign were not greatly different from the issues they had pursued in the previous campaigns. (An exception is M. Riza Sihbudi [1988], who noted that the PDI campaign did contain a new theme in its call for the formation of a "shadow cabinet".) In other words, the parties' programmes appeared to be basically their old programmes packaged in new forms (Ambong 1988, pp. 75–77, 80; *Suara Karya*, 11 May 1992; Haris 1988, p. 91; Sihbudi 1988, pp. 115–16). Harry Tjan Silalahi (1995, p. 32) further concluded that, overall, the objective of the campaign as a means of political education and offering of alternative programmes by the parties was not achieved, because the content of the programmes of the three parties was basically the same, with the differences only found in the emphasis in their "prefatory sentences".

Nevertheless, it is possible to identify certain distinctive characteristics in the campaign themes of the PPP, Golkar, and the PDI.

The PPP

The PPP's self-image remains that of a political party that works to advance the interests of a certain religion, Islam. At a meeting of campaign personnel in Bogor on 24 April 1992, it was explicitly decided that the PPP would continue to use the language of religion (*Media Indonesia*, 25 April 1992). This emphasis was reflected in numerous subsequent statements during the campaign by PPP spokesmen.

For example, Ahmad Sumadi stated that the national leaders must be Muslims; he said this was a logical position for the PPP because it was a fusion of Islamic parties (*Media Indonesia*, 20 May 1992). Dr Ir. Sri

Bintang Pamungkas said the PPP supported having more than one candidate for president, but that the president must be one who defends the Islamic community (*Angkatan Bersenjata* and *Media Indonesia*, 30 May 1992). Mrs Aisyah Amini SH said that the PPP desired that there not be even a single law that hindered citizens from practising the freedom of their religion, and that the PPP wants schools to be given a holiday for the Ramadan fasting month (*Angkatan Bersenjata* and *Suara Pembaruan*, 30 May 1992). Hamzah Haz, campaigning in Bantul, Yogyakarta on 22 May 1992, said that the PPP would increase religious study as well as general studies, from primary school through university level (*Suara Karya*, 23 May 1992). Sumarno Syafei stated that the PPP would endeavour to have the *pesantren* (Islamic religious school) model and religious education included in the Broad Outlines of State Policy (GBHN) so that Islam would be imbedded in the Indonesian education system (*Pelita*, 26 May 1992).

Otherwise, the PPP has presented itself as a political organization which is conservative and defends the status quo. This was reflected in its nomination of President Soeharto for a further term of office from 1993 to 1998. Its rationale was that President Soeharto had succeeded in building the Indonesian nation and country. Although there still were some shortcomings such as asymmetries in the social, economic and political fields, these shortcomings should be resolved by the president over the next five years.[8]

Golkar

As an "experienced" election participant which had won four general elections under the New Order, in the 1992 campaign Golkar strongly projected the image of a party that wanted to maintain the status quo. This was apparent in many statements of Golkar leaders and functionaries.

For example, Golkar General Chairman Wahono, in a campaign speech on Indonesian television explained that, "The system is in place, the structure has been formed, the mechanism is running. We now have all of the equipment that is necessary for the growth and flowering of Pancasila Democracy.... Because of this Golkar is continually developing the political system that exists" (*Kompas*, 14 May 1992). H. Harmoko stated that Golkar will continue to defend the current political order, that is the simplified party system with two political parties and Golkar plus the dual function of the armed forces. This, he said, is because the current political format suits the spirit of the New Order, in accordance with Pancasila and the 1945 Constitution. Therefore Golkar has no interest in adopting any other political format (*Angkatan Bersenjata*, 11 May 1992).

As a status quo party, Golkar also appeared to be basically reactive to the thoughts put forward by other parties, rather than initiating proposals of its own. For example, Golkar spokesman Sudomo made a number of statements responding to suggestions and criticisms that arose during the campaign. In response to proposals that a limit should be set on the number of terms that a president could serve, he said that Golkar holds to the 1945 Constitution concerning the term of office of the president, which is five years with the possibility of re-election. He added that Golkar firmly rejects the idea of changing the 1945 Constitution provisions on the term of the president, but if there is a desire to include the terms of office of the president and vice president in a decision of the People's Consultative Assembly (MPR), then Golkar would agree provided that this was based on a consensus (*Media Indonesia*, 15 May 1992). On another subject, he denied suggestions that Indonesian democracy is sick, asserting that the fact that there are regular general elections demonstrates that democracy is not sick. He pointed out that in the Broad Outlines of State Policy there is a statement that the realization of democracy must be strengthened, but said this does not mean that Indonesian democracy is sick or weak, only that it is challenged in an era and a world that is increasingly broad and complex (*Suara Pembaruan*, 15 May 1992). He also rejected the criticism that national development is only enjoyed by a small group of people (*Angkatan Bersenjata*, 15 May 1992). Similarly, Golkar spokesman Drs Moerdiono rejected as highly unrealistic and irresponsible a proposal that twenty-five per cent of the budget should be allocated to education (*Suara Karya*, 27 May 1992).

The PDI

Unlike the two other parties, the PDI has seen itself as a political party that strongly desires to make changes in the atmosphere and life of national politics, both at the operational and constitutional levels. This was one of the fundamental positions of the PDI's 1992 election manifesto approved at its leadership meeting (*Rapim*) in Bogor on 9–12 April 1992, and one of the points emphasised by its campaign spokesmen.

For example, General Chairman Drs Soerjadi stated that the PDI wished to play a role in bringing about change. Desirable changes included establishing a limit of two terms in the presidency after 1993, making the economic system more equitable, and changing the structure and functioning of the Parliament so that it can be more active by changing the rules of order which have shackled the parliament up to the present (*Tempo*, 16 May 1992).

The theme of change was also reflected in the statement of PDI General Secretary Nico Daryanto in a televised campaign speech in which he said that the PDI desired to bring about changes in a constitutional manner at the operational level, especially where there have been deviations (*Kompas*, 17 May 1992). Similarly, Fatimah Achmad SH in a campaign speech in Palembang on 18 May said that the idea of change reflects the constitutional mandate because the 1945 Constitution provides that changes can be made every five years (*Suara Karya*, 20 May 1992; *Suara Pembaruan*, 22 May 1992).

Impact of Party Programmes on the Election Outcome

As in all previous elections under the New Order, Golkar won the overwhelming majority of votes and of the 400 parliamentary seats contested in the 1992 general election (the other 100 seats being filled by appointed members from the armed forces.) However, the modest differences in the outcome from the previous election did appear to demonstrate an increasing desire for change. The PDI, which clearly offered a programme of change, gained greater voter support and an increase in its seats in the DPR from 40 in the 1987 election to 56 in 1992. The PPP remained almost constant, gaining one seat from 61 to 62. Golkar, the most clearly conservative and status-quo oriented party, suffered a decline from 299 to 282 seats. Although far from conclusive, these changes in the electoral standing of the parties may have reflected the results of societal changes due to economic growth.[9]

THE PARTIES AND THE PARLIAMENT

Another way of looking at the performance of political parties is through the role of the Parliament. Parliament is the arena in which the political parties compete to make their visions of the aspirations and demands of the people reflected in general government policy. Thus the parliament can be seen as an extension of the performance of the political parties.

The principal functions of the parliament are the right to propose laws, to exercise initiative and oversight of government policies through the right to ask the president for information, to conduct research, and to express opinions. However, in many circles it is said that the parliament cannot yet carry out its role and functions in an optimal way. Isbrodroini Suyanto comments:

> It can be said that the power of the Pancasila Democracy parliament to supervise the executive hardly exists, because of the makeup of its membership, in which only the PDI and PPP factions are relatively free from the government but they do not have the power to face the strength of Golkar plus the 100 appointed members who support the government. Also, the deliberative mechanism certainly gives more benefit to the majority, which in this case is an instrument of the executive. (Suyanto 1991, p. 182)

Indeed, Evendhy M. Siregar (1992, p. 64) points out that approximately eighty per cent of the members of parliament consist of government officials or retired officials. It can be expected that these members will feel awkward or hesitant in meetings with the government, the more so with the agencies with which they are associated as officials and subordinates.

The parliamentary right to take the initiative in proposing legislation is very rarely exercised. Indeed, under the parliaments elected during the New Order period (in 1971, 1977, 1982, 1987, and 1992) there has not been a single case in which parliament has initiated a draft law (see Chapter 3, Table 3.1). One major obstacle in this regard is the parliamentary rules of order. According to the rules of order, to propose a draft law by parliamentary initiative requires the support of twenty members, and these members must represent more than one party or fraction.[10] By contrast, during the period of Guided Democracy (which is now so widely criticised), the mechanism of proposing laws by parliamentary initiative only required the signatures of ten members and did not say that they must come from more than one faction.[11]

Thus it is difficult to say that economic growth has had any significant impact to date on increasing the role of political parties in the national parliament.

POLITICAL PARTY AUTONOMY: THE FINANCIAL FACTOR

The final measure of change in political parties caused by the impact of economic growth is autonomy — the degree to which a political party possesses the freedom and capability to produce its own views and actions independent of other people or groups (Salim 1991, pp. 31–32; Alamudi 1991, pp. 4–5). In the Indonesian political system, the autonomy of political parties (including Golkar) is mandated by various laws and regulations. The Broad Outlines of State Policy (GBHN) passed by the People's Consultative Assembly in 1993 stipulates that, "In the framework of political development, the capability, quality and autonomy of social and political organizations must be continuously raised" (Decision No. II/MPR/1993).

The problem of autonomy as it applies to leadership selection and party management has already been considered. Here we consider the issue of funding.

From the perspective of financing the activities of the organization, Golkar has no problems whatsoever, while for the PPP and the PDI this is a big problem. Golkar's ample financing was openly acknowledged by its general chairman for 1983–88, Sudharmono SH, in his report to the Fourth National Congress of Golkar in Jakarta 20–25 October 1988:

> ... Funds gathered by the Head of the Dewan Pembina of the Dana Abadi Karya Bhakti Foundation from aid and contributions from members, cadres and supporters of Golkar clearly was sufficiently large, so that from the interest alone we could assist the Central Golkar organization and the regional organizations at both Level I and Level II each month in carrying out their activities. In addition, in conducting the last election campaign (1987) the Central Leadership Council (DPP) carried out fund-raising from members, business, and donors the results of which have been very encouraging. After these contributions were used efficiently and effectively for campaign purposes both at the centre and in the regions, there was still some left over.

On the other hand, the PPP and PDI suffered a shortage of funds. They have depended for funding of their organizations on dues from party members who sit in legislative institutions and the Supreme Advisory Council, and also on assistance from the president which is channelled through the State Secretariat in the amount of Rp7.5 million per month. To finance the holding of their conferences or congresses, they are almost completely dependent on contributions from the government (Lay 1994a). Thus the Third Conference of the PPP in Jakarta (29 August –

1 September 1994), which was estimated to cost Rp1.5 billion, was primarily funded through government assistance. PPP General Chairman Ismail Hasan Metareum SH argued that this is the way it should be. "The conference should be funded by the state in the same way as the state funds the Congress and National Conference of PDI and the National Conference of Golkar" (*Media Indonesia*, 14 July 1994). Conference co-ordinator Hamzah Haz, however, stated that in order to overcome its general funding problems, the PPP would open a bank account so that those who wished to donate funds could transfer them to that account (*Media Indonesia*, 15 July 1994).

The PDI also faces funding difficulties. Its Fourth Congress in Medan in July 1993, its Extraordinary Congress in Surabaya in December 1993, and its National Conference in Jakarta in December 1993 all received funding assistance from the government. The Medan conference cost Rp800 million, of which Rp600 million was government assistance; the Surabaya meeting cost Rp1.125 billion, with Rp900 million of government aid; and the Jakarta conference was completely funded by the government (*Republika*, 23 and 25 July 1994).

Manuel Kaisiepo, in an article in the daily *Kompas* (1 August 1994) entitled "Uang dan Politik: masalah sumber dana Parpol" ("Money and Politics: the problem of funding sources for political parties"), wrote the following:

> In contrast to Golkar, funding limits are a major problem which has been continuously confronted by the PPP and PDI from their founding in the 1970s up to the present. The funding problem has become more prominent in each general election campaign. In the campaign of 1992, the three participating political organizations received government assistance of Rp250 million each, and another Rp7.5 million in operational funds contributed by the State Secretariat. For the PPP and the PDI, these were their only sources of funds because they do not have their own funding sources.... This situation was clearly different for Golkar: in the 1992 campaign Golkar spent tens of billions of rupiah. From the deposits inherited from the previous Central Leadership Council Golkar had Rp7 billion, supplemented by funds from the Dana Abadi Karya Bhakti Foundation of Rp14 billion, as well as contributions from businessmen which totalled no small amount (one dinner party

in the run-up to the 1992 campaign succeeded in raising as much as Rp50 billion).

Impact of Economic Growth

Logically, with successful economic development the political parties which gain the most financial benefit as a result of development should be able to become more independent. Nevertheless, in Indonesia at this time, this is not happening.

Golkar clearly has benefited from the results of development and economic growth, as indicated by its lack of difficulty in funding its activities. However, it does not appear to enjoy any significant degree of autonomy. Golkar is intimately attached to the leadership of the central and regional executives — the president, ministers who are on its Dewan Pembina, and governors, district heads (Bupati) and mayors who are appointed as heads of its advisory councils. In elections, the leadership of the armed forces and the government bureaucracy, who supposedly should stand above all groups, have always in fact worked for victory by Golkar.[12]

On the other hand, the two non-ruling political parties, which as reflected in their minimal financial conditions have benefited less from the results of development and economic growth, seem more able and willing than Golkar to speak out and to develop and advocate fresh ideas aimed at producing a more democratic political climate. This is also despite outside intervention including continuous interference by the executive in their leadership. For example, in 1995 PPP General Chairman Metareum made a public statement that the political parties had been sidelined and crushed. Minister of Home Affairs Yogie commented that the chairman "may have been sick" when he made that statement, whereupon PPP cadres demanded that Yogie apologize for insulting their party's leader (*Kompas*, 13 and 18 September 1995; *Media Indonesia*, 14 and 16 September 1995). The PPP also publicly threatened not to participate in the 1997 election if there were still fraud and injustice such as had occurred in previous elections (*Media Indonesia*, 29 November 1995).

The thrust for autonomy within the PDI was seen in the courage of the PDI delegates in choosing Megawati Sukarnoputri as their general chairman for 1993–98, despite "sponsor's instructions" from external forces to select another candidate. It was also demonstrated in the stubborn resistance to the subsequent efforts to undermine Megawati's leadership, even though the campaign against Megawati ultimately succeeded.

GROWTH, PARTIES, AND POLITICS: INDICATORS AND PROGNOSIS

Economic growth and development did not appear to have resulted in any significant increase in the role of political parties in the development of democracy or in translating their own visions of the political interests of the public into government policy. Golkar, which has benefited greatly from development in financial terms, is still not capable of playing a role as a democratizing agent. As previously described, Golkar clearly is a conservative party that is not comfortable with change. By contrast, the two opposition political parties, which have benefited less from the results of economic growth, have nevertheless had the courage to propose political concepts which would lead to a more real democracy, but they lack the power to realize these concepts.

The principal cause of the lack of power of the parties (including Golkar) to play an independent political role is excessive government interference in their internal affairs. This includes intervention in the selection of their leadership as well as tight screening of candidates for Parliament by the government through the mechanism of special (security) reviews. The parties are further weakened by the prohibition on organizing at the village level, so that it is very difficult for them to reach out to the people at the grass roots. In practice, the government (executive) apparatus controls the operation of the political process throughout the country, through the designation of the Minister of Home Affairs and the province heads as the overseers of politics.

Because the three formal political organizations do not or cannot fully reflect the political dynamics of the society, the public is finding other channels of political expression. People whose interests are harmed or whose rights are violated make their complaints more often to the National Commission for Basic Human Rights or through the special post office box established in 1988 by then Vice President Sudharmono than to the political parties and Golkar.[13]

Another result has been the appearance of a number of new, quasi-political organizations. These include: Association of Indonesian Moslem Intellectuals (Ikatan Cendekiawan Muslim Indonesia — ICMI), Indonesian Christian Participation (Partisipasi Kristen Indonesia — Parkindo), the Association of Pancasila Development Intellectuals (Persatuan Cendekiawan Pembangunan Pancasila — PCPP), the National Association (Persatuan Nasional or "PNI baru"), the United Council of the Indonesian Moslem Community (Majelis Syarikat Ummat Muslim Indonesia or "Masyumi baru"), and the Foundation for National Harmony and

Brotherhood (Yayasan Kerukunan Persaudaraan Kebangsaan — YKPK) (Suara Pembaruan, 29 December 1995). Dr Riswandha Imawan of Gadjah Mada University in Yogyakarta has described these organizations as providing an alternative to the powerlessness of the formal political actors, and has said that their position is becoming stronger, parallel with the strengthening of civil society and basic human rights (*Kompas*, 6 January 1996). Suggestions have even been made concerning the formation of new political parties.[14]

A final, and potentially most significant, alternative channel of political expression is the increasing resort by the public to direct action. This has been most visible in the urban areas, in the form of labour strikes and demonstrations at the representative bodies and the offices of government departments, governors, *bupati*, etc. (Djadijono 1993*b*). But it has appeared in the rural areas as well. The symptoms can be seen for example in the willingness of village people to protest deviations in the process of electing village heads in various Indonesian villages in 1993. The forms of protest have also varied. Complaints have been made to *Bupati*, heads of district social and political affairs offices, and provincial parliaments. There have even been some instances of violent actions, such as throwing stones at the home of a sub-district head (*camat*) or election committee members (Djadijono 1993*a*). And there have also been incidents in which local people directly confronted the state security forces. (Table 6.1 describes a number of such incidents during 1995 — well before the more widely reported wave of violence around the country starting in mid-1996.)

Clearly, the inadequate functioning of the political parties needs to be remedied. One fundamental requirement is revision of the basic legislation and regulations governing general elections, the legislative structure, the political parties and regional administration,[15] in order to make the process more democratic and to allow an increased role and function for the parties. Such reforms are also essential if the public is to have increased faith in the parties. However, whether and how far these proposals are realized very much depends on the political will of the government, because the government apparatus became the most dominant and determining political actor in Indonesia during the New Order period.

TABLE 6.1
Cases of Public Confrontation with State Security Authorities, 1995

No.	Event	Cause	Source
1	Dozens of workers of P.T. Walet Kencana Perkasa, Surabaya, demonstrate on 10 January at the Rungkut police station demanding the release of two arrested colleagues.	Two workers from the company had been detained on 19 January, accused of inciting workers at the Bagyon insecticide factory on 15 January.	*Kompas,* 23 Jan. 1995
2	Hundreds of workers from a department store in Jember, East Java, complained to the national armed forces commander and the national defence command about the Jember district military command.	The district military command was considered to have intimidated the workers of the store who were in a dispute with the company, by calling 25 workers' representatives to the district military office. The summons was signed by the district commander on 30 June.	*Republika,* 4 July 1995
3	The police chief of the Pademangan Sector, North Jakarta, was killed by a passenger in a *bajaj* mini-taxi on 14 July.	A traffic dispute.	*Kompas,* 17 July 1995
4	Six policemen were seized by members of the public in the Glodok area of Jakarta on 26 August, accused of looting.	The policemen had entered a house without a permit and damaged it. They claimed to be investigating gambling, but had no orders and were not from units responsible for gambling investigations.	*Media Indonesia,* 7–9 Sept. 1995; *Kompas,* 29 Aug. 1995
5	A subdistrict police official in N. Lampung Kabupaten was accused by 19 of 25 village heads in the subdistrict of acting arbitrarily. The village heads asked the province legislation to transfer the official.	The official seized a motor vehicle at a repair shop, searched houses and confiscated motor vehicles without permission. A murder-robbery case had been shelved, but money and a motor-cycle from the robbery had been kept at the police office.	*Suara Karya, Suara Pembaruan,* 11 Sept. 1995

Table 6.1 (continued)

No.	Event	Cause	Source
6	Shortly after a Presidential visit to an earthquake site in Jambi on 10 October, an armed forces member in civilian clothes and a policeman were killed there by a mob. A civilian was also killed, and two other soldiers wounded. The Toyota they were driving was burned by the crowd, and the local police station destroyed as the mob pursued the soldiers.	Stories had spread of the kidnapping of young girls and the escape of 200 prisoners from the jail in Medan who had entered that area. The local people suspected that the soldiers, who invited some young girls to ride on their Toyota and dropped them off at the police station, were kidnapping the girls.	*Kompas,* *Suara Karya,* 13 Oct. 1995
7	A police captain in Padang, West Sumatra, and his family, became victims of brutality by night patrollers on the Padang Bypass in the early morning of 15 October. Stones were thrown at their car by young night watchmen, and as a result the car hit an electric pole and the passengers were wounded, despite the fact that they identified themselves as police.	A story was circulating that there was a wave of robberies in West Sumatra, and that criminals from outside the city were in hiding in the West Sumatra area.	*Kompas,* *Suara Karya,* 17 Oct. 1995
8	On 15 October, hundreds of residents of Pasuruan Kabupaten in East Java demonstrated for the second time against taking over of land by the Air Force. The first demonstration took place on 26 January, blocking the Bangil-Pasuruan road for $3^{1}/_{2}$ hours. Throngs of residents visited the Bupati's office to ask that he press the government to return this land that they had worked before it was taken over by the Air Force.	Taking over of land worked by the people by the Air Force.	*Suara Pembaruan,* 28 Jan. 1995; *Suara Karya,* *Karya,* 19 Oct. 1995

Table 6.1 (continued)

No.	Event	Cause	Source
9	On 20 October, some 800 workers from a shoe factory in from a shoe factory in Jombang, East Java, joined by dozens of student activists, demonstrated at the district legislature, district office and district police and military headquarters, demanding that the Bupati and the district police and military commanders resign.	These officials were considered responsible for the forcible breakup of a demonstration by workers of this factory at the local office of the Labour Ministry on 16 Oct., in which 200 workers were wounded and 13 people left unconscious.	*Merdeka,* *Kompas,* 21 Oct. 1995; *Republika,* 18–19 Oct. 1995
10	On 15 November, demonstrators at PT Cheil Samsung Indonesia in Pasuruan, East Java, attacked a security official. The demonstration continued until 19 November, when it was broken up and order was restored by the local military commander and the Bupati.	Garbage from a spice and fertiliser factory owned by CSI was thrown into a local stream, which local residents considered was causing pollution of their fishponds. A story had circulated that one of the demonstrators had been hit by the security official.	*Republika,* 20 Nov. 1995

Notes

1   There is a substantial literature that argues that economic development will increase interest within a society in politics and also lead to increased democratization, including improved performance of political parties as one of the principal elements of democratic life. On the relationship between economic development and politics, see Organsky 1965 (as cited in Crouch 1982, pp. 52–63); S.M. Lipset (cited in Crouch 1982, p. 118); Lewis 1983, pp. 7–11; Suseno 1991, pp. 340–42; and Salim 1991, p. 25. On the roles and functions of political parties in the political process, see Hardi 1990, p. 55; Budiardjo 1977, pp. 163–64; Macridis 1988, p. 27–31; Ball 1981, pp. 77–79; Kolbe 1985, pp. 5–6; Kuntjoro 1959, pp. 53–61; and Wilson 1990, p. 157.

2   This discussion of political parties includes Golkar because both theoretically and practically Golkar functions as a political party. In fact, in Law (Undang-Undang or UU) No. 3 of 1985 on "Changes in Law No. 3 of 1975 concerning Political Parties and Golongan Karya,"

Article 1, paragraph (2) it is stipulated that: "Political Parties and Golongan Karya, as organizations which are formed by citizens of the Republic of Indonesia on the basis of similar desires, have the same and equal status, functions, rights and responsibilities in accordance with this law, and their sovereignty resides in the hands of their members." See also Dhakidae 1981, pp. 17–18, and Ambong 1988, p. 68.

3   See Article 9, paragraph (1) of Government Regulation (Peraturan Pemerintah — PP) No. 19 of 1986 on the Implementation of Law No. 3 of 1985 on Political Parties and Golkar, and the General Explanation of this regulation.

4   See Article 9, paragraph (1) of Government Regulation No. 19/1986.

5   This is based on the direct observation of the author as an observer at the Extraordinary Congress.

6   "Nasakom" was the ideological formulation developed by President Sukarno in the pre-1965 period that attempted to fuse elements of nationalism, religion and communism.

7   See Article 1, section 5 of Law No. 15 of 1969 (as amended several times, most recently through Law No. 1 of 1985 on General Elections and Presidential Decision No. 8 of 1992), and Article 83 of Government Regulation No. 37 of 1990 on the Implementation of the General Election Law.

8   See inter alia the explanation by the head of the PPP delegation in the Jakarta regional parliament, Dr Djufri Asmoredjo, S.K.M. (*Suara Karya*, 20 May 1992).

9   The results of the May 1997 election did not sustain the trends reflected in the 1992 election. Golkar gained votes and seats, moving from 68 per cent of the votes in 1992 to 74.5 per cent in 1997 and winning 325 out of the 425 seats being contested. (The number of seats at stake rose from 400 in 1992 to 425 1997 because of the reduction in the number of seats allocated to the armed forces from 100 to 75 out of the total 500 seats in the DPR.) The PPP also increased its percentage of the popular vote and its seats, from 17 per cent in 1992 to nearly 22.5 per cent in 1997, and from 62 seats to 89 seats out of the expanded number. The PDI, on the other hand, suffered a disaster (presumably primarily due to the disarray and discontent following the ouster of former party leader Megawati), falling from 16 per cent of the popular vote to 3 per cent and from 56 to only 11 seats (*Kompas*, 24 June 1997). However, because of the situation in the PDI and an all-out campaign by the government to increase its vote percentage back above the 70 per cent mark, the circumstances of the 1997 election were quite different from

those of 1992. Thus the 1997 outcome did not necessarily invalidate the assessment of the 1992 results.

[10] See Article 134, paragraph (1) of the DPR Rules of Order (Peraturan Tata Tertib DPR) promulgated by DPR Decision No. 10/DPR-RI/II/82-83.

[11] See Article 58, paragraph (1) of Presidential Regulation No. 28 of 1960 on Changes in the Rules of Order in the DPR-GR.

[12] Well in advance of the start of the 1997 election process, senior officials were openly acknowledging that the armed forces and government bureaucracy would once again be mobilised to work for Golkar in the 1997 election. Examples include a statement by the army chief of staff on 12 September 1995, and a declaration by the minister of home affairs at a working meeting of officials of North Sulawesi Province Government in Manado on 14 November 1995 (Djadijono 1995).

[13] See "Year-End Political Notes", *Kompas*, 30 December 1995.

[14] See, for example: *Media Indonesia*, 18 September 1995; *Forum Keadilan* 4, no. 18 (18 December 1995), p. 20; and *Forum Keadilan* 4, no. 20 (15 January 1996), pp. 62–63.

[15] The basic legislation governing these matters includes: Law No. 1 of 1985 on General Elections; Law No. 2 of 1985 on the Structure and Status of the MPR and the DPR; Law No. 3 of 1985 on Political Parties and Golkar; and Law No. 5 of 1974 on the Principles of Administration in the Regions.

SECTION III

Mixed Institutions

7

Trade Unions and Labour Unrest

Sukardi Rinakit

In the past decade the number of labour strikes in Indonesia has steadily increased, especially in urban industrial centres. While there were only 48 labour strikes in 1988, this increased to 147 strikes in 1991, and more than 200 strikes in 1994. Moreover, in May 1993, labour strikes took a particularly brutal turn, as evidenced by rioting, destruction of company property, and the murder of a businessman in Medan, North Sumatra. The Indonesian Armed Forces had to be called in to restore order in the wake of this violent labour unrest.

Both of these developments — the increasing frequency of strikes and strike-related violence — contrast sharply with the labour situation in the 1970s and the early 1980s, after which time the government began to more firmly control labour organizing. In those years, although there were a number of labour strikes, the general labour situation was relatively calm (Nursyahbani 1993). Up until the mid-1980s government influence through the officially recognized legal trade union was generally capable of protecting companies against labour strikes. Strikes that occurred were commonly prompted by worker anger at companies over mass dismissals. Additionally, in the early to mid-1980s the Indonesian economy was less expansionary than in the past decade because of the recession caused by declining oil prices. It may be that the lack of economic expansion in those years limited the appeal of strikes as an option for workers.

The sharply increasing number of strikes since the mid-1980s indicates that a serious industrial relations problem has developed in Indonesia. This chapter examines that problem, paying particular attention to the causes of labour unrest in recent years. The linkage between rapid economic growth, structural changes in the economy, and growing consciousness among workers of their rights, is discussed in the first part of this chapter. The second section focuses on the trade union situation during the New Order era. Government control of the legal trade union movement and the political background of trade union management are two significant factors influencing the role of trade unions in industrial disputes. The third part of the chapter discusses the combined impact of government interference in the trade union movement and internal union political problems as a cause of the increase in labour strikes and popular unrest. The emergence of "alternative" labour unions is also addressed. Finally, a strike at Tangerang (an industrial area near Jakarta) in 1991 is analysed as an illustration of the social-economic conditions that cause labour strikes.

EMPLOYMENT AND STRUCTURAL CHANGES IN THE ECONOMY

Continuous economic growth during the New Order has fundamentally changed Indonesia's economic structure. As discussed in previous chapters, among the significant characteristics of this structural change have been economic growth rates higher than population growth rates, the increasing importance of the industrial sector, and the corresponding decline in the importance of the agricultural sector. Other characteristics include an expanding service sector and a declining public sector share of consumption.

These changes have all had direct impacts on sectoral capabilities to absorb labour. The employment structure has changed from heavy concentration in agriculture to a growing role for manufacturing industries. In 1971 the agricultural sector accounted for 67 per cent of total employment. This declined to 56 per cent in 1980 and to 49 per cent in 1990. By comparison, the industrial sector in 1971 was only capable of absorbing 7 per cent of the total workforce, but increased to 9 per cent in 1980 and 11 per cent in 1990 (see Table 7.1).

The increasing capability of the industrial sector, which is primarily urban-centred, to absorb labour, has had a multiplier effect on other urban-based sectors, as seen in the rapid growth of employment in all segments of the economy except agriculture. The proportion of urban workers dramatically increased from 23 per cent in 1971 to 41 per cent in 1990.

The changes in employment from agriculture to manufacturing have created a large new generation of industrial workers whose political consciousness has been formed by their experiences in the industrial centres. For example, workers' relations with management, their fellow employees, and non-governmental organizations (NGOs), have all contributed to enhancing workers' understanding of their rights. Labour analyst Vedi Hadiz argues that the wave of labour strikes in recent years is a direct

TABLE 7.1
Indonesia's Employment Structure, 1971–90

	1971	1980	1990
Employed labour force (millions)			
Total	39.7	51.6	70.2
Manufacturing	2.9	5.8	8.2
Sectoral distribution of employed labour force (%)*			
Agriculture	67	56	49
Manufacturing	7	9	11
Construction, Transport, and Utilities	5	5	10
Trade and Services	21	29	31
Location of employed labour force (%)			
Urban	23	29	41
Rural	77	71	59

Note: * Percentages may not add to 100 due to rounding.
Source: Indonesian Population Census, 1971, 1980, and 1990.

consequence of the growing awareness by industrial workers of their rights (Hadiz 1993). Moreover, because the labour force is much more urban-based today than it was just fifteen or twenty years ago, this urbanization of employment may have promoted a shift from values common to rural, traditional agrarian communities to those more commonly found in an urban, industrial, modern society.

Indonesian workers' growing consciousness of their rights is also due, in part, to a general improvement in educational levels nationwide, and especially in urban areas. For example, in 1985 the number of manufacturing sector workers who had attained at least a primary school education was 4,725,866, but in 1990 this had increased to 5,473,954. From 1985 to 1990, the number of junior and senior high school graduates in the manufacturing workforce doubled from 523,803 and 499,512 respectively to 1,062,484 and 1,049,604. Graduates of post-secondary institutions in the manufacturing workforce increased from 46,698 to 107,221 (BPS, *Statistik Indonesia* 1986, pp. 78–79; 1991, pp. 58–59).

Other awareness-related activities of the workforce, such as reading newspapers or magazines, watching television and participating in social organizations, have increased as well. Government data indicated that 1984 17,448,590 Indonesians regularly read newspapers or magazines, 50,686,080 watched television, and 41,850,630 participated in social or- ganizations. By 1990 the numbers of people involved in each of these activities had almost doubled, reaching levels that could only be possible if these groups included substantial numbers of workers (BPS, *Statistik Indonesia* 1994).

The changes in employment structure, increases in educational levels, and exposure to new ideas and ways of interacting through expanding social activities, have all contributed to the rising level of labour activism. The rapid spread of labour unrest in turn has prompted the government, the private sector, and the NGO community to think more seriously about labour problems, their causes and possible resolutions. Each of these three groups has tried to deal with the changes in the labour structure and resulting problems. But because of its central role in labour unrest, espe- cially in the industrial centres, the trade union movement has been the main focus of attention.

TRADE UNION PROBLEMS

The legitimacy of the official, government-sponsored trade union, the Serikat Pekerja Seluruh Indonesia (SPSI, All-Indonesia Workers' Union), is sharply questioned by many parties. These include the workers them- selves, as well as labour analysts, NGO activists, and international organi- zations.[1] The critics all share the belief that labour unrest occurs, in part, because the government-sanctioned SPSI is unable to carry out its func- tion as an institution which fights for the rights of its members. Noted human rights activist and legal advocate T. Mulya Lubis argues that SPSI, as the only legal trade union, is *loyo* (weak or exhausted) and thereby unable to protect workers (Lubis 1979, p. 16). The weakness of the SPSI — and thus its role in the recent explosion of labour unrest in Indonesia — is deeply influenced by two factors: the focus of the union's management on macro-level industrial policy rather than specific workers' rights, and political and organizational problems within the SPSI.

The involvement of the SPSI in policy debates over macro-level employment policies affecting such matters as social security issues, pensions, and the minimum wage, has made the SPSI's national-level management unpopular among the workers and the people. This is because the union is perceived as being uninvolved in the daily issues and concerns of workers. At the ground level, the branches and the individual SPSI company units are restricted in their ability to fight for labour rights because they are fully controlled by the government (Agrawal 1995, p. 32). However, it is at these lower levels, the regional and company-based SPSI units, that the role of the SPSI *should* be most active and important, because this is where the union is in direct contact with its members. With the SPSI divided in this way — its national management concerned with macro employment and economic policies while its local branches are rendered powerless by government control — it is not surprising that there is a negative perception of the SPSI.

Of course, the efforts of the SPSI in macro policy areas can be viewed as an appropriate union endeavour to elevate the welfare of the workers. But these efforts are often not perceived by workers as being responsive to their concerns. In its central role as a trade union, arguably SPSI should be paying more attention to the problems of workers in the industrial centres than to influencing employment policies at the national level. And it is precisely at the operational level where the union is perceived to be ineffective.

POLITICAL BACKGROUND OF TRADE UNION MANAGEMENT

The weakness of SPSI is compounded by internal organizational constraints and problems. These include the political background of SPSI's management, and government intervention and control (Barbari [forthcoming], pp. 13–15).

During the old order period, and in the initial years of the New Order, Indonesian trade unions were affiliated with political parties. From the 1950s until the mid-1960s there were more than nine political parties in Indonesia, and every party had its own trade union as one of its vehicles for recruiting party supporters. For example, the union of the Indonesian Communist Party was SOBSI (All-Indonesian Workers' Organizations' Union), while the Indonesian Nationalist Party worked through the KBRI (Unity of Indonesian Republic Workers) and GSBI (Association of Indonesian Workers' Unions).

The affiliation of trade unions with political parties was severed in 1973 when the New Order consolidated the nine remaining parties into three political organizations, namely PPP, PDI and Golkar (Sudono 1977, pp. 33–35). After the mergers of the political parties, the government established a single trade union organization, consolidating the unions which were previously affiliated with political parties. In 1973 the Federasi Buruh Seluruh Indonesia (FBSI) was established as the only recognised trade union in Indonesia. At the FBSI's Second National Congress in November 1985, the union's name was changed to SPSI (also translated as All-Indonesia Workers' Union). Beginning in 1985 an effort was made to more clearly formulate the goals and objectives of the union, with the focus placed on improving the welfare of the work-force.[2]

However, some SPSI leaders have become deeply involved in the three political organizations (Golkar, PPP, and PDI) as well as in seeking public office. A number of SPSI officials are members of the national and provincial parliaments, as well as being involved in district-level politics. The interests that these leaders pursue in their political capacities are not necessarily the aspirations of the labour organization. This only strengthens workers' perceptions that the SPSI does not fight to improve their welfare but rather simply provides opportunities for the leaders to advance their personal ambitions.[3]

GOVERNMENT CONTROL OF SPSI

The government's perception of the role of trade unions in Indonesia is central to trade union weakness. As noted previously, the New Order government argued that national political and social stability is a prerequisite for sustained economic growth. Traditional activities of trade unions, such as aggressive advocacy of workers' rights and even strikes, are perceived by the government as fundamentally destabilizing. Therefore, the government developed tight controls on the trade union movement in order to prevent labour activism, in the interest of national stability and development. The government has even been known to use violence against the labour movement (Nursyahbani 1993).

The establishment of control over the national trade union movement by the New Order government started with the formation of FBSI in 1973 as the sole legal representative of workers. However, from 1973 to 1985, the FBSI, despite being the only official trade union, did operate with a certain degree of autonomy. Moreover, during these years the FBSI was a rather loose federation, consisting of 21 semi-independent sectoral unions, Serikat Buruh Lapangan Pekerja or SBLP.

The New Order concept of proper industrial relations (involving labour, government, and private businesses) was developed in the FBSI era. This concept became known as "Pancasila Industrial Relations" (Hubungan

Industrial Pancasila, or HIP). Basically, however, HIP is a tool to prevent strikes. In keeping with the overall New Order conception of Indonesia as a "Family State" (Negara Kekeluargaan), Pancasila Industrial Relations are philosophically based on familial values. Although labour laws recognize the right to strike, HIP deemed them un-Indonesian because they set up conflict (i.e., between management and workers and the state) which was considered incompatible with familial values.

Thus HIP was meant to ensure the smooth, strike-free management of industrial relations. However, the mechanisms used to implement Pancasila Industrial Relations in practice, such as tripartite bargaining, instead became a means for collusion between government and employers at the expense of workers (Nursyahbani 1993).

The continued tendency on the part of union officials to concentrate on their own particular group interests and political activity in the FBSI period provoked the government to intensify its control. In 1985, then Minister of Manpower Soedomo directed that FBSI be transformed from a loose federation into a unitary trade union, which was renamed SPSI.

The centralization of the trade union structure, by reducing the independence of member unions, also tended to reduce their range of activities and effectiveness. For example, during the FBSI period, the individual unions were allowed to maintain direct links with international labour organizations. Under SPSI, all international relationships must be conducted by the central SPSI body. While the old FBSI organizational structure included semi-autonomous unions within the federated body, the unitary structure provided only for standardised "departments" at the national level, "bureaus" at the provincial level and "sections" at the district level, all controlled directly by the national leadership. The unitary model increased the government's ability to control the union, but company level units became ineffective and in some cases virtually nonfunctioning, and the union as a whole has been weakened.

The change of the trade union from a federated to a unitary structure also eliminated the positions of a large number of the managers of the formerly semi-autonomous sectoral SBLPs. The twenty-one SBLPs were integrated into nine nationally-centralised SPSI departments, and the number of management positions was reduced correspondingly. The former SBLP managers and union leaders who lost their positions tended to be those considered by the government to be uncooperative or difficult to control, or who had no personal or political relationships with the governing élite. A similar process occurred at the provincial and district levels.

Although the SPSI receives a significant portion of its budget from the government, SPSI's funding in fact derives from workers' contributions. However, the funds actually received by SPSI from the government are certainly less than the total amount of the workers' contributions. Based on data collected by SPSI's Research and Development Institute, SPSI received about 15 million rupiahs per year during 1990–94. However, in 1993, for example, the total number of SPSI members was 1,786,127. If worker contributions averaged 500 rupiahs per month, total contributions should have reached almost 50 million rupiahs per month or around 510 million rupiahs per year.[4] The discrepancy in these amounts suggests that the union receives only a small fraction of what its members pay in dues.

The combined impact of the outside interests and political activities of many SPSI leaders and the tight government controls over SPSI has weakened the ability of the union to function effectively on behalf of workers' rights. SPSI is almost completely unable to defend the interests of workers in negotiations, especially at the company unit level. This reality is rooted in the workings of the tripartite labour relations structure (labour-government-employer), which is fundamentally unbalanced and heavily weighted in favour of government and employer-supported outcomes. In theory the government should be an intermediary in labour-employer conflict, but instead it tends to defend the employer (Schwarz 1994, p. 259). This inharmonious situation becomes even more turbulent through the involvement of the government security apparatus, which tends to blame the workers for labour unrest, and especially as the cause of strikes (Nursyahbani 1993).

Interestingly, despite the tight government controls, in the early 1990s there was an effort within SPSI to restore a greater degree of union independence. In 1993, then SPSI head Imam Soedarwo proposed that, as a means of increasing its effectiveness, SPSI once again become a federation with autonomous sectors. This effort was ultimately unsuccessful, but it demonstrated that some union leaders were aware of, and dissatisfied with, the negative impact of the previous organizational changes.

Soedarwo had an additional, more lasting impact on SPSI. He recruited a new group of skilled, independent activists, which increased the educational level of SPSI's management. Approximately forty per cent of SPSI's national officials are now university graduates.[5] It is unlikely that the staffs of any of the NGOs operating in the labour field are as well educated. However, a superior educational background does not necessarily result in greater attention to workers' rights. It is the NGO workers who are more active in this area, especially at the plant level.

ALTERNATIVES TO SPSI

In the vacuum of effective labour representation due to SPSI's weakness and unpopularity, two other trade unions have appeared in Indonesia in recent years. These are the Serikat Buruh Sejahtera Indonesia (SBSI, or Indonesian Prosperity Trade Union) and the Serikat Buruh Merdeka Setia Kawan (SBMSK, or Solidarity Free Trade Union). The appearance of these unofficial unions was greeted enthusiastically by workers. However, the government rejected the new labour organizations as illegal, and therefore did not recognize their attempts to represent workers or seek improvements on their behalf.

The basis of the government's rejection of the SBSI and SBMSK was that they were not recognized in the Pancasila Industrial Relations (HIP) system. The HIP system does not recognize the right of workers to set up new organizations which are concerned with labour problems. Yet it is precisely these "illegal" unions which have helped workers expand their understanding of their role and position in Indonesia's changing society through education, discussion and social activities. The previously-noted higher educational level of workers enables the work-force to more easily absorb the information provided by labour activists who are based in the illegal trade unions. As a result, workers are generally more aware of conditions that are detrimental to them, such as low wages, social security problems, and the ineffective and biased nature of the tripartite bargaining structure.

CAUSES OF LABOUR STRIKES

The sharp increase in labour activism and strikes in industrial zones in recent years is the consequence of the convergence of societal conditions — improving educational levels, urbanization, and increasing social awareness — and the political/internal weaknesses of SPSI, together with the New Order's conception of proper industrial relations. While in the first part of the New Order (through 1980) there were only 73 strikes, the number of the labour strikes dramatically increased to 1248 between 1981 and 1994 (see Table 7.2).

The most common cause of strikes between 1987-1994 appears to have been low wage levels (see Table 7.3). One of the workers' main grievances is that government regulations stipulating a Regional Minimum Wage have not been implemented by many companies.[6] Additionally, child labourers generally receive a lower wage, often only 50 per cent of the

TABLE 7.2
Labour Strikes, 1971–94

Year	Strikes	Workers Involved (thousands)	Manufacturing Strikes (as % of total)
1971–80	73	12	83
1981–90	304	86	87
1987	40	14	87
1988	37	15	83
1989	23	6	68
1990	92	31	89
1991	147	60	96
1992	177	67	78
1993	323	89	63
1994	297	77	80

Source: Research and Development Institute of the All-Indonesia Workers' Union (SPSI), 1994.

TABLE 7.3
Causes of Labour Strikes, 1987–94

	1987	1988	1989	1990	1991	1992	1993	1994
Number of Strikes	40	37	23	92	147	177	323	297
Causes: (as % of total)*								
Wages	32	61	69	58	63	67	61	61
Working conditions	41	21	26	31	17	14	15	13
Collective labour agreement	–	–	–	3	4	3	3	4
Annual bonus (Idul Fitri allowance)	19	5	–	–	8	9	11	8
Formation of union	8	10	5	6	6	6	9	12
Social insurance	–	3	–	2	1	1	1	2

Note: * Percentages may not add to 100 due to rounding.
Source: Research and Development Institute of the All-Indonesia Workers' Union (SPSI), 1994.

minimum wage, even though children work as hard as adults. In 1982, the regional minimum wage in Jakarta was Rp750 per day; outside Jakarta (including outside Java) it was Rp500–Rp700 per day. In 1991, the minimum wage was increased to Rp2.500 per day in Jakarta and Rp1,350–Rp1,930 per day in the other regions (BPS, *Indikator Ekonomi* 1982–91). However, this regional minimum wage only met approximately 80 per cent of what the government calculated to be the minimum physical needs (*kebutuhan fisik minimum*) for the average single worker.[7] This indicates that the socio-economic conditions of labour in the industrial zones have been very distressed (Schwarz 1994, p. 259).

Government minimum wage regulations were amended in 1994 with the aim of equalizing minimum daily wages with the officially-determined basic sustenance needs (*kebutuhan hidup minimum*) for single workers. Minimum daily wages increased to Rp4,600 for Jakarta and Rp4,100 for outside Jakarta. However, implementation of the increase was very slow. Many companies, especially in the textile and garment sectors, urged the government to postpone implementation of the new minimum wage policy on the grounds that it would be too expensive (*Media Indonesia*, 3 December 1994). (Nevertheless, even though labour *costs* involve more than just wages, Indonesian daily wages remain among the lowest in Asia — see Table 7.4.)

TABLE 7.4
Manufacturing Labour Wages in Asia,
1991 and 1993
(US$ per hour)

Country	1991	1993
Japan	13.23	16.91
Taiwan	4.35	5.35
Singapore	4.39	5.12
South Korea	4.13	4.93
Hong Kong	3.47	4.21
Malaysia	1.69	1.80
Thailand	0.60	0.68
Philippines	0.64	0.67
China	0.27	0.54
Indonesia	0.22	0.28

Source: Morgan Stanley in *Business Times* (Singapore), 22 June 1993.

The New Order government's reluctance to enforce its own minimum wage regulations highlights an acute dilemma faced by policy-makers. On the one hand, the government is aware that low wages are a main cause of labour unrest. On the other hand, the government has sought to maintain Indonesia's low wage levels in order to encourage foreign investment which was seen as essential for Indonesia's continued economic growth. From 1985 to 1990, the low cost of labour in Indonesia was officially promoted as one of Indonesia's comparative advantages. And, in general, the reality of low wages was tied to the fact that Indonesia's workers remained relatively unskilled. Furthermore, Indonesia has a labour surplus so it is difficult for trade unions to improve their bargaining position. For example, approximately 2.5 million persons were entering the labour force every year while there were jobs for only about 2.1 million. This means that total unemployment was increasing by about four hundred thousand persons per year, and that there has been a huge pool of unemployed who can take the places of workers who quit or are terminated (Sukardi Rinakit 1993). Thus, the government is most interested in job creation, not necessarily *well-paying* job creation.

However, the wave of labour strikes in the recent years indicated a fundamental change in workers' attitudes and consciousness. Workers were rejecting low wage levels because they no longer accepted government and company assertions that they are too unskilled or unproductive to merit higher wages. Based on information they have received from NGOs, the workers understand that their productivity is actually quite high (*Media Indonesia*, 2 February 1994).

Moreover, the increasing trend of labour strikes indicated that the government's tight control over trade unions, which was intensified after 1985, was not necessarily effective. In fact, strict government regulation of the trade union movement may have contributed to strikes by forcing an unresponsive and ineffective SPSI on workers as their only legal representative body. It is now clear that the government is facing demands for devising a new approach to labour unrest.

CASE STUDY: STRIKE AT TANGERANG

A survey[8] of workers involved in a strike in 1991 in Tangerang, an industrial area west of Jakarta, provides a good illustration of the background causes of labour unrest, such as the poor socio-economic conditions of workers and the relationship between employer and employee in the factory. It also demonstrates the importance of relatively "small" issues (such as non-payment of traditional allowances for the annual Islamic holiday Hari Raya Idul Fitri) as key flashpoints in igniting labour strikes.

Respondent Characteristics

The Tangerang survey involved some 200 persons between the ages of 21 to 30, 85 per cent of whom were women and 15 per cent men (see Table 7.5). All of the male respondents were monthly, or permanent, employees of the company. Fifty per cent of the female respondents were weekly workers and 50 per cent monthly workers. All male respondents were senior high school graduates, while only 3.7 per cent of the female respondents had graduated from high school, with the remainder of the women having graduated from either junior high or elementary school (a higher percentage being junior high school graduates).

A large portion of the respondents (male and female) had been employed for between one and three years. The male workers had been employed longer than the female workers. The female workers were generally "new workers" and on average had been working for about 1.5 years. The respondents worked an official average of eight hours per day. The effective normal working hours were between 7:30 a.m. and 3:30 p.m., with a one hour unpaid break. While the eight hour workday was the official company requirement, the respondents said that in practice they generally "must" work overtime (compulsory overtime) for at least two hours each day. After the compulsory overtime they could work ordinary overtime. Compulsory overtime occurred between 3:30 and 5:30 p.m., and ordinary overtime was from 5:30 to 8:30 p.m. The respondents generally lived near the company and the majority of them were

TABLE 7.5
Tangerang Worker Sample: Gender and Work Status

Gender	Employment Status						Total	
	Daily		Weekly		Monthly			
	No.	(%)	No.	(%)	No.	(%)	No.	(%)
Male	–		–		30	(15)	30	(15)
Female	3	(1.5)	85	(42.5)	82	(41)	170	(85)
Total	3	(1.5)	85	(42.5)	112	(56)	200	(100)

drawn from the local population. Most of the respondents from other areas of Java lived in the company's rental "huts",[9] in which one room was usually occupied by three to six persons and the monthly rental cost for one room was about Rp40,000.

Background and "Ignition" Factors in the Tangerang Strike

The strike was due, in large part, to several factors related to broad-based social and economic problems. Low income and a growing gap between income and the cost of living was a primary factor. Most of the respondents received a salary between Rp51,000 and Rp70,000 per month depending on their length of employment (interestingly, there appears to be no correlation between workers' educational background and their wage levels). Workers in an initial probation period received Rp1,200 per day, whereas the monthly (permanent) workers received wages at least equal to the official minimum wage regulation, which was Rp1,600 per day in May 1991.[10] The compulsory overtime wage was calculated at 1.5 times the basic hourly wage, while the ordinary overtime was calculated at two times the hourly wage. Only with overtime was it possible for the workers to earn close to the official minimum income necessary for meeting basic needs. (One additional source of earnings was a monthly premium of about Rp5,000 per month, but this bonus was only given to workers who were never absent in the preceding month.)

In Tangerang in April 1991, the minimum income for basic human needs was about Rp70,000 per month. Starting in July 1991, however, the minimum income necessary for basic needs was revised upwards to about Rp95,000 per month (*Media Pekerja* 6, no. 412 [July-August 1992], p. 15). Therefore, the government policy to increase the minimum wage from Rp1,600 per day to Rp2,100 per day in 1991 was clearly appropriate, even though this new wage minimum was still insufficient to meet the standard of minimum human needs.

There was also a striking differential in income between the workers in the survey, who barely earned enough to survive, and management. The differential between an ordinary worker and a foreman was 1:25; that between a worker and a section head was 1:60; between a worker and the manager 1:130; and between a worker and the president director 1:225. These sharp wage differentials added to the volatility of the situation.[11] The extreme difficulties in meeting their basic needs made the workers keenly sensitive towards any issues related to bonuses, allowances or other supplements to the basic wage.

Another factor that may have played a role in the Tangerang strikes was poor communication between the workers and company management (see Tables 7.6 and 7.7). Although only 123 respondents (out of 200 surveyed) elected to answer the question on communication, by a nearly 2-to-1 margin these respondents expressed the view that worker-management communication was poor.

TABLE 7.6
Tangerang Worker Sample: Views on Worker-Management Communication, by Education Level

Education Level	Assessment of Communication				Total Responding		Total in Group
	Good		Poor				
	No.	(%)	No.	(%)	No.	(% of Group)	
Primary School	–	–	3	(10)	3	(10)	29
Junior High School	11	(14)	19	(24)	30	(38)	78
Senior High School	31	(33)	59	(63)	90	(97)	93
Total	42	(21)	81	(42)	123	(62)	200

Note: Totals may not add due to rounding.

TABLE 7.7
Tangerang Worker Sample: Views on Worker-Manager Communication, by Income Level

Income (monthly) (Rp 1000s)	Assessment of Communication				Total Responding		Total in Group
	Good		Poor				
	No.	(%)	No.	(%)	No.	(% of Group)	
30–50	–		3	(17)	3	(17)	18
51–70	38	(22)	66	(39)	104	(61)	170
71–90	4	(33)	8	(67)	12	(100)	12
Total	42	(21)	77	(39)	119	(60)	200

According to the respondents, they found it difficult to meet directly with the management. If there was a problem and a worker wished to meet directly with management, managers tended to become suspicious. Furthermore, the respondents perceived the managers' attitudes as generally unhelpful, especially in the case of the personnel manager.

An extreme example of workers' frustrations was seen in a protest by female workers, who destroyed two cars and office rooms. In Indonesian communities, according to Javanese political culture scholar Franz Magnis-Suseno (1991), it is very rare for women to engage in violent behaviour. For example, in the survey many female workers declined even to answer a question concerning the behaviour of the manager. According to Magnis-Suseno, their violent protest in this case must have been caused by very high feelings of frustration and injustice.

Of particular interest in the data in Tables 7.6 and 7.7 is the relationship between workers' education and income levels and their views of communication between workers and the company's management. The higher the level of their education and wage, the more likely workers were to express the opinion that communication between workers and management was poor. In addition, higher-income workers also tended to evaluate the attitude of the manager as less positive than other workers.

These background factors — stress in meeting basic needs and poor views of management — had existed for a reasonably long time. A more immediate explosive factor was required to ultimately provoke the strike action. The triggering factor in this case was the small allowance given by the company to the workers at the time of the Idul Fitri celebration (marking the end of Ramadan, the Islamic fasting month). The Idul Fitri allowance was between Rp5,000 and Rp15,000, depending on the employee's position and length of employment with the company.

According to the workers, the allowance was very small and was insufficient to buy anything. This angered the workers because they had expected to receive an allowance sufficient to buy clothes and other items necessary for the 1991 Idul Fitri holiday. The previous year they had received a minimum bonus of Rp50,000. It was this gap between the workers' expectations and the actual 1991 allowance that ignited the Tangerang strike.

CONCLUSIONS

This chapter has traced the labour unrest phenomenon in industrial zones as an integral part of the changing characteristics of the Indonesian political economy. Government approaches that place political stability as an absolute precondition for economic development have prevented trade unions from playing an effective role in defending workers' rights, especially in the unitary trade union era of the SPSI (1985 to the mid-1990s). Government control of trade unions has been tighter in this period and it has made the trade union a weak and unequal player in genuine collective bargaining at the plant level. However, tight government control has not necessarily been more effective in preventing strikes. In fact, government controls may even have exacerbated conditions that led to strikes.

Three major conclusions emerge from the survey:

First, the wave of labour strikes in industrial areas has been due the changing social-economic conditions of the Indonesian labour force, such as higher levels of education and expanding awareness of workers' rights, plus the specific problems of the labour movement itself (weak, poorly managed, and controlled by government). Unlike a decade earlier when dismissals were the major reason for labour disputes, concerns over wages and working conditions have been the main causes of the recent unrest. Strikes have primarily been associated with lack of compliance with the minimum wage laws, unsatisfactory working conditions, and failure to pay bonuses, such as the Idul Fitri allowance.

Second, the obsession of government with creating political stability has ensured the powerlessness of the trade union movement. Pancasila Industrial Relations does not work as had been intended: disputes are *not* harmoniously resolved in accordance with family-like values. The government's conception of labour relations has indirectly encouraged wildcat strikes and walkouts as the only option available because of the inability of workers to engage in productive and fair negotiations with employers. Additionally, efforts by the legal trade union (SPSI) to modernize its organization and became somewhat more autonomous (as in the pre-1985 period), have not been successful.

Third and finally, based on the field data, workers not only regard their socio-economic position as weak, but also believe that their personal stress is very high because of the employers' distrustful attitudes towards them. This poor communication between management and employees is a factor which makes the working environment conducive to labour unrest.

Notes

[1] In 1987 the International Confederation of Free Trade Unions (ICFTU) lodged a complaint with the International Labour Organization (ILO) in

Geneva about trade union freedoms and roles in Indonesia. Although this complaint focused primarily on the lack of union representation for public sector workers, it also concerned the role of trade unions. See Sukardi Rinakit 1994.

[2] For a comprehensive description of the SPSI programme and goals, see the SPSI constitution (SPSI 1988), Article (*Pasal*) 8.

[3] The acute differences between the interests of the union as an independent institution and the political orientation of many union leaders can be seen when SBSI holds its national congress or other national deliberations. These meetings are invariably coloured by the disagreement over whom to elect to the leadership positions. Disagreements are sharp precisely because by becoming part of the union management the officials increase their chances for appointment to government bodies.

[4] For additional explanation, see Decree No. 16/DPP SPSI/11/1986 in SPSI 1986, pp. 33–34.

[5] This data is reprocessed from SPSI 1991, pp. 33–34.

[6] A survey by the Asian Free Labour Institute indicated that fifty-six per cent of Indonesian companies were paying less than the minimum wage.

[7] "Minimum physical needs" are calculated by adding the costs of forty-seven separate items consumed by a single worker. These items are categorized under food, energy, transportation, recreation, clothing, and housing. In 1991, the category totals per day for a worker in Tangerang were: food Rp1,000, energy Rp250, transportation Rp300, recreation Rp40, clothing Rp100 (based on the assumption that a worker would need to buy one set of clothing every three months), and housing Rp350. The overall total came to Rp2,040 per day (the equivalent of just over $US1 at the prevailing exchange rate). However, the official minimum wage in Tangerang at that time was Rp1,700 per day, only 80 per cent of the minimum physical needs. (It should be noted that since 1993 the minimum wage has been set at a level equivalent to the minimum physical needs, so the situation has improved in the mid-1990s.)

[8] The following section is based on research on labour strikes in Tangerang conducted by the author and J. Babari in May 1991. The research results were used by SPSI, either for internal distribution or for a report to the Asia Pacific Regional Office of the International Confederation of Free Trade Unions (ICFTU-APRO) at a seminar on Economic Development and Manpower Problems held in Singapore in 1991.

[9] In the questionnaire the respondents' region of origin was not asked. This explanation is based on secondary data obtained through unstructured interviews with two respondents selected for in-depth interviews.

[10] The minimum wage in West Java, where Tangerang is located, was increased to Rp2,100 per day in 1991 (through the Decree of the Minister of Manpower No. 338/Men/1991), to Rp3,100 in 1993, and in January 1995 to Rp4,100 per day.

[11] A number of psychology and criminology theories discuss the relationship between social and economic difficulties and deviant behaviour. For example, see Barlow 1984, pp. 37–39; and Conklin 1981, pp. 181–212.

8

Education: Access, Quality, and Relevance

Onny S. Prijono

Rapid economic growth increases the supply of educational services by increasing the resources available for education. It also increases the demand for education, both in terms of the numbers of potential students with the necessary income and/or aspirations, and in terms of the numbers of employers seeking a better educated and trained work-force (World Bank 1996a, p. 1). Education is also recognized as one of the basic requirements for the functioning of a modern, complex society (Boediono and Adams 1992, pp. 125–26). Likewise, access to education is essential to any individual's opportunity to participate successfully in modern society, and thus is also a measure of the degree of equity in a society (Priest 1974, p. 28).

In Indonesia, the New Order government's basic educational development strategy was set in 1969 (Beeby 1979, pp. 8–9). Three broad problem areas in education were identified:[1] curricula, infrastructure, and financial resources. Other important issues included the growing numbers of students, the quality of education, the relevance of education to the labour market, low government spending on education, efficiency, and unclear educational objectives (Prijono and Pranarka 1979, pp. 3–6). (Regarding the last category, twenty years later a law on the National Education System was passed [Law No. 2 of 1989] which provided guidance on the objectives of education from pre-school to tertiary levels.)

Under the New Order policies and with the success of economic growth, the next three decades saw a dramatic expansion in Indonesia's education system. The effects of economic growth can be seen in structural changes at all educational levels, and the emergence of a more educated and skilled society. However, overall expansion has been accompanied by growing discrepancies in educational opportunities and achievements within the society, and a widening gap both between urban and rural areas and between regions. There has also been a growing imbalance between the output of the education system and the requirements of the nation's economy and labour market. Thus the fundamental problems identified at the start of the period persist, at all levels of education.

This chapter examines the change in the Indonesian educational system from a supply orientation, emphasizing the production of graduates, to a demand orientation directed towards development needs — how to produce graduates that meet the needs of development in general and the labour market in particular (Boediono 1994). This institutional change includes greater participation by the private sector and the business community in providing education and training. The changes, and the issues associated with them, are discussed on the dimensions of access, quality, and relevance.

ACCESS TO EDUCATION

Access is a critical factor not only in determining the output of the educational system but also in social equity (Boediono, McMahon, and Adams 1992, p. 11). Social equity requires equality of opportunity to obtain an education, regardless of socio-economic status, religion, or geographic location. This concept is enshrined in Indonesia's basic law on the national education system (Law No. 2 of 1989). However, in practice equality of opportunity in education is very difficult to achieve. The poorer segment of the population still often has little access to education opportunities (Department of Education and Culture 1993b, pp. 1–2). Even an extensive scholarship system has not been able to compensate for differences in access to quality education among various socio-economic groups. The current five-year development plan is attempting to address this problem by achieving the goal of nine years of universal education, and by seeking ways to reduce the cost of junior secondary school in order to enable the children of less well-to-do families to enrol.

Pre-school Education

At the lowest level of the process of education, one result of economic growth has been a rapid increase in recent years in the number of pre-school institutions — kindergartens, play groups, and day care centres. These institutions have appeared largely in response to the demands of the growing and more affluent middle class, and to the increasing recognition of the educational value of pre-school experience (Pranarka 1991, p. 88). In 1990, the government issued Regulation No. 27 establishing rules for pre-school institutions. However, to date this remains largely an urban phenomenon, dominated by private sector institutions of widely varying quality.

Primary Education

The New Order government viewed expansion and improvement of basic education in the country as a necessity for successful economic develop-ment and modernization. In 1974, the government launched a nationwide school building programme to expand primary education, known as SD Inpres (for Sekolah Dasar Instruksi Presiden, the Presidential Instruction on Primary Schools). In 1984 primary school education became com-pulsory for all children between the ages of seven and twelve. As the programme was implemented, six-year old children were increasingly admitted. In 1987, children reaching the age of five-and-a-half to six years were officially allowed to enter primary school because the expansion of primary schools provided sufficient space (Prijono 1991, p. 4). By 1990/91 the number of primary schools had vastly increased, from 65,910 in 1973/74 to 146,558. During the same period, the number of pupils enrolled doubled, from 13.1 million to 26.5 million. In the early 1970s gross enrollment was 75 per cent, but it increased to about 90 per cent by the end of that decade. By the mid-1980s, gross enrollment rates exceeded 100 per cent and by 1994/95 had reached 112 per cent (World Bank 1996b, p. 1).

The expansion of educational facilities and opportunity was an extra-ordinary accomplishment, particularly since the growth occurred prima-rily in rural areas where the bulk of the Indonesian population lives (sixty-nine per cent, according to the population census of 1990). As a result of this programme, the proportion of children in rural areas with primary education rose dramatically (in urban areas, the percentage of children with *only* a primary education actually fell in the same period, but only because more children were educated beyond the primary school level). The proportion of the labour force in both urban and rural areas with no formal education at all continued to decline.

The SD Inpres programme is now limited to maintenance and rehabili-tation of existing schools, as well as construction of teachers' housing.

However, demand for education beyond the primary level continues to rise and far exceeds the available facilities. The focus of the government has therefore shifted from the primary to the secondary school level.

Secondary Education

In 1990, Government Regulation No. 28 expanded compulsory education to nine years, consisting of six consecutive years of primary school followed by three years of lower secondary (junior high) school. The nine year compulsory education programme was actually only implemented starting in May 1994, to be carried out in steps. The crude participation rate in this programme (the percentage of eligible children actually enrolled for the full nine compulsory years) is projected to rise from 43.4 per cent in 1993/94 to 66.2 per cent in 1998/99, and to 87 per cent by 2003/04 (Booth 1994, p. 29).

An additional impact of attaining nearly universal basic education has been the phasing out of vocational and technical schools at the lower secondary level.[2] The vocational and skill programmes of the former vocational and technical schools are now included in the local content portion of the general education curriculum of the lower secondary schools. This is in keeping with evidence that suggests vocational training is most cost-effective if trainees have a solid base of primary and secondary education (World Bank 1993b, p. 198). It is also in line with the role of secondary schools in educating entrants to the labour force, enhancing the trainability of workers, and providing qualified inputs into higher levels of education (World Bank 1996b, p. 1).

The government intends to gradually increase access to upper secondary education. In 1993–94 gross enrolment rates were 111 per cent, 54 per cent, 34 per cent, and 11 per cent in primary (elementary), lower secondary (junior high school), upper secondary (senior high school), and higher education, respectively (World Bank 1996a, p. 1).

Tertiary Education

Another government objective was to expand access to public higher education. At least one university was established in each province. This policy not only promoted regional equity, but it also provided all provinces with a local source of teachers, professionals, and specialists (World Bank 1996a, pp. 1–2). As of 1994, the total number of public higher education institutions was 78.[3] Meanwhile, there has been rapid growth in private institutions of higher education since the 1970s, with the total reaching 1,159 in 1994.[4] In 1984 student enrolment in higher education, both public and private, numbered 815,000. This figure increased to approximately 1.61 million in 1994, almost a hundred per cent increase in a single decade. However, compared with other Asian countries such as the Philippines, Korea, and Taiwan, Indonesia's higher education enrolment rates are still relatively low.

There has been a shift in the government's higher education policy from quantitative to qualitative improvements. Under this policy, public institutions are expected to concentrate on quality improvement, while private institutions are to be the vehicle for expanding access (World Bank 1994*b*, p. 7).

Higher education in Indonesia, as elsewhere, is expensive. This means that most of the students in both public and private institutions come from better-off families. Greater access by children from poorer families is hampered by the fact that large numbers of them must enter the labour market even before completing secondary school. Differences in investment in education between regions have also resulted in large variations in the quality of public higher education. These constraints also tend to perpetuate existing social and regional disparities (Oey-Gardiner 1991, p. 84).

THE QUALITY GAP

One of the consequences of rapid growth in school enrolment has been a drop in educational standards, or at a minimum, a lack of improvement in educational quality. The compulsory education programme focused only on increasing the numbers of the students rather than on educational performance and standards. Most primary schools have poor educational standards, except for a few private and public schools where parents provide financial support. There is a strong impression that the best private primary schools are still better than the best public schools (Buchori 1996). Moreover, schools in rural areas tend to show poorer performance than urban schools. Despite the success of the SD Inpres programmes, there remain significant discrepancies in the quality of instruction between regions, between urban and rural areas, and also between Java and regions outside Java.

Out of 20,838 public and private junior high schools throughout the country, only 18 (0.23 per cent) fulfill the criteria for category A classification (the highest of five categories). Six hundred junior high schools

(2.89 per cent) fall in category B, while more than 50 per cent fall in category E (the lowest category). Almost all of the E category are private schools; a rough estimate puts the worst public schools generally in the D category.

At the senior high school level, after the first year students are split into four streams: (1) physics, (2) biology, (3) social sciences, and (4) language and arts. In many municipal senior high schools, the fourth stream is not established at all. By contrast, in suburban and rural senior high schools, the first stream is often not available or has the lowest number of students (Nasoetion 1991, p. 69). The national examination scores achieved by students of rural high schools are also lower than those of urban high schools (Fidhiawan 1991).

The growth in educational institutions has not always been accompanied by improvements in quality. Therefore, the government is now focusing on qualitative improvements. The current emphasis is on curriculum improvement (Government Regulation No. 28 of 1990). Starting in the 1994/95 school year, a new curriculum replaced the 1984 previous standard for primary and secondary schools. In addition to the standard national requirements, the curriculum allows for "local content" that reflects the local environment, specific conditions, and needs of the local community.

The high cost of quality education is a serious problem. Quality education is costly because it requires good textbooks, equipment, and teaching materials, as well as properly trained and adequately compensated teachers. In general, poor quality stems from inadequate spending on education.[5] Consequently, a school that wants to provide a reasonable quality of education must assess additional charges on its students (the amount of the charge usually depends on the economic status of the parents).

Another shortcoming is a continuing lack of qualified teachers. Many unqualified teachers are being produced by the nation's colleges. This is due, in part, to the fact that the teacher training institutes do not attract the brightest students. The very low salary of a public school teacher is clearly one deterrent. Given their low income, teachers are usually forced to hold more than one job and therefore cannot concentrate fully on teaching. Additionally, they often miss opportunities to improve themselves either by in-service training or by attending upgrading courses.

A further problem is that, while the supply of graduates from teacher training institutes may be high, a considerable number of graduates never actually enter the teaching profession. One of the motivations for students to enrol in teaching training institutes is simply to obtain an academic degree as a stepping stone for entering other professions. Although empirical data is unavailable, it does appear that a large number of primary school teachers shift from teaching to administrative work. In fact, there is still an absolute shortage of primary school teachers, especially in remote areas. Teacher shortages at secondary schools persist in some specialized subjects, such as art and music, in provinces where the local teacher training institute does not run an appropriate training programme (World Bank 1996c, p. 5).

The problem of maintaining quality in private schools is further aggravated by the fact that some teachers, especially mathematics teachers, are lured away by the business community. Schools and training programmes managed by the business community offer higher salaries and better working conditions.

Not only are the better secondary schools located in Java, but so are the better institutions of higher education. It is generally accepted that the older, more established institutions are the best, and these are mostly located in Java. The top four of these are the University of Indonesia in Jakarta, the Bogor Institute of Agriculture, the Bandung Institute of Technology, and Gadjah Mada University in Yogyakarta. While some private higher education institutions are of reasonable quality, none of them is comparable to the four major public institutions (Oey-Gardiner 1991, pp. 84–85).

Most Indonesian universities also suffer from a shortage of academically qualified teaching staff. In 1995, the majority of teaching staff held only the equivalent of Bachelor's degrees, and only thirty per cent of the teaching staff in public institutions and eleven per cent in private institutions held the equivalent of Master's or Ph.D. degrees (World Bank 1996a, p. 4).

Changes in law and regulations in 1989-90[6] granted financial autonomy to all public higher education institutes, which permitted them to retain direct earnings. Although precise data are not available, it is likely that financial autonomy will further widen the disparities between the stronger and weaker institutions (Oey-Gardiner 1991, p. 94).

RELEVANCE : MISMATCH BETWEEN GRADUATES AND LABOUR FORCE NEEDS

Education is considered relevant if it fulfills the needs of consumers and users (Babari and Prijono 1996, pp. 76–77). The issue of relevance in the

Indonesian education system is acute, as the present system, especially the higher education, is not producing graduates with the types and level of knowledge and skills that are needed by the rapidly growing and structurally changing economy. One indicator of this mismatch is the long waiting period between graduation and employment. One study of ten universities found that graduates in humanities and social sciences and those from universities located in regions with lower levels of economic development had difficulties in finding jobs and were unemployed for periods of up to three years following their graduation (World Bank 1996a, pp. 5–6).

Labour-intensive manufacturing tends to need more workers with primary or lower secondary education than upper secondary or tertiary education. As shown in Table 8.1, through the year 2003 the projected demand for workers with a general basic education (lower secondary and primary school) will be higher than the supply. Assuming that more students will continue on to upper secondary education and tertiary education, there will be an absolute decline in the supply of lower secondary school

TABLE 8.1
Labour Demand and Supply, by Education Level, 1988–2003
(per cent)

Education Level	1988–93		1993–98		1998–2003	
	Demand	Supply	Demand	Supply	Demand	Supply
Primary & below	48	29	27	16	20	3
General lower secondary	22	21	25	21	27	15
Vocational upper secondary	13	20	17	18	19	21
General upper secondary	12	21	24	30	24	39
Tertiary	3	4	4	5	6	7
University graduate	2	6	2	10	3	15
Total (%)	100	100	100	100	100	100
Total Number (millions)	11.5	11.9	12.6	13.0	13.3	13.7

Note: Percentages may not add to 100 due to rounding.
Source: National Development Planning Board (Bappenas).

graduates in the years 1998–2003 as compared to the years of 1993–98. At the same time, the projected demand for workers with higher education will be lower than the projected supply.

Another indicator of the mismatch is the unemployment rate. National labour force surveys and population census data show that unemployment rates are higher for those who have completed upper secondary education, especially for those living in urban areas. In rural areas the number of upper secondary graduates is also increasing, although in most rural areas available jobs are still limited to family businesses and farming. This leaves only a small share of job opportunities outside the agriculture sector.

A similar increase in unemployment can be seen among those with tertiary education. This is in line with the skill structure of the industrial sector, which requires only 1.5 per cent middle level managerial employees, compared with 66.3 per cent skilled production line workers and 17.9 per cent unskilled workers (*Kompas*, 12 March 1994). Growth in tertiary graduates is much faster than the growth in job opportunities (Setiawan 1991). Those who have completed tertiary education (and many upper secondary school graduates as well) are often members of the middle class and can afford to wait until an appropriate job comes along. However, in the long term mismatches not only result in higher unemployment rates among university graduates, but cause a reduction in their relative wage rates and consequently encourage employers to substitute them for non-university educated workers. Graduates often have to adjust their career expectations and accept lower quality and lower paid jobs (Glytsos 1989).

The changing structure of the economy is also changing the mix in the types of skills required at the high-education end of the spectrum. In particular, there is a growing need for scientists, engineers, and technicians. There are already significant shortages of personnel in fields such as biotechnology, electronics, metallurgy, and computer science (Ranuwihardjo 1991, p. 54). Based on predictions for the period of Repelita VI (1994–1999), there will be an increasingly serious shortage of graduates in pure sciences (Table 8.2). By contrast, colleges and universities are producing far more graduates in law and the social sciences than there are jobs in these specialities. According to UNDP (1990), 63.1 per cent of university students are enrolled in social sciences, which includes education, social studies, economics, business, and administration, whereas only 23.3 per cent of the students are enrolled in natural sciences, including medicine, engineering, physics, and agriculture.

TABLE 8.2
Projected Labour Supply and Demand for
University Graduates, 1994/95–1998/99

Discipline	Supply	Demand	Difference (%)
Humanities	41,663	12,922	69
Social Sciences	435,689	144,871	67
Law and Judicial	226,618	40,125	80
Pure Sciences	5,563	263,795	–97
Agriculture & Forestry	27,721	92,129	–70
Mass Communication	6,253	2,347	60

Sources: Higher Education Graduate Manpower Studio (*Studio Tenaga Kerja Lulusan Pendidikan Tinggi*); National Development Planning Board (Bappenas); Department of Education and Culture; Department of Manpower; Central Bureau of Statistics (BPS) 1990/91.

Indonesia also lags behind almost all other Asian countries in the production of science graduates. Comparative data show that the percentage of all twenty-three year olds in Indonesia with natural science and engineering degrees was only 0.4 per cent compared with 0.8 per cent in China, 1.1 per cent in India, 4.2 per cent in Taiwan and Singapore, and 6 per cent in South Korea and Japan (BPPT 1993, pp. 120–21).

The high cost of establishing science and technology faculties may have a bearing on the tendency for concentration in the social sciences, rather than hard science and technology programmes. Only an estimated fifteen per cent of tertiary education institutes offer a science and technology programme (*Kompas*, 3 September 1994).

Research and development in science and technology at the tertiary education level is also far from satisfactory, both in terms of quantity and quality. In fact, even at those universities which consider themselves research universities research remains far from adequate. The main problem, as in primary and secondary schools, is the lack of qualified teachers and appropriate facilities. Basic research and development — essential for an industrializing society — at the university level is also rare. Although investment in science and technology research is not always immediately profitable for government or private enterprises, since the results are usually seen only in the long term, investment in research is still necessary in order to develop the human resources to meet Indonesia's current and future needs.

GOVERNMENT INITIATIVE: "LINK AND MATCH" AND THE "DUAL SYSTEM"

In 1993, in response to the mismatch problems being experienced in the labour market, the Department of Education and Culture introduced the concept of "link and match". The goal of the link and match policy was to increase the relevance of education to the needs of development in general, and to the labour market and the business and industrial world in particular. The policy was to be applied to all levels of education, from primary to higher education.

As an initial step, in 1994 a "dual system" (*sistem ganda*) of education was established at vocational secondary schools, to provide structured on- and off-the-job training tailored to specific needs of the labour market. The programme was introduced at 247 vocational secondary schools through-out the country, involving 36,788 students and 6,078 small and medium sized companies. In order to gain support from the private sector and to obtain information on the requirements of business (both now and in the future), the department has been attempting to establish a co-operative relationship between the education sector and the business community (Department of Education and Culture 1993c). The department is co-operating with the Chamber of Commerce and Industry, business associa-tions, and companies in implementing this programme.

The goals of the dual system are: (1) to improve vocational education; (2) to strengthen the link and match between school and work; (3) to increase efficiency in the education and training of qualified workers; and (4) to recognize and appreciate work experience as part of the educational process (*Business News* 7, no. 350, 1994).

The dual system integrates off-the-job education provided by schools with on-the-job training acquired in the workplace. Industries provide training places for students in a real setting, and co-operate in the develop-ment of an appropriate curriculum and in the formulation of examinations and testing that measure actual skills acquisition. Trainees therefore gain experience in real work situations in industries, and the length of training (around three to four years) is commensurate with the time needed to acquire the skills required by industry. The on-the-job work undertaken by trainees is related to the education and training in basic skills taught in the classroom. In this way there is a closer link between formal education and real, applicable skills.

The success of the dual system of course depends very much on the degree of interest and co-operation on the part of the business and industrial world. Vocational schools must to take the initiative in approaching industries or enterprises. However, a number of companies have expressed reservations about participating in the dual system because of previous negative experiences with apprentices. Large companies face risks of costly disruptions in production or damage to equipment by poorly prepared student workers. Small companies, on the other hand, face financial constraints which limit their ability to participate.

The Minister of Education and Culture has openly acknowledged the difficulties in implementing the dual system (*Kompas*, 6 April 1995), and the number of interested students still exceeds the number of available training facilities. Thus while this is a potentially promising initiative to solve the mismatch problem, it is still too early to determine if it will succeed in preparing significant numbers of students for the workforce.

ENTERPRISE AND EDUCATION

The shortage of qualified personnel such as managers and technicians is recognized as a major constraint on further development (CSIS 1990). In anticipation of the need for more qualified human resources in the private sector, and to attract both foreign and domestic investment, the laws on foreign investment (Law No. 1, 1967) and domestic investment (Law No. 6, 1968) state that both types of investors are allowed to employ foreign executives and professionals for positions that cannot be fillled by Indonesians. However, investors are obliged to provide education and training to Indonesians in order to prepare them to eventually take over the jobs of expatriates. Foreign investors are also obliged to provide education and training facilities in the fields of management and business administration, and domestic and foreign marketing (Prijono 1993, p. 4).

One of the government requirements for establishing a private educational institution in Indonesia is that it must come under the formal auspices of a foundation (*yayasan*) or some other social institution. This reflects the official philosophy that education is a not-for-profit endeavour (Government Regulations Nos. 27, 28, 29 and 30 of 1990). In keeping with this legal framework, a number of firms have set up foundations to provide education in the general area that the company is involved in, but do so in an explicitly charitable fashion. The following examples illustrate the variety of business projects and approaches.

Yamaha Group

The Yamaha Training Center enrols senior high school graduates who do not continue on to the tertiary level. Students are trained to become entrepreneurs or independent skilled workers in an eleven month course. In keeping with the business orientation of the Yamaha group, the Yamaha Center provides motor cycle technical education and training, free of charge. The curriculum is forty per cent theoretical and sixty per cent practical.

Gobel Group

The Masgobel Educational Foundation is an in-house training activity established in 1984 in Jakarta by the Gobel Group, an electronics firm, and its joint venture partner, Matsushita of Japan. The foundation's main activities are education, training, research, and information. Its purpose is to improve the quality of human resources of the seventeen companies within the Gobel Group. The foundation supports and assists these companies in personnel recruitment and in providing education and in-service training to employees.

The foundation also provides a social service through vocational training for school dropouts in an apprenticeship project, sponsored by the Chamber of Commerce and the Department of Industry. There is a possibility for those involved in apprenticeship training to be recruited as employees of the Gobel Group enterprises or other companies.

Other organizations also use the Masgobel Foundation's training facilities, including the Department of Manpower, the General Directorate of Customs Duties, and other private companies. These programmes run from three days to three months. The average number of students is 2,000 per year, with educational backgrounds ranging from senior high school diplomas to academy and university degrees.

Mercu Buana Group

Another example is the Mercu Buana Group, whose main business is general trade and animal husbandry. This group founded the Menara Bhakti Foundation, which established Mercu Buana University in 1985. The university sets reasonable tuition fees so that students from low income families can afford a university education (*Media Indonesia*, 10 August 1992).

Mercu Buana University has four faculties: Engineering (with Departments of Civil Engineering, Architecture, Mechanical and Electrical Engineering, Planning, and Informatics Engineering); Agriculture (with Departments of Cultivation and Social Economics); Economics (with Departments of Management and Accounting); and Communication (with Departments of Journalism, Public Relations, and Advertising). The initial enrolment was only 125, but as of 1993 this number had grown to 2,599 students. In 1992/93 the university produced 171 graduates, of whom 24 were technical engineers, 25 agricultural engineers, and 122 economists.

The main characteristic of Mercu Buana University is the application of a learning-by-doing programme. Apprenticeship programmes have been established with companies and development projects managed by the Mercu Buana Group. The university also provides supporting programmes, such as English courses in co-operation with the Indonesia-America Institute and computer courses in co-operation with Mercu Buana Raya Contractor, Ltd.

Sahid Group

Another major firm, the Sahid Group, primarily involved in the hotel industry, founded the Sahid Jaya Educational Foundation in 1988. This foundation established the Sahid Academy of Hotel and Tourism, and Sahid University, which as of March 1995 had faculties of Economics (Departments of Economics and Development Studies, Tourism, and Hotel Management), Communication (Departments of Public Relations and Information), and Engineering (Departments of Food Industry, Industrial Management, and Environment Technology). Other departments are Accounting, Marketing and Trade, Journalism, Business Communication, and Mechanical and Informatics Engineering.

Co-operative Programmes

An alternative approach to meet specific labour skill needs is through co-operation by groups of firms. For example, in 1980 114 entrepreneurs (76 of them belonging to the 200 largest business groups in Indonesia) established the Prasetya Mulya Foundation. In 1982 the foundation established the Prasetya Mulya Graduate School of Management. Prasetya Mulya conducts management education and training, research, and public services, in addition to special programmes in the form of courses, seminars, and workshops. As a public service, Prasetya Mulya offers assistance, especially to small-scale entrepreneurs, in various aspects of business management.

The education and training programmes organized by the business community both reflect the needs of the labour market in general, as well as companies' particular needs. This explains the heavy emphasis on business schools and engineering programmes in business-sponsored education ventures at least at the tertiary level.

In-house training activities, however, are still relatively uncommon. Although the government has encouraged the business sector to participate in organizing education and skill training programmes by providing tax incentives,[7] implementation continues to be a problem, even in providing upgrading courses for employees. A small number of large companies is free from this problem because these companies have sufficient facilities and resources, either at the parent company or regional branch companies. However, the majority of companies, particularly small and medium-sized firms, are reluctant to commit time and resources to structured in-house training. This is partly because firms frequently lose trained personnel to "poaching" by other companies offering better compensation. Thus, although programmes run by businesses in pursuit of their own interests can help to bridge some of the education and training gap, they cannot substitute for broader government-sponsored programmes.

EDUCATION AS A COMMODITY

Quality education is costly. The high admission and tuition fees limit access to students who can afford to pay, denying academically qualified but poor students. In line with the rise of an affluent middle class in Indonesia, education — particularly pre-school and tertiary education — has become a lucrative commodity guided by market forces, which responds to consumer demand represented by employers as well as by students. According to John D. Stanford, "education is a private economic commodity" (UNESCO 1988, p. 103).

The extent of the market's and community's demands for education are illustrated in the following examples of educational institutions established by the Lippo and Jaya Groups. Both are in the real estate and finance businesses (Prijono 1995, pp. 469–70).

Lippo Group

The Lippo Group was ranked in 1991 as the sixth largest business group in Indonesia. In 1993 Lippo established Pelita Harapan School, an elaborate, extremely expensive private school located on a ten hectare site in the midst of the sprawling, exclusive 1,000 hectare Lippo Village real estate project in Karawaci District, Tangerang (25 kilometres west of Jakarta).

The school is intended to be a profit-making venture. It was introduced simultaneously with the launching of Lippo Village, a luxurious housing and condominium project. The 1.6 hectare plant was built at a total cost of around US$10 million for the primary and secondary schools, and was estimated to return the investment in five to ten years. Five hundred students enrolled at Pelita Harapan in the first year (based on an initial target of 600 students) despite very high admission fees and tuition. The school has since expanded from pre-kindergarten up to university levels.

Pelita Harapan is outfitted with high quality facilities and supported by expatriate teaching personnel. Distinguishing characteristics of the school are the mastering of English at an early stage, encouragement of creative thinking, and a variety of extracurricular activities. It has sports facilities (a horse track, swimming pool, gymnastic centre), art studios (painting, music, and dancing), science labs (language, physics, and research), computer terminals, library, and a dormitory.

Pelita Harapan University was established in 1994 and enrolled 270 students in its first academic year. The university has three faculties: Economics (Departments of Management and Accounting); Civil Engineering and Planning (Departments of Architecture, Civil Engineering, and Design); and Industrial Engineering (Departments of Electrical, Informatics, and Industrial Technology).

In 1994 Pelita Harapan built another school on a 10 hectare lot in the 2,000 hectare Sentul Royal Highland development project in Bogor (50 km south of Jakarta), with an investment of Rp20 billion (US$10 million). In its first academic year Pelita Harapan Sentul enrolled 200 students in the lower and upper secondary schools. After construction is completed, enrolment is projected to reach 2,000 students. Pelita Harapan plans to extend its schools to other locations in the north, east and west districts of Jakarta, as well as to Bandung and Surabaya (*Media Indonesia*, 5 June 1994).

Jaya Group

Another real estate development conglomerate that has entered the education field as a profit-making endeavour is the Jaya Group. Jaya has a long-standing involvement in education through Tarumanagara University, a private university specializing in business and engineering courses. In addition to helping supply the needs of the growing business sector in general, the Jaya group recruits Tarumanagara graduates to work at its numerous constituent firms.

In 1995, the Jaya Educational Foundation established the Global Jaya Kindergarten and Primary School. As in the case of the Lippo Group's school, Global Jaya is connected with a new residential community being developed by Jaya outside Jakarta. English is the medium of instruction. The school planned to add lower and upper secondary education levels in 1996.

CONCLUSION

The role of education in preparing people for life is becoming much more complex, with rapid social changes affecting the world of work, especially with the application of modern technology and the rising demands of industrialization. One visible contribution of education to both economic growth and poverty alleviation in Indonesia has been the universalizing of primary education. By the early 1980s, Indonesia had attained a net enrolment rate (the percentage of children from the relevant age group who are enrolled) of over 90 per cent in primary education. Having achieved universal primary education, the government is now working towards universal lower secondary education, with the objective of reaching this goal by 2010 (World Bank 1996a, p. 1).

At present, the main challenge is to improve the efficiency of educational institutions, the quality of processes and outputs. Quality improvements needed include: better teacher training programmes; improved teaching in math, the sciences, and languages; better textbooks and teaching materials at all primary and secondary schools; teacher pay incentives and career paths; improved classrooms; new curricula; and higher achievement standards at all education levels (Boediono, McMahon, and Adams 1992, p. 11). At the university level, the main task is to improve the qualifications of academic staff and the development of laboratories and research. This includes financial incentives so that academic staff can devote more time and energy to teaching and unpaid research. Regulations setting limits on supplementary earnings may be needed as well (Arndt 1991, pp. 152–53).

Indonesia's formal educational institutions are being challenged by the demands for higher quality graduates emanating from the business community. Specifically, a "mismatch" has developed between the graduates produced by educational institutions and the needs of the industrial sector. Employers complain that graduates do not fulfill the requirements of the labour market, and blame the educational system for producing poor quality graduates. In fact, education's responsibility is to prepare students for *working life* that will ease their transition to the world of work, and not for the preparation of an *occupation*. In this respect, programmes have been introduced in general secondary schools to provide pupils with the mastery of one or more practical skills. However, truly effective preparation for working life requires a major change in the structures and processes of the education system (Singh 1986, pp. 144–47).

Employers also tend to prefer graduates from abroad, especially graduates of prestigious universities, rather than domestic graduates. This is due to the better quality of education, better communication and foreign language skills, and greater independence and initiative of foreign graduates. Domestic graduates from favoured universities, such as the University of Indonesia (UI), the Bandung Institute of Technology (ITB), and Gadjah Mada (UGM) are preferred to graduates of other Indonesian universities for the same reasons. The challenge is to improve education at all Indonesian universities to meet the perceived needs and desired qualifications in graduates.

As it is unlikely that the government will be able to raise substantially the budget levels for the education and training system, the private and business sector will play an increasing role both in financing and in directly providing education and training.

Some businesses are involved in education through public service initiatives, for example through the establishment of vocational and technical schools with reasonable tuition fees. These undertakings also fulfill the company's own needs for qualified human resources. Other business initiatives in education are intended as profit-making ventures, and are characterized by more elaborate facilities, international standards and high fees. Such initiatives provide domestic alternatives to overseas study, especially at the primary and secondary level, as well as preparation for continuing studies abroad or to meet other future needs. In addition, the government has sponsored business co-operation with public educational institutions through the dual system of education.

The emergence of education as a for-profit business and the establishment of expensive schools present a dilemma for government policy. On the one hand, there is a need for high quality education (which is expensive) which the government cannot provide. On the other hand, the proliferation of élite schools, which further accentuate disparities in the quality of education, may heighten inequality and perceptions of a social gap in Indonesian society. The principle of equality and equity in Indonesia's constitution and national development plans requires that gifted children who come from less fortunate families be given the opportunity of high quality education. One possibility for achieving this objective, modelled on regulations for the construction of luxury housing projects, would be for investors in education to be required to provide places for low-income students. An alternative is for the state to establish schools for gifted children, such as the armed forces' Taman Taruna Nusantara (senior high school) which provides education at no charge.[8] A related and even more challenging problem is how to provide better education opportunities to people in the more remote areas.

Thus the involvement of the private sector in improving the quality of education appears promising, but also raises a number of questions and uncertainties. What is clear is that the government will continue to bear the responsibility of ensuring that the poor are given increased opportunity to participate in the educational and training process, and that the educational system develops in a way that meets overall national objectives, including equity.

Notes

[1] At a seminar on the Identification of Educational Problems, in Cipayung (28–30 April 1969).

[2] Between 1976 and 1993, 800 vocational schools at the lower secondary level were closed, with others scheduled to be closed in 1994–95.

[3] There are five types of tertiary education institution: *Academy* (a three-year, professional diploma-granting institution); *Polytechnic* (same as an academy, but primarily in the fields of engineering, agriculture and some areas of business); *College of Higher Education* ([Sekolah Tinggi], an institution granting degrees up through Ph.D. in one sub-speciality within a broader academic discipline, such as banking or the performing arts); *Institute* (an institution granting degrees up through Ph.D. in one discipline or field such as engineering or agriculture); and *University* (an institution granting degrees through Ph.D. in multiple faculties

and disciplines). The 78 public tertiary institutions in 1994 consisted of: 2 academies, 27 polytechnics, 4 colleges of higher education, 14 institutes, and 31 universities.

4   The 1,159 private institutions included: 380 academies, 8 polytechnics, 476 colleges of higher education, 47 institutes, and 248 universities.

5   Estimates of public spending on education in Indonesia vary widely, but several published estimates for the 1980s and 1990s are in the range of three per cent of Indonesia's GDP (see World Bank 1993*b*, pp. 198–99). This is roughly comparable to the percentage figures for other rapidly-growing Southeast Asian countries such as Thailand or even Singapore. However, the per capita GDP of these other countries is significantly higher than Indonesia's, so actual spending per student in Indonesia remains considerably below the level of most of its neighbours.

6   Education Law No. 2 of 1989 and Government Regulation No. 30 of 1990.

7   Department of Finance Decree No. 770 of 1990 stipulates that all costs accrued by taxpayers for in-service training, apprenticeships, and scholarships can be deducted from a firm's gross income for income tax purposes. The training may be provided by training institutions in or outside Indonesia.

8   For a further discussion of the Taman Taruna Nusantara School, see Chapter 5.

9

Mass Media: Between the Palace and the Market

Dedy N. Hidayat

The mass media in any country operate in a field of multiple forces that compete to define what the media do, as well as for access to and control of the media. The impact of economic growth on mass media institutions in a country in any period of time depends therefore importantly on the distribution of political power within that country.

This chapter discusses the impact of economic growth on the Indonesian mass media during the thirty years of the New Order. Discussion of this topic will, in part, be framed with reference to the much hypothesized causal relationship between capitalist economic development and democratization.

In Indonesia under the New Order administration, the media are frequently referred to as "partners in development" and have been used both to facilitate the functioning of development policies and to create a political climate conducive for economic development. Under the official New Order label of "developmental journalism" or "development supportive communication" both government-owned and private media are intimately involved in a variety of development processes, promoting development programmes from agriculture to family planning.

The Indonesian mass media under the New Order have also been, for the most part, important economic institutions in their own right. They help generate surplus value in other sectors of commodity production through advertising, and thus contribute directly to the economic growth of the country.

At the same time, the current condition of the mass media in Indonesia is also a byproduct, or in part, a creation of economic development. Mass media, as a capitalist venture, is part of the market economic system in which it operates. Mass media institutions (newspapers, magazines, television and radio stations) are thus influenced by the logic, operation, and evolution of the Indonesian market economy.

The first section of the chapter examines the ways in which the institutional structures, content, style, personnel and organization of the media have changed as a result of economic growth during the New Order. The second section analyses the "vertical political integration" of the media industry, that is, the multifaceted business and political relationships between the ruling élites and the private media industry. The third part of the chapter considers the impact of capitalist economic development on the media industry and whether and how this has created an impetus towards greater democratization. Finally, the fourth section offers some conclusions on the relationship between diversity in the media industry (in terms of opinions and ideas) and market forces, and on whether we can aptly identify media "diversity" as evidence of democratization.

ECONOMIC DEVELOPMENT AND THE GROWTH OF THE MEDIA INDUSTRY

In economic terms, the media industry is unusual because it operates in what is called a *dual product market* (Picard 1989, p. 17). It creates one product but participates in two markets: the audience market and the advertising market. Consequently, the growth of the media industry can best be observed as a dual process that depends on economic growth: the evolution of an audience *and* the expansion of the advertising industry.

On one hand, the relationship between the growth of media industry and audience is one of supply and demand for two basic social commodities: information and entertainment. Rapid economic growth in the Indonesian market economy has brought into being a new middle class with relatively higher education and income levels. This new middle class consists of entrepreneurs, private companies' employees, foreign enterprises' workers, middle level government employees, and other professional, technical, and administrative workers. The growth of the middle class means greater opportunity for the media to find large "serious" audiences who have real purchasing power as a result of the country's growing economic and cultural sophistication. This is reflected in increases in circulation figures. Before the New Order, the largest newspaper was *Harian Rakyat*, an organ of the Indonesian Communist Party, with a claimed circulation of 55,000 (Dhakidae 1991, p. 46). During the first decade of the New Order administration (1966–76), most Indonesian newspapers sold less than 20,000 copies per day and only four dailies had a circulation exceeding 40,000 (Hill, D. 1994, p. 36). Today, however, many daily newspapers enjoy a circulation of more than 100,000 with at least two dailies (*Kompas* and *Pos Kota*) over 500,000.[1]

On the other hand, the relationship between the growth of media industry and the growth of advertising expenditures is one of supply and demand for "access to consumers". The growth of the advertising industry during the early years of the New Order, particularly in the 1970s, was in part made possible by the New Order's open door policy for international trade and foreign investment. Transnational advertising agencies arrived *en masse* during the 1970s, the two largest being Lintas and Ogilvy & Mather International — the latter with US$5 million in billings in 1977 alone (Lent 1982, p. 184). Of the ten largest advertising agencies in the world (by gross income), five established offices in Indonesia (Anderson 1980, p. 1259). The growth of the advertising industry is directly reflected in the growth of advertising expenditures. Available data show that from 1988 to 1992 alone the total advertising expenditures increased from Rp314 billion to Rp978 billion (PPPI 1993, p. 47). Despite the Indonesian Press Council regulation to limit the amount of space devoted to advertising (not more than thirty per cent of a daily's pages), the growth of advertising expenditures has meant greater opportunity for country's media industry to become a most profitable business by selling their "access to audiences" to advertisers.

Clearly, media performance in the audience market affects performance in the advertising market. The amount charged for bringing readers and viewers into contact with advertisers' messages — that is, the price of the audience as a commodity — is dependent upon the size and characteristics of the audience to which access is provided.

Since the late 1960s, the Indonesian media industry has entered a new historic phase. According to a senior journalist who experienced this transition, the development of a commercially-oriented Indonesian press began when the New Order regime launched its series of five-year economic development plans in 1969 (Oetama 1987, p. 26).

However, it is also true that the current shape of the Indonesia media industry is not entirely a result of economic growth. One media analyst, Wibisono (1992*b*), has estimated that about 100 out of 260 publication permits are currently held by 10 major media conglomerates. The emergence of these giant media groups (especially the Gramedia Group, the Pos Kota Group, and the Tempo Group), which signifies a tendency towards the concentration of capital, has in part been facilitated by a series of economic crises — not simply rapid growth — that took place during the course of economic development under the New Order. Daniel Dhakidae (1991, p. 69) suggests that concentration and centralization of capital under the ownership of a few huge media groups accelerated at each recurrence of a specific or temporary economic crisis — newsprint short-age, devaluation of the rupiah, oil crisis. The growth of the media industry was also a byproduct of state intervention, in the forms of subsidies and protection, especially during the early years of the New Order administra-tion. Nonetheless, the Indonesian media industry has in general benefited from the economic growth and the resulting expansion of both audience and advertising-based markets under the New Order.

POLITICAL AFFILIATION, ORGANIZATIONAL STRUCTURE, AND PERSONNEL

One of the most fundamental changes that has accompanied Indonesia's economic growth is the change in the political affiliations and political outlook of most media in the country. Previously, the Indonesia media functioned primarily as "political media" that aligned their editorial policies with particular politicized segments of the population. Except for a few newspapers, most media now aim at achieving a broad readership across social, cultural, and political distinctions in order to have as large circulation as possible and hence attract more advertisers.

The depoliticization of the media began in 1966 when the New Order government annulled a regulation that stipulated that all newspapers had to be formally affiliated with a political party or mass organization of their choice.[2] Most of the partisan and politically activist newspapers from the 1960s (such as *Nusantara*, *Pedoman*, *El Bahar*, *Suluh Marhaen*, *Duta Masyarakat*, *Abadi*, and *Harian Kami*) ceased to exist. Some were closed down by the New Order government for political reasons, while the rest went out of business simply because they could not meet market demands. Several remaining newspapers which retain an image as political or partisan, such as *Merdeka*, *Pelita*, *Suara Karya* and *Berita Yudha*, were financially struggling for their existence. The strong survivors are those papers that have successfully depoliticized their contents in line with the political criteria of the new ruling élites, and with the changing market conditions which have been shaped by the emergence of a critical middle class who demand independent accounts of social and political realities — not just partisan views.

The growth of the media industry has affected the organizational struc-ture of many media institutions in the country. In the days before rapid growth, according to Jakob Oetama (chief editor of *Kompas*, the largest daily newspaper in the country), the press consisted of only a board of editors controlling the process of news production, whereas the printing equipment was owned by other companies, and circulation and advertisements were also limited. The publication of a newspaper merely required a consensus between a man of ideas who had a "pen" and a man of means who had a "heart". The technicalities of the business side were treated almost as an unpleasant interruption; what was important was the idea behind the newspaper (Makarim 1978, p. 273). Nowadays, many Indonesian news media have developed into integrated organizations with control over editorship, printing, and management (Oetama 1987, p. 25). A newspaper is for the most part a capitalist venture that involves large investments of capital, technology, and organizational skills. There has also been widespread adoption by the print media of modern marketing and promotion methods or strategies, through hiring professional media consultants from the United States, applying audience research, and sponsoring various public events, from seminars to sports.

The changes in the organizational structure and the political affiliation of the media also led to changes in media personnel. Prior to the New Order, journalism seldom drew the solid "backbone-of-the-nation" type of person who had the privilege of an outstanding higher education; the latter rather become lawyers, research economists or consultants, businessmen, government executives or minister's assistants. University dropouts and "free" intellectuals made up the bulk of most newspapers' editorial staffs (Makarim 1978, p. 272). Today, as salaries of reporters have risen to relatively respectable levels, young university graduates from various fields of study, including many with degrees from outstanding universities abroad, seek employment in media enterprises. At the same time, the growth of the media industry and the intense competition among the media have imposed demands for increases in the skill levels of media personnel. Consequently, most media organizations now tend to employ more university graduates than in the past. The proportion of university graduates among Indonesian journalists has significantly increased, from 28.2 per cent to 45.3 per cent during 1988–93 alone.[3] In addition, more and more Indonesian journalists have gained opportunities to participate in professional training programmes abroad through scholarships offered by foreign institutions or governments.

The changes in the organizational structure, the political affiliation, and the economic orientation of the media can be directly observed in the media's content and style. As soon as the country geared itself towards economic development, there was a marked shift in mass media content from a preoccupation with "national prestige and national identity" during the period of Guided Democracy, to a concern with a clean and efficient government for economic growth under the New Order administration.[4] Increases in the proportion of university graduates among Indonesian journalists may also have contributed to changes in media content. In contrast to their senior colleagues who tend to be "politician" journalists, many of the young graduates prefer to perform as "professional" journalists. The new breed of editors in the Indonesian media industry is more preoccupied with journalism's professional standards and pursuing impartial and balanced reporting, avoiding normative analyses, separating facts from opinions, applying academic analytical tools and conducting scientific public opinion polls, etc.

Some observers argue that the new breed of editors tends to be more apolitical out of fear to write straightforward news on sensitive political matters. However, there certainly have been various critical and militant individuals among them. There seems an inherent critical impulse among some of the young journalists, as many of them believe in the idea of the press as the "fourth estate". In many cases, their older colleagues have prevented them from reporting critical issues. A young journalist from a leading newspaper, for example, mentioned that his chief editor had warned him not to proceed with his news gathering on a sensitive matter involving the Soeharto family's businesses. Another young journalist, from a prestigious national daily newspaper, revealed that he was not allowed to make a critical report involving products sold by a chain of stores owned by the newspaper as part of its corporate diversification strategy.[5]

CHANGING STRUCTURE OF THE MEDIA INDUSTRY

Another important impact of economic growth on the structure of the media industry is the emergence of specialized media sectors. The needs of the growing business and financial community for up-to-date business and economic information can now be easily satisfied by a growing number of newspapers and magazines specializing in economic news, business and trade issues, or property development. Prominent among these specialized publications are *Bisnis Indonesia, Swa, Properti, Info Bank, Info Bisnis, Warta Ekonomi, Indonesian Business and Economic Review*, and *Indonesian Business Weekly*.

In addition to print media, Indonesia also has a growing electronic media sector. Radio, including private stations (especially in the larger cities such as Jakarta) has long been a popular medium with a large audience. A major new development occurred in November 1988 when RCTI (Rajawali Citra Televisi), the first private television station in Indonesia, started broadcasting. In the subsequent years, four more private television stations have been established: SCTV (Surya Citra Televisi), TPI (Televisi Pendidikan Indonesia), AnTeve, and INDOSIAR.

Further changes in the structure of the Indonesian media industry can be projected on the basis of a growing tendency among some media enterprises to spread their financial risks into a wider range of products. For example, the media enterprise that publishes *Kompas* has diversified into a series of related activities in media and non-media sectors. It now publishes more than twenty magazines and journals (including *Jakarta-Jakarta*, a pictorial magazine, *Bola*, a sport tabloid, *Bobo*, a magazine for children, and *Info Komputer*, a specialized magazine on computers). The Kompas Group has also invested in book publishing through its Gramedia and Grasindo publishers, in a chain of bookstores (Gramedia Books), and even a chain of supermarkets (Grasera).

These past few years have also been marked by a trend towards horizontal integration of media companies. For example, the Kompas Group collaborates with several regional newspapers, including *Sriwijaya Pos* in Palembang, *Serambi Indonesia* in Aceh, *Berita Nasional* in Yogyakarta, and *Mandala* in Bandung. The Tempo Group has gained control of over more than ten regional newspapers, including *Manuntung* in Balikpapan, *Jawa Pos* in Surabaya, *Fajar* in Ujung Pandang, *Independen* in Jambi, and *Manado Post* in Manado.

The newest entrant in the print media industry is Media Indonesia Group — which is owned by Surya Paloh, a founder of the influential lobby group, Forum Komunikasi Putra-Putri Purnawirawan ABRI (Communication Forum for the Sons and Daughters of Retired Members of the Armed Forces). This group took over ten regional publications (including *Mimbar Umum* in Medan, *Yogya Post* in Yogyakarta, *Cahaya Siang* in Manado, and *Nusatenggara* in Denpasar).

A more recent trend involves another form of horizontal integration in which media groups jointly control several print media. For example, Kompas Group and Pos Kota Group control the daily *Surya* in Surabaya.

As some media groups have expanded beyond the media sector, correspondingly some large companies in other spheres of operations have moved into the media industry. One example is Bimantara Group, owned by one of President Soeharto's sons. Predominantly a general products corporation, in 1988 Bimantara Group penetrated the media sector with the first commercial television station, RCTI. Another example is Salim Group, a business empire that entered the media arena in 1994 with a commercial television station, INDOSIAR.

The entrance of non-media firms has brought a new breed of entrepreneur into the Indonesian media industry. Prior to the 1980s, successful media companies were mostly owned by journalists who successfully managed their media as businesses. Jakob Oetama, head of the Kompas Group, has vast experience as journalist and is still the chief editor of the daily *Kompas*. Goenawan Mohammad of the Tempo Group is also a prominent journalist, even though he was financially backed by successful business persons (including Eric Samola and Ciputra, a real estate entrepreneur). Even former Minister of Information Harmoko, who owns the Pos Kota Group, was also a journalist. Today, however, many businessmen without any background or prior experience in journalism have invested in the print media sector and even dominate the private television sector in the country. With their footing in various lucrative business sectors, they are potentially able to risk slow returns in the print media industry.

Rapid growth of the media industry also means more intense competition, both within and between media sectors. The intensity of competition can be inferred from the fact that even though total newspaper circulation increased from 1.5 million in 1973 to 7.6 million in 1985, the number of newspapers decreased from 122 to 95 over the same period (Department of Information 1986). During 1990–94, the number of newspapers climbed again, from 64 to 74, but the total paid circulation went down from 5.3 million to 4.7 million (*Media Indonesia* [Editorial], 29 March 1995).

The entry of private television stations into the Indonesian media arena may be one of the factors responsible for the decrease in newspaper circulation. In the advertising market, competition between newspapers and television is also becoming more apparent. During 1989–94 alone, advertising expenditures in newspapers decreased from 50.5 to 33.3 per cent of the total advertising expenditures in the country, whereas the share of television increased dramatically from 6 to 49.1 per cent over the same period (SRI 1995; PPPI 1993, pp. 47). The total amount of advertising expenditures rose markedly over this period (from Rp481 billion in 1989 to Rp1,345 billion in 1993 and an estimated Rp1,600 billion in 1994), so spending on print media advertising as a whole actually inceased (from Rp315 billion in 1989 to Rp555 billion in 1993, and an expected Rp603 billion in 1994). Advertising revenues of some leading print media popular with middle and upper-middle class readers, such as *Kompas* and *Femina*, rose significantly over this period, but other print media suffered as their advertising revenue steadily decreased. Among these were *Pos Kota*, the second largest paper by circulation and the most popular for the middle to lower class, *Suara Karya, Suara Pembaruan*, and also *Media Indonesia* (which had only begun publication in 1991).[6]

Despite the fact that various dimensions of the Indonesian media industry have been changed by economic growth, one dimension remains untouched. The 1966 Press Act stipulates that "the capital of a Press Corporation shall be wholly national, whereas all its founders and Board Members shall be Indonesian citizens". The government opened various sensitive economic sectors to foreign investment, but the Indonesian media industry is still fully in the hands of indigenous economic actors.[7]

VERTICAL POLITICAL INTEGRATION

The growth of the media industry has attracted participation by many members of the ruling élite. These new investors in the media industry have included members of a web of politically well-connected business people that surrounded former President Soeharto's family and friends, or heads of conglomerates who have strong ties with powerful officials. Thus, even though the government itself does not invest in the growing media industry, several members of the ruling élite have built up large portfolios of shareholdings in media companies. Former Minister of Information Harmoko, the official who had the authority and the power to grant or to withhold the crucial Press Publication Business License (Surat Izin Usaha Penerbitan Pers, or SIUPP), himself controlled significant shares of various print media and commercial radio stations.

The economic integration previously discussed is thus in part also a vertical political integration between the media and certain segments of the Indonesian ruling élite. With vertical political integration, the economic and political resources necessary for the media professionals to maintain their existence and to attain their publishing and media goals are coming under the control of the ruling élite.

This is especially visible in the commercial television sector. Two of five commercial television stations in the country have been under the control of giant business enterprises owned by members of the Soeharto family. As previously mentioned, Soeharto's son Bambang Trihatmodjo controls RCTI. Bambang's elder sister, Siti Hardijanti Rukmana, controls TPI through her holding company, Cipta Lamtoro Gung Persada. Another commercial television station, SCTV, is owned by Soeharto's step brother, Sukamdani Gitosardjono. The owner of INDOSIAR, the latest entry in the television sector, is Liem Sioe Liong (Sudono Salim), one of Soeharto's business associates who is ranked among the forty richest persons in the world. Thus, the commercial television sector in the country is practically dominated by members of the ruling élite and their business associates.

In the print media sector, the process of vertical integration between media and ruling élites can be observed from the fact that various "men of power" act as patrons for, and at the same time control significant shares of, various print media. As previously noted, the Pos Kota Group is owned by Harmoko, former Minister for Information and chairperson of the ruling party, Golkar. Abdul Gafur, a deputy chairperson of Golkar, and Sudwikatmono, Soeharto's cousin, are the business patrons and advisors of *Sinar*, a news magazine with a circulation of around 30,000. Sudwikatmono also reportedly invested several billion rupiahs in a 24-page weekly tabloid, *Bintang* (with a claimed circulation of around 200,000). Another of Soeharto's step brothers, Probosutejo, controls the dailies *Kedaulatan Rakyat* in Yogyakarta and *Kartika* in Semarang. Siti Hardijanti Rukmana, the eldest daughter of Soeharto, is general chairperson and publisher of *Wanita Indonesia*, a popular thirty-two-page tabloid for women with a claimed circulation of 250,000. Two new entrants in the magazine sector that began publication in early 1995, *Gatra* and *Tiras*, both have important patrons. *Gatra* is controlled in part by prominent businessman Bob Hasan, one of Soeharto's close associates, while the patron of *Tiras* is Abdul Latief, Soeharto's Minister for Labour. In 1985, ten prominent leaders of Golkar bought sixty per cent of the shares of *Pelita*, a daily newspaper that was previously aligned with the Development Unity Party.

The investments made by members of the ruling élite and their business associates in the media industry can be explained in terms of both political and financial purposes. David Hill (1994, p. 103) observes that the involvement of Sudwikatmono in *Bintang* and *Sinar*, and of Siti Hardijanti Rukmana in *Wanita Indonesia*, may represent a "calculated move by members of the presidential family to establish a foothold in the print media, after their success in the electronic media". Michael Vatikiotis (1993, p. 108), former *Far Eastern Economic Review* correspondent in Jakarta, went even further, asserting that "one way in which Soeharto appeared to be trying to curb the press by early 1990 was by having members of his own family buy into the media". Several Indonesian journalists and observers also tend to believe that the driving intention of the First Family and its business associates to enter the media industry was to strengthen their political position.

Christianto Wibisono (1992*a*, p. 33), head of the Indonesian Business Data Center (PDBI), believes that the conglomerates were entering the media industry both for financial and political advantage. His view is supported by Goenawan Mohammad (1995, p. 9), former chief editor of the then-banned *Tempo* magazine. Goenawan noted that only ten days after the closure of *Tempo*, a new publication company under the control of Bob Hasan, was established to publish another news magazine, *Gatra*. *Gatra* was modelled on *Tempo*, and was staffed by approximately thirty former *Tempo* journalists. Bob Hasan could make greater profits in other sectors of the economy. This led Goenawan Mohammad to believe that political motives were more important than financial motives for Bob Hasan when he invested in the print media industry.

Such vertical integration of the private media and the ruling élite is a rare phenomenon in the world's market economies. A general trend in developing market economies is the attempt by national governments to gain control of mass media. This is usually accomplished through the establishment of mixed-ownership in which the government shares with private interests the responsibility for media operations (see, e.g., Vasquez 1983, pp. 274–75). In neighbouring Southeast Asian market economies Singapore and Malaysia, the media have been under state-controlled holding companies. However, in the Indonesian case, it is the individual members of the ruling élite and their business associates who personally own the media as part of their business empires.

The launching in 1993 of *Republika*, a daily newspaper staffed by members of the Association of Indonesian Muslim Intellectuals (Ikatan Cendekiawan Muslim Indonesia or ICMI), is also part of the vertical integration of the media and ruling élite. ICMI, headed by then Minister for Research and Technology Habibie, was formed in December 1990 with President Soeharto's blessing. This organization — largely dominated by Muslim government bureaucrats and other well-educated devout Muslims — has been a major political resource for Habibie, and thus the main thrust behind the publication of *Republika* is more political than economic (money-making).

DEVELOPMENT, THE MEDIA, AND DEMOCRACY

The vertical integration of the media and the ruling élite in Indonesia has been facilitated by the fact that the basic relationship between the media and the ruling élite has not been changed fundamentally by economic growth. The East Asian evidence provides weak support for the proposition that successful capitalist development generates pressures towards democracy (see, e.g., Berger 1987, p. 161). On the contrary, the South Korean and Taiwan cases even have led some scholars to conclude that there is an inevitable trade-off between democracy and development, and that authoritarianism contributed to economic growth, at least in the initial stages of development.

The Indonesian political scene from the late 1980s until the early 1990s was marked by demands and promises for more democracy, giving the impression that economic growth had at last produced the political conditions conducive for democratization. In December 1989, General Edi Sudradjat, the then army commander, said that Indonesians were now better educated, therefore they want more active participation in the decision-making process. Sudradjat also called for an end to the "foot-stomping, father knows best style of leadership" and warned that the military did not wish to be "mere fire-extinguishers" for those in power (*Indonesian Observer*, 5 December 1990). President Soeharto, in his national address of August 1990, called on people not to be afraid to express different views. In March 1991, when Abdurrahman Wahid, one of the most respected Muslim leaders in the country, formed the Forum for Democracy, the military did little to oppose the move and may even have lent some tacit encouragement (Vatikiotis 1993, p. 97). In June 1993, the government announced the formation of the National Commission on Basic Human Rights, to be headed by a former chief justice of the Supreme Court. June 1993 was also marked by an initiative approved by the president towards reconciliation with the most prominent group of political dissidents, the 'Petition of 50' group *(Tempo*, 12 June 1993).

Over the same period, there was also an air of relaxation of restrictions on the press. In August 1990, then Co-ordinating Minister for Security and Political Affairs Admiral Sudomo went even further by assuring that there would be no more banning of newspapers. A foreign journalist and observer recounted that the military had become less hostile towards the press, and actively encouraged journalists to write about selective social and economic issues (Vatikiotis 1993, p. 108). The extensive press coverage of the deadly November 1991 incident between the Indonesian Army and East Timorese, in Dili, East Timor, was also believed by many observers as signalling a new era of openness and press freedom as formerly off-limits issues were exposed in detail. Friction between military and civilian factions within the government was analysed by various leading publications during the early part of 1993. In mid-1993, newspapers headlines were filled with news about, and interviews with, members of the 'Petition of 50' group. Workers' demonstrations and unrest made front-page news.

Those signs and events led ordinary Indonesians to believe in the prospect of more openness, more democracy, and a freer press. Memory of wholesale bannings of the press that had taken place prior to the 1990s seemed to have been erased from the minds of Indonesian journalists.[8] As previously taboo topics began to be brought up with greater boldness, there developed a sense among Indonesian journalists that the very magnitude of the media industry and the growing diffuseness and fragmentation of power within the New Order regime would no longer enable the government to undertake the kind of mass bans that typified the 1970s (Hill, D. 1994, p. 41).

However, the sudden and dramatic closure in June 1994 of two leading news magazines, *Tempo* (with an estimated pre-closure paid circulation of 180,000), and *Editor* (with a claimed circulation of 80,000), and on political tabloid, *Detik* (with claimed sales of 400,000), again brought home the fact that the government retained the power to revoke permission to work in or run a business in the media sector. The closure of the three publications — described by David Hill as an anachronistic act (Hill, D. 1994, p. 41) — clearly proved that the power relationship between the ruling élite and the media remains asymmetric, and that the president's interpretation of what is or is not permissible in the media supersedes the Indonesian Press Act of 1982 that stipulates (in Chapter II, Article 4): "No censorship or bridling shall be applied to the National Press".[9]

It may be true that the New Order's power was gradually fragmenting as market pressures were overriding the old military obsession with nebulous and ill-defined "national security" (Hill, D. 1994, p. 1). However, the bans clearly suggested that economic growth had not — thus far — generated sufficient pressures towards more democracy and freer press, and that after nearly thirty years of economic development, Indonesia remained a bureaucratic polity in which power was concentrated in the hands of the president and the highest élite echelons.[10]

This helps explain Dhakidae's statement that the closure of media is not a mere journalistic affair alone, but rather a "meta-journalistic" affair (Dhakidae 1994, p. 51) which cannot be understood simply in terms of the problems of gathering and reporting of news. Instead, it should be analysed within the larger political-economy framework of mass media under New Order Indonesia. The fact is that the limits of press freedom have been subjectively defined by the ruler according to shifting socio-political conditions.[11]

Clearly, control over the permission to run media enterprises is an effective instrument of power. The government has been in a strong position through its ability to grant publishing licenses only to politically and economically favourable parties, and to revoke permission from those who fail to meet certain political and economic criteria. Article 5, Section 1 of the 1984 regulation of the Minister for Information concerning press publication permits states that Press Publication Business Licenses (SIUPP) are "granted to bonafide, free and responsible press companies/publishers". In addition, Article 19, Paragraph 1 of the regulation stipulates that "the working capital earmarked by a press company/ publisher shall be sufficient for the financing of its regular publications for the duration of at least one year".[12] On the one hand, this means that a publisher with small working capital and without political credentials (or with a known reputation as a critic) has virtually no chance to get a publication permit. On the other hand, members of the ruling élites and their crony businesspersons always have a good chance to get permission to enter the media sector.

In the print media, the government's selective distribution of SIUPPs clearly contributes to the integration of the private media and the ruling élite. In 1987, when 267 licenses had already been issued, Minister for Information Harmoko declared that the government would not issue any new SIUPP. The official reason was that the print media sector was already saturated. Several applications for SIUPP were therefore turned down; among them was the application from Surya Paloh — former chief editor of the banned daily *Prioritas* — to publish a new daily, *Realitas*. However, the minister did issue a SIUPP for a different new daily, *Republika*, the mouthpiece of the Association of Indonesian Muslim Intellectuals (ICMI) headed by the then Research and Technology Minister Habibie, and to the new magazine, *Gatra,* financed by the president's close business associate Bob Hasan.[13] Several banned publications have been granted new publication permits, under altered names, only after they agreed to accept some pro-government individuals as shareholders, senior editors, or editorial advisers.[14] Goenawan Mohammad, after the closure of *Tempo*, asserted that trying to run an Indonesian news magazine was like being a "pilot in a hijacked plane" — even if the government was prepared to issue *Tempo* a fresh publishing license, he would only end up with "a new plane complete with new hijackers" (Hill, D. 1994, p. 157).

Thus, it seems that the publication of a newspaper in Indonesia today requires a consensus between a man of ideas who has a "pen", a man of means who has political "access" to the centres of power, and a man of power who need have nothing but power. This contributes to a process whereby market forces and political power work to exclude not only media institutions that lack the capital base required to survive the market competition, but also those that lack political connections and protection.

The demands and promises for more democracy and freer press, however, continued after the June 1994 triple bans. The bans themselves did not go unchallenged. For the first time in the history of the Indonesian press, the bans triggered widespread social protest questioning the constitutional authority of the Information Minister to ban mass media. More than that, the chief editor of *Tempo*, Goenawan Mohammad, brought suit in the State Administrative Court (PTUN), alleging that the Information Minister had acted illegally in revoking the magazine's publishing license. In May 1995, PTUN Chief Judge Benjamin ordered the Minister for Information to reissue the magazine's publishing license. Harmoko appealed the decision to the Appeals Court, and in November 1995 that court also found in favour of *Tempo*. As noted in Chapter 3, Harmoko then successfully appealed to the Supreme Court. However, for a time at least, these court decisions bolstered a public spirit pressing for more democracy and a freer press.

DIVERSITY, DEMOCRACY, AND THE MARKET

Diversity — in terms of opinions, ideas, viewpoints — is often regarded as a desirable goal of media activity. It is a necessary condition for rational choice by its audience, and is often considered as essential to democratic systems where alternative political ideas and policy options are offered competitively and discussed publicly.

To assert that the current trend towards the vertical integration of private media and ruling élites contributes to a higher degree of homogeneity in the content of mass media may be overstating the case. There is persistent social, cultural and political diversity in Indonesian society. This may lead to constant demands for diversity in media content, based on the tastes, political orientations, socio-economic backgrounds, life styles, ethnicity, and regional origins of Indonesians. Thus, as a result of market demand, the media industry is always structured to take account of this diversity. Nor can the ruling élite who control the media be conceived of as a homogeneous or monolithic entity; they may have different views, opinions, and strategies; they may even engage in a series of intra-élite frictions. In fact, ownership does not necessarily mean total control over the day-to-day news producing activities. Also, unlike the Guided

Democracy period when most papers were affiliated with political parties or groups, much of the media today is actually more independent in editorial policy, and thus relatively free to take sides according to their editors' judgment of which side they wish to support.

In July 1994 for instance, the news magazine *Sinar*, owned by Sudwikatmono, the president's step-brother, and backed by some prominent leaders of Golkar, was one of several publications that received written warnings from the Department of Information in the weeks after the bans of *Tempo*, *Editor*, and *Detik* for their reporting of the bans and subsequent demonstrations. There are several possible explanations as to why *Sinar* carried such reporting. First, tabloid papers like the banned *Detik* had demonstrated the market demand for investigative, politically critical publications; therefore *Sinar* could have been attempting to capture the readership vacuum left by *Detik* by increasing its bold reporting of events of public interest (Hill, D. 1994, p. 101). Second, public acceptance of any publication associated so transparently with the presidential family may be slow, and *Sinar* may have been trying to gain credibility by providing politically critical reports. Third, *Sinar* may have been taking a stance in a factional split within the ruling élite.[15]

Diversity and dissenting views, however, do not necessarily mean democracy. A variety of pressures from the markets, and from ongoing intra-élite frictions, may lead to the appearance of differing perspectives, conflicting opinions, or competing ideas in the media. The diversity nevertheless tends to focus on a narrow set of problems, especially as defined by the government or as framed within the ruling élite's horizon of thoughts and interests. The diversity of opinions on the bloody November 1994 incident in Dili, East Timor, for example, was framed within the context of the sincerity of the government to hold a public inquiry into the incident.

The extent of government control over permission to enter the media industry, and the degree of vertical integration between the media and ruling élite, determine the degree to which issues reported by the media represent the "population" of issues that exist in Indonesian society. Government control over licensing and the growing media-ruling élite integration clearly operate in favour of the exploitation of certain issues and the suppression of various unfavourable issues in the media. The closure of newspapers and magazines is part of a mechanism in which some issues — along with groups or individuals who try to publicly present these issues — are eliminated from the spheres of public discourse. Under current conditions, public discussion of a number of issues is discouraged, and there are several highly sensitive issues that media are prohibited from touching. These include issues dealing with Marxism, and also those that may generate ethnic, religious, racial, group or class conflicts. However, until the upheaval of 1998, one issue stood out above all for its sensitivity: the business activities of the Soeharto Family. This meant that dissenting ideas, differing views, and conflicting opinions on issues dealing with what lay beneath the surface of the New Order regime was a commodity that the Indonesian media industry was unwilling to produce, even though there was always a high demand from the market for such a commodity.

Under the constellation of political power in the New Order, Indonesian journalists had to develop a skill for reading between the palace and the market, to find the formula for reporting politically sensitive news that maximized sales and minimized the risk of closure. On one hand, according to a former journalist, reporters and editors had to develop "sensitivity to the government's approval and disapproval conveyed through an intricate and culturally conditioned network of subtle gestures and signals" (Makarim 1978, p. 279). On the other hand, journalists have also had to be sensitive to the market's demand for independent critical reporting.

Notes

[1]   The estimated sales figures of some newspapers in 1991 were as follows: *Kompas* ± 522,872, *Pos Kota* ± 500,000, *Jawa Pos* ± 350,000, *Suara Pembaruan* ± 338,802, *Media Indonesia* ± 302,000, *Pikiran Rakyat* ± 180,600, *Kedaulatan Rakyat* ± 105,000, *Surya* ± 127,983, *Suara Merdeka* ± 170,700 (Department of Information 1991/1992).

[2]   The earlier pattern, under which media were affiliated with certain political parties or groups, had been formalized on 25 March 1965 — a few months before the end of the Guided Democracy era — in a Department of Information regulation requiring that all newspapers be affiliated with a political party or mass organization of their choice (Decision of the Minister for Information, No. 29/SK/M/65 on the Basic Norms for Press Enterprises). Under this regulation, editorial staff had to be nominated by the party, which was regarded as having responsibility for the contents of the paper.

[3]   Data from the Department of Information (*Departemen Penerangan RI*), 1988 and 1993.

[4]   See Makarim (1978, p. 259). However, a study by Robert Crawford (1967, p. 486) suggests that there was no significant change in newspaper content during the last years of the Guided Democracy era and

the first year of the New Order administration: interest in political affairs remained high. (Nevertheless, Crawford's study might have yielded different results had it covered a longer period of the New Order era, especially the period after the wholesale banning of newspapers in 1974.)

5   This was revealed openly by a young journalist in a discussion on "A Journalistic Code of Ethics" organized by the Soetomo Press Institute in Jakarta on 19 December 1994.

6   *Kompas'* advertising revenues rose from Rp50,258 million in 1989 to Rp85,916 million in 1993, and *Femina's* rose from Rp5,284 million to Rp13,194 million over the same period. *Pos Kota's* revenues fell from Rp8,035 million to Rp5,400 million, *Suara Karya's* from Rp4,214 million to Rp2,641 million, *Suara Pembaruan's* from Rp28,510 million to Rp27,550 million, and *Media Indonesia's* from Rp17,927 million in 1991 to Rp9,367 million in 1993. These figures are based on data from the Indonesian Advertising Companies Association (PPPI 1992, 1993, 1994).

7   Government Regulation No. 20 of 2 June 1994 included the mass media sector among previously off-limits sectors to be opened to foreign investment and majority foreign ownership. Information Minister Harmoko sharply criticized the regulation, asserting that it contradicted the 1966 Press Act which explicitly prohibited any kind of foreign investment in the press industry. Harmoko declared that, irrespective of the regulation, he had the full support of the president in keeping foreign investment out of the press industry. Despite having earlier signed the regulation, the president endorsed Harmoko's exemption of the press from the regulation. This suggested to some observers that the president was losing touch with the increasingly complex web of government policy. However, there was also speculation that the pressures for foreign investment in the media sector came from politically-connected business interests in television, specifically television companies owned by members or associates of the Soeharto Family, who wanted to bring in foreign partners. This speculation was in part related to the signing of a cooperative agreement between Rajawali Citra Televisi (owned by Bambang Trihatmojo, Soeharto's son) and international media magnate Rupert Murdoch, in March 1994. But if this speculation were true, it would have meant a conflict between the Minister for Information and members of the Soeharto Family, which was very unlikely. An alternative line of speculation was that the minister's statement was intended only to calm small media enterprises

which would suffer more if giant foreign investors co-operated with local media conglomerates. Sceptics within the print media argued that "well-connected conglomerates in the television sector will deftly evade restrictions on foreign investment; outside funds could easily be disguised by a series of transfers between media and non-media branches within these giant conglomerates" (Hill, D. 1994, p. 152).

8   During the New Order era, there were at least two wholesale mass media bannings. The first occurred in January 1974, when thirteen newspapers and news magazines were closed following student demonstrations and riots in some major cities. Encouraged by the scale of demonstrations and riots, the press gave heavy coverage and editorial support. Again, in 1978, the government banned fourteen newspapers for their coverage of student demonstrations directed at President Soeharto.

9   President Soeharto had signed the 1982 Press Act. However, many observers believe that the order to close down the three publications came directly from the president, based on the fact that the bans were issued shortly after the president, in early June 1994, asserted that some publications were jeopardizing national stability by provoking political controversy over such issues as the purchase of former East German warships (see Hill, D. 1994, p. 42).

10   In 1978, Karl Jackson (1978, pp. 3-5) suggested that, at least since 1957 when parliamentary democracy ended with the declaration of martial law, the basic form of government in Indonesia had been a presidential variant of a bureaucratic polity. The concept of a bureaucratic polity means a political system in which, among other things, the national decision-making process is insulated from social and political forces outside the highest élite echelons, and thus the main arena for political competition is interpersonal competition within the élite circle. In Jackson's presidential variant of a bureaucratic polity, power is more concentrated in the hands of the president.

11   For example, in 1983, *Ekspo*, a news magazine, lost its publication permit for publishing a report on "Indonesia's 100 Millionaires", a list that included an embarrassing number of New Order business associates. In what has been termed by observers as a suicidal act, another news magazine, *Fokus*, also lost its publication permit in 1984 for publishing a similar list of Indonesian millionaires. However, according to David Hill, "it was symptomatic of the changing attitudes towards capitalism that such listings had become common by the 1990s, when it was no longer politically embarrassing to be ostentatiously rich." The

official explanation for closing down *Tempo* in June 1994 was that some of its contents did not reflect a "free and responsible press", without referring to any specific reason. However, there is a widely shared view that the true cause was *Tempo* reports on a controversy over the purchase of thirty-nine East German warships that implied a factional split between the camp of Research and Technology Minister Habibie and the military. The reports included critical comments by some military leaders over the purchase, which had been managed by Habibie. This may have been seen as a direct challenge to the president, since the purchase had been made with his approval.

12 This in practice requires that press companies/publishers that apply for publishing licenses possess at least Rp500 million (around US$250,000), proved by a bank statement.

13 See "Media", *Independen* 1995 (10), p. 4. After the closure of *Tempo*, the editors applied for a license to publish a new magazine, *Berita*. Their application was turned down. However, less than two weeks after *Tempo*'s closure, the government granted a license for *Gatra* to a group in which Bob Hasan was a principal investor.

14 For instance, *Sinar Harapan*, a leading evening newspaper with estimated paid circulation of 350,000, was shut down on 9 October 1986 for commentaries on economic policies. This newspaper was permitted to reappear under a new name, *Suara Pembaruan*, after its publishers agreed to accept a prominent leader of the ruling party as its general chairperson. Another example is the case of *Pelita*, a daily newspaper which was previously considered a voice of Islamic opposition to the ruling élite. *Pelita* was shut down in May 1982, and subsequently reopened under new, pro-government leadership.

15 Several senior military officers publicly mentioned that they did not approve the use of ministerial authority to close down *Tempo*, *Editor*, and *Detik*. For example, Lieutenant General Harsudiono Hartas, then chief of the armed forces social and political affairs office, declared that if the government believed certain articles had breached press guidelines, it should rather have taken legal action against the particular journalists or editors responsible for any contravention.

SECTION IV

Other Institutions

10

Social Organizations: Nahdlatul Ulama and Pembangunan

Douglas E. Ramage

SOCIAL ORGANIZATIONS AND THEIR ROLES IN INDONESIAN SOCIETY

In the early twentieth century, a variety of self-consciously modern, mass-based, organizations emerged in the Netherlands East Indies. These organizations have been central to the development of Indonesia as a modern society and an independent national state. Many of these organizations are now identified as fostering the origins of Indonesian nationalism and were key to the germination of the idea of independent Indonesia. These institutions included, for example, the Sarekat Islam (Islamic League), Budi Utomo (Noble Endeavour), the Taman Siswa education movement, Muhammadiyah (modernist Islamic organization), and Nahdlatul Ulama (traditionalist Islamic organization).[1]

The principal feature of all these organizations was that they were primarily indigenous associations that grew up in the late colonial era to provide services of various kinds to Indonesians. In the decades prior to World War II these organizations were the exemplars of civil society in the colonial era. They concentrated primarily in fields of religious welfare, social work, education, business, and health. Although these organizations eschewed explicit participation in politics (leaving that to the independence-oriented political parties), they often developed an important nationalist orientation or engaged in activities that were to have important consequences for strengthening the nationalist movement.

This chapter is concerned with how these early "modern" mass-based societal organizations have adapted to the rapidly accelerating rate of industrialization and economic development that has been a hallmark of the New Order. Of the organizations mentioned above, only two — Muhammadiyah and Nahdlatul Ulama — remain very active as large, mass-based nation-wide organizations which have sought to adapt and change in response to rapid economic development. Although these organizations are "social" organizations they are, perhaps most importantly, largely *Islamic* organizations dedicated to religious issues. Yet it is these Islamic organizations which remain the largest mass-based social institutions in the country, with millions of members. Therefore, the ways in which these ostensibly non-political organizations, have adapted to Pembangunan (the New Order's programme of economic development) is worthy of analysis in this study of how Indonesian institutions have adapted and responded to development.

This chapter primarily considers the Nahdlatul Ulama (Revival of Religious Scholars, or NU) as a case study. Nahdlatul Ulama is today the largest socio-cultural organization in the country, with approximately twenty to thirty million members and followers. The specific purpose of the chapter is to analyse how NU has dealt with — and proposes to deal with — the social, political and economic changes in Indonesia that have accompanied, and possibly been caused by, the New Order's programme of Pembangunan. However, it is first necessary to review NU's organizational structure, origins and political behaviour.

NU'S ORGANIZATIONAL STRUCTURE[2]

Authority and leadership of NU is formally vested in the hands of the *kiai* (a title meaning religious scholar, but increasingly used for any leader of the Islamic movement regardless of the leader's level of religious knowledge) and *ulama* (religious scholars, also often community leaders). According to Andre Feillard, NU is "an association of ulama *fiqh* (ulamas knowledgeable in Islamic jurisprudence) and ulama *tarekat* (ulama involved in the sufi brotherhoods), within a relatively centralized and well-managed organization" (Feillard 1993, p. 1). The base of education and training of NU's leaders has traditionally been the *pesantren*, Islamic boarding schools where future *kiai* study under senior religious scholars and spiritual leaders. The NU is governed and managed by a form of dual leadership. Its religious head is the Rais Am (President-General) who is assisted by a deputy Rais Am. The Rais Am is the ultimate authority in spiritual matters for NU. Religious issues are the primary responsibility of NU's supreme Islamic law council, the Syuriah. Additionally, the organization is run on a day-to-day basis by a Ketua Umum (General Chairman), the head of the NU's Executive Board, and in reality, often the most powerful leader in the organization. NU holds a congress every five years to elect the Rais Am, deputy Rais Am, and Ketua Umum. Abdurrahman Wahid has been selected three times to lead NU as Ketua Umum (1984, 1989 and 1994). NU is also organized into provincial and district branches, each with a leadership structure mirroring the national structure.

NU'S PURPOSE AND OBJECTIVES

Nahdlatul Ulama was established partly in response to the arrival and vitality of the modernist/reformist Islamic movement in Indonesia in the early twentieth century, most prominently represented by the formation of the modernist organization, Muhammadiyah, in 1912. NU's ulamas conceived of NU as a forum primarily for the reassertion and articulation of "traditionalist" Islam in Indonesia. Its primarily goal has always been to protect the *umat* (community of believers), especially in terms of traditionalist values and beliefs.

NU was established in 1926 by a group of *kiai* who were alarmed at the attacks on Islamic traditionalism by the growing modernist movement, typified by Muhammadiyah.[3] The interests that the NU *kiai* set out to defend and maintain were based on Sunni orthodoxy, in particular the loyalty to Sunni Islam's four legal schools. As Greg Fealy has pointed out, "maintaining orthodoxy meant maintaining the privileged position of the *kiai* because as 'doctors of law,' they were the only ones capable of interpreting Islamic law".[4] And the traditionalist *kiai* saw the modernists as threatening their key socio-religious roles. Moreover, there were also economic interests the NU *kiai* sought to maintain, as traditionalist *kiai* often held élite socio-economic positions as well, particularly in Java.

While NU has always maintained as its priority defence of traditionalist Islamic interests, the means NU chose to defend "traditionalism" and orthodox Islam was the development of an organization characterized by modern strategies and operations. And although NU has primarily been concerned with matters of faith, it will be shown below that NU's leaders have also given much consideration to how NU *as an institution* could best function in, and adapt to, Indonesia's rapidly changing political economy, especially in the New Order. For Indonesia's traditional Islamic leaders in NU, defence of traditionalism has never meant incompatibility with, or rejection of, modernity and development.

POLITICAL BACKGROUND OF NU

NU co-operated with the nationalists in the struggle for Indonesia's independence in the 1940s. Although NU joined with Masyumi, the modernist Islamic political organization, to present a united Islamic political grouping for a number of years, it broke away to form its own political party in 1952. Importantly, in the interest of national unity, NU's leaders decided that it was acceptable for independent Indonesia *not* to be an Islamic state.

From 1952 to 1973 NU functioned as an independent political party, garnering as much as eighteen per cent of the vote in the 1955 general elections. From 1973 to 1984 NU was the largest component of the PPP (Development Unity Party), the New Order's forced amalgamation of Islamic parties. In 1984 NU abandoned formal political activities and rededicated itself to religious, cultural and social activities in accordance with the organization's original purposes. Although NU is an ostensibly non-political organization dedicated to the social, economic and cultural improvement of its followers and the Indonesian *umat* in general, it has been recognized by the New Order government as one of the country's single most important institutions. The intense controversy and government involvement in the December 1994 NU Congress in Cipasung, Tasikmalaya testifies to the importance of Nahdlatul Ulama and the degree to which the government seeks to influence NU's direction, policies and leadership.[5]

ADAPTATION TO *PEMBANGUNAN*

It is extremely difficult to prove direct causal links between *Pembangunan* and NU's institutional changes and activities. However, if the New Order's three decades of Pembangunan are also taken to include political changes and various social trends, then it is possible to sketch out the ways in which NU has sought to accommodate, respond to, and even anticipate such changes. It is apparent that the major impetus for change in NU's institutional behaviour and in the political and economic thinking of its leadership has been political and other pressures from the New Order government and its development programmes.

As noted above, only for a part of NU's nearly seventy-year existence has it behaved explicitly as a political party — from 1952 to 1984. By the late 1970s many NU members, especially its younger activists and intellectuals, perceived that NU's political behaviour on the national stage had only distracted the organization from its initial purposes — to protect the *umat* in traditionalist religious matters and to encourage the social and economic improvement of the Muslim masses. Abdurrahman Wahid, the general chairman of NU since 1984, argues that thirty years of political activity at the national level only served to deepen government interference in NU's internal affairs and denigrate the organization's original social purposes. Moreover, during this period of political party activity NU's leadership atrophied and seemed unable to address the genuine social, economic, and educational concerns of the NU *umat*.

CHANGES IN INSTITUTIONAL BEHAVIOUR

The single most important change in NU's institutional behaviour and organization came as a result of decisions taken at its 1984 National Congress (or Muktamar) in Sitobundo. At this congress NU declared that it had abandoned formal participation in the New Order's political structure and was returning to its original mission — to cater to the religious, social, and educational needs of its followers. This decision was formulated as the "*Kembali ke Khittah* 1926" (Return to the Commitment of 1926). Kembali ke Khittah is NU's response to the pressures — political and economic — on the organization, particularly during the first fifteen years of the New Order. The Khittah strategy is NU's way to respond to government pressure, to recuperate from political exhaustion experienced after years of political manoeuvring, to protect the institution against further deterioration and outside interference. In general, NU's young leadership in 1984 — most prominently represented by Abdurrahman Wahid — argued that participating in a political system that provided few visible benefits to the NU *umat* was self-destructive and, moreover, not in accordance with NU's original mission and goals.[6]

The Khittah strategy was formulated to respond to both political and economic pressures that have accompanied the New Order's programme of Pembangunan. While the initial reasons for withdrawing from formal politics were political (outlined below), NU leaders were also acutely aware that NU must, according to Said Budairy, former head of an NU research and development institute (LAKPESDAM), "change itself to accommodate far-reaching social, economic, and cultural changes that have been unleashed by economic development".[7] However, the social-economic thinking of NU leaders as to how to reorient NU towards contemporary economic and social issues first required the internal consolidation and revitalization of NU as an independent non-political organization.

POLITICAL FACTORS

NU was an ardent early supporter of the New Order. Particularly the dynamic NU leader in the 1960s, Subchan Z.E., urged NU to actively fight against Sukarno and the PKI. NU's men's youth wing (ANSOR) carried out violent operations against suspected PKI sympathizers, particularly in Java. NU, along with other early New Order supporters, considered itself to be worthy of greater participation in national affairs than it had been under Sukarno. The New Order government however, sought to "depoliticize" society and ensure that all political activity was strictly controlled in accordance with a strategy to maintain "political stability" so that national economic development could be carried out. NU, along with all other political parties and actors, soon found itself constrained by an unsatisfying political format, particularly after NU was forced to amalgamate with the other existing Islamic-based political parties into the PPP in 1973. Moreover, in the 1970s NU found itself in opposition to the Soeharto government over a number of issues (for example, civil marriage laws and Pancasila education programmes). Although NU has always sought to protect the religious interests of the *umat*, it was unused to finding itself perceived as an "opposition" party.

Abdurrahman Wahid explained that the more NU allowed itself to stay in the New Order's restrictive political structures, the more its independence and integrity would wither away. Additionally, Abdurrahman Wahid argued that as long as NU remained a "political" actor its voice was increasingly *not* heard on the national stage and "NU found itself unable to clearly articulate alternative visions for national development".[8] This was due, in part, to the ability of the government to deeply involve itself in the internal affairs of the formal political parties. Therefore, according to Wahid, the only solution to NU's increasingly marginalized position and weakened institutional structure was to withdraw from politics and return to its roots and pursue goals of religious, social and economic improvement of its followers without direct participation in national politics.[9]

At its 1984 Congress, in addition to withdrawing from formal politics, NU also decided to embrace the five-point Pancasila doctrine as its philosophical foundation (*asas tunggal*), as the government was pressing all political and mass organizations to do. For Muslims, the major significance of Pancasila was its principle of "belief in god", which implicitly allowed other religions than Islam and meant Indonesia would not be an Islamic state, a long time goal of many Indonesian Muslims. Abdurrahman

Wahid and Achmad Siddiq argued that only by recognizing that Indonesia was based irrevocably on a nationalist (not an Islamic) ideology could Indonesian Islam flourish unmolested in the Indonesian state.

NU's abandonment of formal politics and embrace of Pancasila in turn had a very tangible political impact. That is, according to Abdurrahman Wahid, "NU left politics in order to participate more effectively in politics". The politics that NU engaged in were then much more grass-roots based. NU politics in the post-1984 era were the politics of the long term, the politics of education and culture. It has not been an élite political approach. The "Kembali ke Khittah" has allowed NU to find intellectual and institutional space to develop as a more democratic, socially-minded institution with nation-wide reach down to the grass roots. Many of the NU delegates at the December 1994 Congress argued that NU's successful resistance to outside interference in its congress proceedings and its democratic procedures exemplify a mass-based awareness of the meaning of democracy and accountability of leadership. Moreover, some NU congress delegates, such as Fajrul Falaakh who became a member of the NU Executive Board (PBNU) in December 1994, argue that NU will help expand the movement towards a civil society for all Indonesians. NU leaders and especially younger NU activists, argue that NU is helping to create and reinforce certain philosophical and principled arguments about what Indonesian society should look like (i.e., not based on Islamic politics, but instead seeing religion as a private matter to guide one's social interactions and behaviour).[10]

The NU initiative to "Return to the Commitment of 1926" was not fully embraced by all segments of the NU leadership or its followers. Thirty years of national politics had created vast patronage networks and a sense of political entitlement that were not easy to shake off. Yet at the 1989 and 1994 congresses the "Khittah" group prevailed again and Abdurrahman Wahid was re-elected general chairman. However, NU branches and members began to demand more concrete evidence of the appropriateness of the abandonment of politics. Greater attention was therefore paid to how NU should help its members adapt to the economic changes wrought by Pembangunan. NU's leadership pledged to focus on economic and community-based issues rather than national politics.

ECONOMIC FACTORS

It was not politics alone that provoked far-reaching institutional change within NU and in terms of its social activities. Abdurrahman Wahid has explicitly argued that NU must also ensure that its membership — and indeed all Indonesians — benefit from the country's rapid economic growth, especially in the 1990s (van Bruinessen 1991; Feillard 1993). Towards this end, NU initiated some small-scale pilot projects in the fields of banking, agro-industry, co-operatives, and education.

The most prominent of these NU initiatives has been the scheme to create 2,000 Peoples' Credit Banks (Bank Percreditan Rakyat, or BPR) throughout Indonesia. Abdurrahman Wahid and Mustopha Zuhad (former Secretary General of PBNU and responsible for the BPR scheme) argue that a nation-wide rural banking system can help develop a new generation of Indonesian entrepreneurs. These new entrepreneurs will then be better poised to ensure that rising incomes and standards of living accrue to the rural Muslim masses and not simply to urban dwellers in the major cities.[11] According to Zuhad, the BPRs will provide credit and modern banking facilities to ordinary, small-scale businesses throughout Indonesia. Abdurrahman Wahid adds that this will also naturally create a populace more committed to national economic development. Interestingly, the NU BPRs are intended to function as ordinary, interest charging banks. In other words, NU has concluded that interest can be accommodated by Islam in the context of a modern state with modern economic practices. The NU banking scheme has not progressed very far, however. By the time of the 1994 Congress, only twelve BPRs had been established. Indeed, the failure to move more rapidly to the stated goal of 2,000 branches was cited by opponents of Abdurrahman Wahid as evidence of why he should not be re-elected as general chairman. Although Abdurrahman Wahid claims government support for the NU BPR scheme, Adam Schwarz reports that former Finance Minister Sumarlin was instructed to place obstacles in the path of the NU banking project (Schwarz 1994, p. 189).

Based on interviews with Mustopha Zuhad, Abdurrahman Wahid, Gafar Rahman (former NU Executive Board member), Said Budairy, Fajrul Falaakh, and others, NU's thinking about its economic needs and participation in national economic development does not reflect zero-sum type arguments that NU's members suffer from the economic success of non-Muslims. These kinds of arguments are heard more often from others, including some activists associated with ICMI, the government-sponsored Association of Indonesian Muslim Intellectuals.[12] Instead, as Mustopha Zuhad explains, NU seeks to finds ways to "jump into" the economic prosperity enjoyed by others, but not to deny others' successes. The BPR scheme was first launched in a highly public co-operation with the non-Muslim, Chinese Indonesian-owned Bank Summa, and the BPR scheme was initially called "NUSumma". After the financial collapse of the Soeryadjaya family (owners of Bank Summa), NU decided to retain the name "Bank NUSumma" — but stated that the name now stands for "Bank Nahdlatul Ulama Sumber Manfaat Masyarakat" ("Bank NU — Source of Benefit for the People"). Moreover, according to Mustopha Zuhad, the new Bank NUSumma's motto is "From NU, by NU, but for *all* the people".[13] Therefore, NU's banking scheme is underlain by an inclusive vision of society and is cognizant of the realities of economic development including recognizing the potential benefits of co-operating with Chinese-Indonesian capital and banks.

THINKING ABOUT THE FUTURE, OR HOW NU COPES WITH "MODERNITY"

As an organization dedicated to a "traditional" form of Islam, some observers may be tempted to view NU as *kolot* (old fashioned) and therefore not modern and uninterested in designing strategies to cope with rapid societal change. Yet NU traditionalists have always been capable of adapting to their times — for example, by reforming *pesantren* education and adding secular subjects to the traditional religious curriculum. Clearly Abdurrahman Wahid and his colleagues have done much to attempt to depict NU as a fully "modern" organization, prepared to adjust to and anticipate the political, economic, and social demands of the current era.

It is often said that Abdurrahman Wahid stands alone — that his ideas are not shared by his followers and by NU as an institution. Yet it is precisely an increasingly large group of younger generation NU followers that have been implementing programmes and thinking about how NU should "change itself" to adapt to the multiple issues confronting Indonesia as a modern, industrializing society. Many of these young generation NU activists and thinkers are associated with various non-governmental organizations (NGOs), some of which are loosely connected to Nahdlatul Ulama, while others are directly under the general supervision of the NU Executive Board.

For example, LAKPESDAM is one of NU's main research institutes and NGOs dedicated to community-based development. LAKPESDAM is also NU's official documentation centre as well as a publishing house. LAKPESDAM was established after the Situbondo congress. Its original mission was to work for the improvement of the *lapis bawah* (poorest masses) of NU. Its former director, H.M. Said Budairy,[14] stated that

LAKPESDAM was designed to spread information that will actually "help" NU members throughout NU's branches across Indonesia. Said Budairy stated that part of the mission of LAKPESDAM was to encourage NU to change itself and adapt to new circumstances and challenges facing Indonesia.[15]

A concrete example of how NU has been trying to adapt to the demands of a changing society can be seen in a major educational and leadership training initiative begun by LAKPESDAM with funding from USAID and the Asia Foundation. The initiative is a "Post-Pesantren Leadership Training Project" in which exceptional *pesantren* graduates will be identified and given additional, specific education and training in various skills to make them more effective as future NU leaders. The current task in this project is to carry out research to identify exactly what are the needs of the potential future leaders and what kinds of skills — managerial, financial, administrative — they require. LAKPESDAM will then contract out to experts to prepare the curriculum. The curriculum will then be disseminated throughout all NU branches for instruction.

Other issues that LAKPESDAM is trying to incorporate into NU's internal discourse include the role of women in development and AIDS awareness. Said Budairy also notes that LAKPESDAM is working on various issues in co-operation with other religious groups including health and sanitation projects, the role of women in development, and joint co-operation with the Asian Institute of Health in Japan. LAKPESDAM also publishes the monthly *Bulletin Lakpesdam* which contains articles on the role of NU in economic development at the village level, changes in NU as a socio-cultural movement, and other issues. The *Bulletin* also contains articles and explanations of "appropriate level technology" for use at the village level.

Two other foundations or institutes loosely associated with NU deserve brief mention: "Yayasan 164" (the "164 Foundation," named after the address of NU's Executive Board headquarters in Jakarta, at No. 164 Jl. Kramat Raya) and LKiS. Ellyasa KH Dharwis, a young NU activist associated with both "164" and LKiS argues that NU's strength is that it seeks to defend the faith in a broad, expansive fashion. Ellyasa argues that by seeking an economically equitable, democratic society (and he cites the BPR scheme as a positive example), NU members defend traditional Islam in a sophisticated fashion. That is, he argues that the NU will remain relevant only if it seeks the development of a modern civil society in which all Indonesians, Muslim and non-Muslim, live in a nation characterized by a economic prosperity and democracy. Only in such a civil society can all Indonesians follow the teachings of their respective faiths by their own volition.[16]

Shortly after Abdurrahman Wahid's re-election as general chairman of NU on 5 December 1994, Wahid publicly acknowledged that much of his support came from the younger generation of NU activists who are most interested in ensuring NU's relevance for a modern society.[17] Many of these younger activists involved in Yayasan 164 and LKiS endorse Wahid's vision of a religiously tolerant, pluralist nation in which NU functions as a proponent of a democratic civil society.[18] Indeed, one of the most impressive young generation NU leaders and scholars, Fajrul Falaakh, has been elevated to the NU Executive Board for the 1994–99 term. The appointment of Fajrul, a lecturer in law at Gajah Mada University in Yogyakarta, is indicative of NU's awareness of the need for regeneration of leadership that shares the conception of NU as an institution relevant to a modern, industrializing Indonesia.

IMPACT OF ISSUES GENERATED BY ECONOMIC CHANGE ON NU

The major factors influencing and initiating most of the changes in NU outlined above derive primarily from political factors, not economic ones. However, as also noted above, this has not meant that economic issues have been altogether absent. (Indeed, some economic factors may have motivated the initial establishment of NU as some *kiai* sought to preserve traditionalist Islam as a means of maintaining their own privileged élite socio-economic positions in Indonesian society.) The NU leadership has clearly expressed a desire to establish programmes (such as the BPR scheme) that will be of direct economic benefit to the *umat* and allow them to participate more fully in rapid national economic growth. Additionally, LAKPESDAM for example, undertakes a wide variety of activities consciously designed to deal with issues generated by economic change and development. Abdurrahman Wahid has specifically argued that the NU masses should not be left behind in the rapidly growing prosperity enjoyed by urban-based conglomerates.

Much of this discussion has already dealt with the general institutional, political, and economic ways in which NU has responded to development. However, it may be helpful also to comment briefly on the impact on NU of a number of more specific changes that have resulted from rapid economic development.

The Emerging Middle Class

First, NU has been affected by the growth of the middle class in Indonesia. Although this has been primarily an urban phenomenon, growing numbers of NU followers are not solely rural peasants. Furthermore, an increasing number of NU branch leaderships are being filled by people who work as civil servants. More and more middle class civil servants are identifying themselves as NU followers. Andre Feillard argues that this is because by abandoning formal politics NU has made itself more attractive to people who otherwise did not want to be associated with an "oppositionist" group (Feillard 1993). It may also be the case that middle class urban NU activists find Abdurrahman Wahid's civil society ideas most appealing. Their membership may reinvigorate the organization regardless of how long Wahid may continue as general chairman.

Values

As previously indicated, NU has embraced the idea of Indonesia as a nation based on a religiously neutral national ideology (the Pancasila). At the 1994 NU Congress firm support was given to Abdurrahman Wahid's exhortation for NU as an organization to be tolerant and respectful of other religions and respectful of minorities in Indonesia. Issues raised by other, usually "modernist" Muslim organizations in Indonesia in the 1990s, such as fears of "Christianization" and the need for Muslims to be given a portion of political and economic power in accordance with their percentage of the population, were not heard at the NU Congress. Although NU *kiai* are committed to defending their faith, they tend not to identify non-Muslims as the cause of their problems. Indeed, numerous *kiai* and NU-affiliated NGOs reported that they encouraged inter-faith dialogue and co-operation.[19] Djohan Effendi, a senior researcher in the Department of Religious Affairs, has argued that one of Abdurrahman Wahid's biggest contributions to NU is that he has helped to create an intellectual environment within NU in which progressive, tolerant attitudes and values appropriate to Indonesia's ethnic and religious diversity, have been encouraged and nurtured.[20]

Finally, Nahdlatul Ulama has also been something of a pioneer in advocating co-operative business endeavours between the *umat* and the Chinese-Indonesian business community. While NU members have long co-operated with Chinese-Indonesians, it is particularly the NU-Summa Bank links that some observers felt greatly advanced racial harmony.

Institutional Relationships

In keeping with its own evolution as well as the broader change in society, NU's relationships with other institutions and the government have also changed dramatically. NU no longer sits in Parliament as a faction in the PPP. Nor do any NU members receive government posts or ministerial positions. Most significantly, NU has distanced itself from the only ostensibly "Islamic" political party — the PPP. In so doing, NU members have been free to vote in whatever way they wish. Many NU members in the 1987 elections opted to support Golkar, rather than the PPP. In 1994 Abdurrahman Wahid, as well as NU *kiai* such as KH Alawy Muhamad in Madura, suggested that in the 1997 election NU might encourage its followers to vote for the PDI.

NU's relationship with the government, however, remains extremely important to NU. Despite his advocacy of democracy and human rights (and the attempts by some parts of the government to dislodge him from the NU leadership at the 1994 Congress), Abdurrahman Wahid strongly argued that he has a good relationship with the President and the government in general. Even though this is not always entirely the case, Abdurrahman Wahid felt it necessary to reassure the ulama that NU is still on good terms with the government.[21]

The rapid increase in global communications and institutional connections has also impacted NU. NU has been increasingly linked to international organizations and institutions in the past ten years. Abdurrahman Wahid himself is a frequent contributor to international conferences and seminars whose topics range from religion to democracy and human rights. He was also the 1993 Recipient of the Ramon Magsaysay Foundation Award for Community Leadership, and has been elected as a co-president of the World Council on Religion and Peace. Other NU followers are also increasingly part of international discourse on Islam and community development.

CONCLUSION

NU was established to defend traditionalist Islam and it has often sought to do so in a pragmatic, flexible, and "modern" fashion. Defence of traditionalism has not meant rigidity and extreme orthodoxy in face of new challenges. Indeed, visionary leaders of NU such as Wahab Hasbullah, Hayshim Ashari, and Abdurrahman Wahid used modern organizational methods and importantly, *ideas*, to create and motivate a mass-based association precisely in order to adapt to the ways society was changing around them. While NU and its leaders have historically been primarily concerned with advocacy and defence of traditionalist Islam, in so doing they have also often acted as much as a genuine national organization, eschewing extreme religious demands for the sake of national "Indonesian" unity.

Under the New Order, NU has begun to search for the most appropriate activities to benefit the *umat*, including an ambitious banking scheme explicitly designed to integrate the *umat* into the rapidly growing national economy. Although the NU leadership was severely criticized at the December 1994 Congress over its failure to thus far widely implement the BPR scheme, it exemplifies the leadership's thinking about how NU can remain both relevant to its members and institutionally and economically relevant to Indonesian national development. Whether NU is ultimately effective in ensuring that an organization devoted to defence of traditionalist Islam continues to have a central role in a rapidly industrializing society will depend, in part, on the success of schemes such as the NUSumma Bank and the successful translation of other ideas into concrete programmes.

Notes

[1]   On the Sarekat Islam, Budi Utomo, and Muhammadiyah, see, for example, Boland 1971 and Noer 1973. On the Taman Siswa movement see Tsuchiya 1987. On Nahdlatul Ulama see Sitompul 1991 and Fealy [forthcoming].

[2]   The following section is based on Fealy 1994, p. 89.

[3]   Note should be made here of the key distinction between Muslim modernists and traditionalists. Traditionalists sought to adhere to the interpretations of the Qur'an by the classical Mideast scholars (particularly in matters of the four schools of Sunni law), whereas the modernists sought to "cleanse" the faith of these post-Qur'anic interpretations and teachings and advocated a return to the Qur'an itself. See for example, Barton 1994.

[4]   Fealy, interview, 12 December 1994.

[5]   Author's personal observations, 1–5 December 1994, Tasikmalaya, West Java. On the December 1994 Congress, see Fealy 1995.

[6]   On the *Kembali Ke Khittah* 1926 see, for example, Jones 1984; and Mudatsir 1985.

7 Said Budairy, interview, 12 December 1994.
8 Abdurrahman Wahid, interview, 17 September 1994.
9 Interviews with Abdurrahman Wahid, 18 and 24 June 1992 and 3 May 1993.
10 Fajrul Falaakh, interview, 2 December 1994.
11 Interviews, Wahid, 3 May 1993 and Zuhad, 14 December 1994.
12 On ICMI, see Ramage 1995.
13 Mustopha Zuhad, interview, 14 December 1994 (original emphasis).
14 Budairy was replaced by KH Masykur following the December 1994 Congress.
15 Said Budairy, interview, 12 December 1994.
16 Ellyasa KH Dharwis, interview, 3 December 1994.
17 Abdurrahman Wahid's speech at the President Hotel, 7 December 1994.
18 See for example, the journal *Tashwirul Afkar* whose inaugural issue (December 1994) includes articles on the "implications of modernity for socio-religious NU activism," the "future of the NU community," and "the *umat* as a civil society."
19 Based on personal observations and interviews at the NU Congress, 1–5 December 1994.
20 Djohan Effendy, interview, 3 December 1994.
21 Historically, NU has always sought to remain on good terms with government. NU's preference for accommodation with established authority is underpinned by its conception of the medieval Sunni Islamic law thinkers who argued that living under a tyrannical government was always infinitely preferable to anarchy (see Fealy 1994, p. 90).

11

Non-Governmental Organizations and the Empowerment of Civil Society

Muhammad AS Hikam

Non-governmental organizations (NGOs), better known in Indonesia as LSM (Lembaga Swadaya Masyarakat), have emerged as an important social force in contemporary Indonesia. Some have even gained prominence in both national and international fora through their activities in various community development projects, human rights advocacy, environmental protection programmes, etc. Thanks to the work of such leading NGOs as LP3ES (Lembaga Penelitian, Pendidikan dan Penerangan Ekonomi dan Sosial, or the Institute for Economic and Social Research, Education and Information), Bina Desa (Village Guidance), LSP (Lembaga Studi Pembangunan, or the Institute for Development Studies), LBH (Lembaga Bantuan Hukum, or the Legal Aid Institute), and Walhi (Wahana Lingkungan Hidup, or the Indonesian Environmental Forum), to name only a few, grassroots-oriented activism has become known at the national level, making possible the proliferation of hundreds of other medium and small NGOs at the regional level.

Many observers believe that the role of NGOs in Indonesia will become more decisive in the years to come, given the current global and national trends towards debureaucratization and decentralization of decision-making processes in society. Also, NGOs are expected to play an important role in strengthening and empowering civil society, which in developing countries such as Indonesia is still weak.

That being said, however, there are also some problems that need to be addressed and resolved by NGOs in Indonesia, and in the meantime it would be wise to avoid too much optimism over their eventual role in the country. Some of these problems originate within the NGOs themselves, having to do with their basic visions and practical choices. They may also come from outside the NGOs, namely the existing structural constraints imposed on them by both the state and dominant groups in the society.

To make a balanced assessment of Indonesian NGOs, it is important to examine them in the context of the structural and institutional transformations taking place in Indonesian society. More specifically, the growth and development of Indonesian NGOs should be seen as one aspect of the societal response to the rapid structural transformations brought about by economic development and modernization, coupled with the particular political restructuring carried out by the New Order regime.

Non-governmental organizations are not a recent phenomenon in Indonesia. Historically, there have been many institutions and organizations in society whose functions are similar to those of modern NGOs, that is as social empowerment agencies. The traditional neighbourhood mutual assistance (*gotong-royong*) associations, religious charitable organizations, village co-operatives (e.g., *lumbung desa*), agricultural irrigation groups (e.g., *subak*), and some education institutions (e.g., *pesantren*) are among the most well known. The common characteristics of these traditional institutions include their loose organizational structures, small size, local base, and survival orientation (Billah and Nusantara 1990, p. 59). In addition, they are usually organized according to primary relationships such as ethnic, religious or racial groupings.

The origin of modern NGOs in Indonesia can be traced to the 1920s, when many social and economic organizations were established in conjunction with the emergence of the nationalist movement in Indonesia. The leaders of these early NGOs mostly came from the middle class, and had modern education. Thus, the modern NGOs were characteristically urban-based organizations led by professionals, with broad ideological bases, objectives and membership. The fact that some of these organizations eventually transformed themselves into political parties only further demonstrates their transitional nature.[1]

It was not until the late 1960s and early 1970s that NGOs focused on specific development-related issues began to be established in Indonesia. This was primarily stimulated by the accelerated economic development that took place under the New Order government, and its subsequent impact on subordinate groups in society. As in the case of the previous group of NGOs, the leaders and members of the new NGOs tend to come from middle class families. However, their educational background is relatively higher than that of the previous generation and encompasses various fields and disciplines, including natural and social sciences as well as the humanities. As a generation of Indonesian society which was born and grew up in the post-colonial era they have, obviously, different experiences and expectations from their predecessors. Nevertheless, there is one commonality between the two generations of NGO leaders in that both see themselves as idealists who are concerned with the oppressed and disadvantaged people in the society. Also, activists of both generations have consisted mainly of respectable figures in the community and intellectuals, who share a similar perception of their obligation in the emerging society.

What are known as issue-oriented NGOs have emerged partly as a societal response to the development strategy of the New Order government. NGO activists believe that the current strategy of development has placed too much emphasis on macro-economic growth and has been biased towards the élite's interests. Furthermore, it has been a top-down approach; these activists argue that bottom-up approaches aimed at empowering society, especially those at the grass-roots level, are more viable. At a minimum, the activists demand that the prevailing model should be balanced by giving more opportunities to the people to get involved in the decision-making process.

Programmatically, the issue-oriented NGOs share some basic objectives. These include providing assistance to the target groups, especially the poor (charitable objectives), designing and implementing programmes with people (service objectives), promoting self-help projects designed and implemented by people (participatory objectives), and empowering the people in social, economic and political affairs (empowering objectives) (see Korten 1990; Lee 1994). As Eldridge (1990, p. 36) has pointed out, the NGOs' role is to "enhance the capacity for self-management among less advantaged groups, enabling them to deal with government agencies and other powerful forces on more equal terms", and, as a consequence, "they are serving to strengthen civil society *vis-à-vis* the state."

The NGOs' strength lies in their flexibility and diversity as organizations as well as their local origin. These factors enable NGOs "to retain a measure of autonomy from bureaucratic control" (Eldridge 1989, p. 3). The potential for NGOs to become alternative channels for the grassroots populace is even greater when one considers that in many developing countries, the existing channels in society are generally originated and dominated by the state. The state-sponsored channels usually function "less as an institution encouraging political participation and delivering basic services [than as] a machinery controlling the population and enriching powerholders" (Magno 1993, p. 12).

This chapter focuses on the efforts of Indonesian NGOs over the past two decades to bring about changes through implanting consciousness among the people and promoting participation in social, economic and political development. It does so through an examination of three well known non-governmental organizations whose main concerns are with empowerment issues: LBH (Lembaga Bantuan Hukum, or Legal Aid Institute); Fordem (Forum Demokrasi, or Democracy Forum); and Walhi (Wahana Lingkungan Hidup, or Indonesian Environmental Forum). The LBH is representative of human rights NGOs. Fordem represents democratization-oriented NGOs. (Although it does not regard itself as a formal organization, let alone as a regular NGO,[2] the author views Fordem as essentially an empowerment NGO because of its objective to serve as an open forum for those who are concerned with questions related to democratization.) Walhi has been a leader among environmental groups in Indonesia and is well known both nationally and internationally.

NGOs UNDER THE NEW ORDER

The New Order period has been marked by a fundamental restructuring of Indonesia's society, economics and politics. One of the results has been the emergence of the state, especially the executive branch, as a powerful agency where social, economic and political decisions are ultimately formulated and executed. Similar to the experiences of some other countries in Asia and Latin America, in Indonesia a strong state is seen as a condition *sine qua non* to facilitate the process of economic development, at least during its early phase. This view largely derives from the past failure of both the liberal democracy and Guided Democracy regimes to establish a united and strong authority at the central level. It is argued that strengthening the state would lead, if only gradually, to a greater sense of unity, legitimacy and authority in the society.[3]

No doubt, the idea of strong state has been highly compatible with a growth-oriented development strategy. The establishment of a strong state system has been achieved through corporatization of political and social organizations and the depoliticization of the grassroots population, especially in the rural areas where the majority of the Indonesian people lives. Corporatization is a powerful instrument, involving both co-optation and repression. Depoliticization was viewed as a means of preventing a potentially destabilizing force in society.

It is in this context of restructuring of the polity that NGOs have had to carry out their activities. Starting in the early seventies, development-oriented NGOs began to grow in the form of grassroots organizations concentrating on such practical development matters as cooperatives, health care, small industries, agricultural innovation, etc. Their objectives were to narrow the uneven development in society, balance the top-down approach, and lessen, if not eradicate, some of the negative consequences of the growth-oriented development process.

At this point, the NGOs were largely involved in designing and implementing small scale development programmes, either sponsored by the state agencies or by outside sponsors. They were influenced by the popular concept of community development already practised in some Asian and African countries such as India, Sri Lanka, Tanzania, and Kenya.[4] Examples of NGOs that gained prominence through involvement in community development projects are Bina Desa, LP3ES, LSP, YIS (Yayasan Indonesia Sejahtera, or Prosperous Indonesia Foundation), and P3M (Perhimpunan Pengembangan Pesantren dan Masyarakat, or Association for the Development of Pesantren and Society). They conducted their own programmes, such as co-operatives, small industry assistance, health, improvement of *pesantren* (religious schools), etc., and sometimes even provided assistance and advice to government agencies to help the government make better use of its scarce resources through promoting grassroots development. Because of the close relationship between this type of NGO and the government, they were well regarded by the government and treated essentially as partners (Hannam 1987, p. 23).

At the same time, continuous analysis and reassessment within the NGOs led to a broadening of their areas of activity. Some NGO activists moved beyond the conventional model of community development and began to look at the redefinition of institutional roles, emphasizing notions of power-sharing between the national and local levels as well as popular participation in their action programmes. This trend was reinforced by increasing pressure from the state in the late seventies on formal political groupings in the society. Many activists began to see NGOs as a new arena for political activism. For example, Mulya Lubis, a former director of LBH, has noted that NGOs "served as think-tanks or frontier posts" for student activists. He maintains that "by setting up NGOs, the students renewed their activities", possibly in the absence of adequate channels for their aspirations following the clampdown on campus political activity in the late seventies (Lubis 1993, p. 209).

The new wave of political activism also broadened the subject matter of NGO activities to include current macro social and political issues such as human rights, the environment, consumer protection, labour relations, gender issues, etc.[5] NGOs began to consider themselves as being capable of offering alternative models to the predominant government-centred approach to development (Billah, Hakim, and Nusantara 1990, p. 58).

It is fair to say that LBH, Fordem and Walhi represent this new trend among Indonesian NGOs. Their activism has been directed towards focusing attention on critical topical issues such as human rights, democratization, and environmental destruction. This both directly and indirectly challenges the prevailing approach to development supported by the state, counterposing the notion of popular participation and mobilization to the corporatization strategy pursued by the government.

THREE CASE STUDIES

The Legal Aid Institute (LBH)

The Legal Aid Institute (Lembaga Bantuan Hukum or LBH), established in the early 1970s, has been active in monitoring human rights protection and promoting democratization in Indonesia. According to its constitution, the goals of the LBH are "to provide legal assistance, in the broadest sense, to those whose civil, political, socio-economic and cultural rights are violated, ... in particular for those social groups lacking wealth and political power"; "to uphold and defend human rights and the values of the rule of law within the legal and political system"; and "through constitutional means to carry forward social transformation in order to realise a just, equitable, and democratic society" (Nasution 1994, p. 117).

What makes the LBH distinct from other legal aid organizations has been its commitment to fight for issues or causes and "not solely on behalf of individual clients" (Lubis 1993, p. 248). In so doing, it adopts what is popularly known as a structural approach to legal aid, namely taking on important cases "that offer an entree into a pressing issue and provide occasions for community organizing and education" (Nasution 1994, p. 119). The goal of this approach is to "focus domestic and international attention on abuses and to mobilize people to press for the reform of laws or procedures that discriminate against the poor and vulnerable" (Nasution 1994, p. 119).

In the context of the political system under the New Order, the LBH's structural approach has been directed more towards raising people's awareness of their political position *vis-à-vis* the powerful than to "achieve technical victory in court". According to long-time LBH leader Adnan Buyung Nasution, such an approach, even in the course of failing, has been able to organize and train people and communities to defend their rights under the constitution and laws.

Seen from the perspective of empowerment of civil society, what the LBH has been doing is to expose the abuses of power in society and to undermine the legitimacy of undemocratic forces (see Diamond 1994, p. 6). It also implants and maintains the sense of responsibility among the citizens which tends to be eroded in an authoritarian political system. This has been done primarily through educating people about their rights and the ways in which they can defend themselves against the powerful.

In order to enlarge its scope of activities, the LBH has worked together with other NGOs through its Network Development Programme (Nasution 1994, p. 118). It has forged ties with local and national NGOs representing various elements in society such as farmers, students, women, environmentalists, and workers. It has also developed relationships with the international organizations concerned with human rights protection such as the International Association of Legal Aid Associations, Human Rights Watch/Asia, Amnesty International, Greenpeace, etc.

The LBH has given high priority to legal reforms in Indonesia. Chief among these are reforms in the Criminal Code Procedures (KUHAP), the acceptance of the universality of human rights, and ratification of some key international human rights instruments such as the Convention Against Torture and other Cruel, Inhuman or Degrading Treatment or Punishment.[6]

In the field of democratization, the LBH together with other pro-democratic forces in the country has closely monitored and critically scrutinized abuses of power by the state and state apparatuses which hinder the process of democratization in society. Examples include LBH involvement in such high-profile cases as the murder of a young East Java labour activist (Marsinah), efforts to organize an independent labour union (SBSI), and military excesses in East Timor. Other LBH activities include the formation of legal teams to defend students and activists imprisoned for political statements, banned publications, and people who have experienced harassment and physical abuse by government apparatuses throughout the country.

Given its level of political involvement and activism, it is not surprising that the LBH has often faced pressures from the government. One of the most effective weapons employed by the government has been the strict regulation of financial contributions to the LBH from foreign countries. Like many Indonesian NGOs, the LBH has been the recipient of financial support from various institutions in foreign countries. When the

Indonesian Government curtailed all Dutch financial aid to Indonesian NGOs, LBH suffered the most because eighty-eight per cent of LBH's US$650,000 annual budget came from Novib, a Dutch-based NGO (Nasution 1994, p. 120).[7] Pressures have also been directed at LBH staffers, especially lawyers in its regional offices. Many instances of harassment and physical threats have been reported by the regional lawyers.

Financial dependence on outside support has undoubtedly been the Achilles heel of the LBH. It certainly affects its programmes and future projects. It is indeed ironic that NGOs strive to implant the idea of autonomy and self-reliance among the people, while at the same time being vulnerable themselves because of financial dependency on external donors.

The Democracy Forum (Fordem)

The Democracy Forum, (*Forum Demokrasi,* commonly known as "Fordem"), was established following a two-day meeting in Bogor on 16 and 17 March 1991. The meeting ended with the signing of the Cibeureum Accord (*Mufakat Cibeureum*) by forty-four pro-democracy activists who became the founders of Fordem. According to the accord, the essence of the forum is first and foremost the spirit to fight, without resorting to violence, for the principles of freedom and democratic structure as the basis of administering the state and as a means for social communication.

As a loosely organized grouping, the forum maintained that it has no intention to become a formal organization since its purpose was only to provide a space to allow various people to express concerns about the condition of democracy in the country. According to Fordem's working group leader, Abdurrahman Wahid, the participants and supporters of the forum were united in the belief that the maintenance of national unity could only be achieved through the development of a more mature and progressive nation and the creation of a democratic atmosphere (Wahid 1991, p. 1).

Fordem has been seen by both political observers and scholars as an important experiment that could pave the way for genuine democratic discourse and practices in the country. Its prominence has been greater because it was launched at a time when the political atmosphere in Indonesia seemed to be moving towards sectarianism and particularism. This could be seen in the return of politicization of Islam in the late eighties, despite the claim that the New Order has attempted to eradicate the legacy of *aliran* (group/ideology)-based politics and the unification of ideology under Pancasila.

Thus, when such prominent intellectuals from different persuasions established Fordem in 1991, there was widespread speculation that this action was a response to the recent establishment of ICMI (Association of Indonesian Muslim Intellectuals). This speculation was reinforced by several statements and critical comments by Abdurrahman Wahid that could be easily interpreted as a critique of the growing power of political Islam in the country. Wahid's relentless critiques of sectarianism, for example, have been considered by his adversaries as a direct attack on ICMI and those who support that association.

However, it is misleading to understand Fordem as just another political organization or movement in the ordinary sense. For, far from being a solid and well organized association, Fordem has no unified ideological basis upon which its members could generate a movement similar to a progressive political party or mass-based organization. Compared to the Czechoslovakian Civic Forum, to which Fordem apparently owes its inspiration, Fordem is at best still in an embryonic stage. The amalgamation of intellectuals and activists within Fordem seems to be much weaker than that of the Civic Forum, and the differences among the members of Fordem regarding its goals and objectives are still too great to create a strong and significant political movement which could challenge the establishment.

Nevertheless, Fordem has had an impact on the political configuration under the New Order. Fordem's principal significance lies in its ability to expand the free public sphere and to generate critical attitudes and symbolic resistance against the otherwise overwhelming power of the state. Through its regular meetings and statements in the mass media, and especially through the figure of Abdurrahman Wahid, Fordem succeeded in providing a voice for critical minds in the society which tend to be emasculated by the dominant, official political discourse.

Another important contribution of Fordem is in developing the notion of a free public sphere which makes it possible for genuine dialogue to take place among different political and social groupings. Such dialogues, limited as they are within the forum's regular meetings and very informal setting, can be expanded to promote what Habermas (1979 and 1981) calls the "communicative competence" of the people which is essential for the establishment of a democratic polity in the future.

Still another contribution of Fordem is as a political alliance of pro-democratic forces in the society. This is part of the process of empowerment of civil society. Like LBH, Fordem also functions as a civic organization which protects society from the abuse of power. While Fordem has yet to develop concrete programmes, its presence in the current Indonesian political arena has energized the democratic impulse through its public defence of those who become victims of undemocratic forces. In one of his critiques of the New Order's ruling élite, for instance, Abdurrahman Wahid warns of the increasing gap between people's political aspirations and those of the élite groups. He contends that such a condition would eventually undermine the latter's power base (*Jakarta Post*, 7 October 1992). Therefore, the need for a change in political life is a pressing one.

The avenue for political reform intended by Fordem is not a radical one, for in Wahid's view that would be a futile exercise, since radicalism only invites repressive measures from the state. The most realistic avenue is through enlarging dialogues to make it possible for different opinions to flourish. This eventually will lead to the disappearance of monopolistic tendencies in politics.

Since 1991, Fordem has represented the critical minds in society, commenting and assessing current developments in social, economic and political affairs. So far the response from the government towards Fordem's activities has been cautious. The government has not reacted strongly towards the members and their activities. This is especially true by comparison with the government's treatment of the members of the *Petisi 50* group (of former senior figures who issued statements critical of the New Order government). Even though there have been some instances in which Fordem has not been allowed to conduct mass gatherings, the government has not put its members on the list of those prohibited to travel abroad or to give speeches in seminars and other public meetings.

There are reasons for this leniency. One is Fordem's loose membership among small numbers of intellectuals, principally in Jakarta and several other cities on Java. Also, their activities are limited to informal meetings and public statements that are capable neither of mobilizing the masses in society nor of directly challenging the existing power. Further, compared with the *Petisi 50* group, Fordem has been less vocal in criticizing political practices in a way that can be interpreted as a direct attack on the existing political system. Fordem's informal structure has enabled it to bypass the existing regulations regarding social and mass organizations. Therefore it is difficult for the government to openly control its movements by imposing restrictions such as denying permits and other legal measures.

Government activity has been largely restricted to the monitoring of Fordem's public activities.

The problem in the future for the forum is how to continue to develop its influence in Indonesian politics without being too dependent upon one figure. It is important for the forum to resolve this problem, since such a dependence would only weaken its ability to face external and internal pressures.

The Indonesian Environmental Forum (Walhi)

Established in October 1980, the Indonesian Environmental Forum (Wahana Lingkungan Hidup, commonly known as "Walhi")[8] is intended to be an umbrella organization for individuals and groups who are concerned with environmental problems in Indonesia. It now includes approximately 400 organizations on its membership list, some 120 of which are considered active.

Walhi's main activities have been in the fields of training, research, information dissemination, and advocacy on environment-related issues. One of its main objectives is to encourage "local groups to become involved in their own research, and play similar advocacy and communication roles, calling on the services of Walhi where necessary" (Eldridge 1989, p. 38). In addition, Walhi also "acts as a lobby group with respect to policy and legislation". In this respect, the organization has been in the forefront of those pressing the government to become more assertive in implementing environmental regulations to protect the nation's natural resources from being overexploited in the name of development.

Walhi played an important role in drafting the environmental laws, especially the law of 1982. One of its main achievements has been the legal acknowledgement of the role of NGOs in the implementation of environmental policies, through Article 19 of the 1982 law. Walhi especially emphasizes advocacy and education programmes. These are targeted on associated local groups, "placing particular emphasis on encouraging them to undertake locally and regionally oriented action-research" (Eldridge 1989, p. 39).

Walhi has been involved in several actions that have forced it to directly confront the existing political and economic powers. For instance, Walhi has brought several law suits against corporations that have been negligent in implementing environmental regulations. One of the most prominent cases was a law suit against the pulp company IIU (Inti Indorayon Utama) in North Sumatra for violating environmental regulations regarding reforestation and waste management (Zulkarnaen 1995, p. 259). This case attracted national and international attention, primarily through substantial media coverage.

Walhi has also formed networks at both the national and international levels to disseminate information and strengthen its advocacy efforts. According to one of the current Walhi leaders, Zulkarnaen, the organization has forged a strong alliance with environmental groups and NGOs in the other ASEAN countries through the formation of SEACON (Southeast Asian Coalition) in 1990. Domestically, Walhi has been working together with influential NGOs such as LBH, SKEPHI (Sekretariat Kerjasama Perlindungan Hutan Indonesia, or the Joint Secretariat for the Protection of Indonesian Forests), YLKI (Yayasan Lembaga Konsumen Indonesia, or the Foundation for the Indonesian Consumers Institute), LP3ES, and many others. These networks have become especially important as Walhi's activities have begun to enter areas beyond strictly environmental issues, such as human rights and democratization.

This enlargement of Walhi's scope of activities was evident in Walhi's agenda for 1992–95 (Zulkarnaen 1995, p. 259). In this agenda, the notion of the people's rights to natural resources occupies a pivotal position. Its underlying philosophy is the conviction that the people should have sufficient resources to enable them to support their lives. To guarantee this right, democracy and decentralization are seen as prerequisites, in order to avoid monopoly and centralization of resources in the hands of the few. Thus Walhi views the empowerment of civil society as a fundamental element of its overall mission.

From this discussion it is clear that Walhi envisions a more people-oriented approach. This will create antagonisms between Walhi and the government, particularly when environmental issues arise in connection with development plans. The government will tend to perceive environmental advocacy by Walhi in such situations as an obstacle to development, particularly foreign investment. This is not unlike the situation of LBH, whose human rights advocacy is considered inimical to development.

On the other hand, Walhi also has considerable value to the state's environmental agencies, primarily the Department of Environment. The department needs Walhi's extensive networks and its ability to mobilize its resources in the society. The department's capability to implement its own programmes of environmental protection is quite limited. This can be seen in numerous cases in which violations of governmental regulations on waste management have gone unnoticed or there has been no enforcement to rectify them. It is through NGOs like Walhi that such violations are brought to public attention and that demands for justice can be aired.

However, like other Indonesian NGOs, Walhi has yet to develop into an autonomous organization. The organizations under Walhi are mostly dependent for funding on other agencies both from inside and outside the country. Politically, they are also very vulnerable to government pressure. However, as a loose umbrella organization, Walhi has more flexibility in its internal co-ordination and administration than LBH. Also, its political content is less discernible than that of Fordem, although some officials see its activities as being politically motivated.

The strength of Walhi, in this writer's view, lies in its broad networks, both domestic and international. Also, given that environmental issues will occupy a pivotal position globally in the future, the existence of Walhi can be extremely valuable for Indonesia. It remains to be seen, however, whether Walhi's effectiveness will grow in the years to come. For the time being, it is performing a major and badly needed function in a country that has been undergoing ecological transformations as a result of industrialization.

CONCLUSION

The emergence and development of modern Indonesian NGOs have been inseparable from the processes of economic development and modernization. Although similar organizations have existed in Indonesia in earlier periods, the new-type NGOs discussed here only emerged following the rapid institutional changes brought about by political, social, and, especially, economic developments since the early 1970s. LBH and Fordem exemplify NGOs that respond to and anticipate the increasing demands for democracy and the protection of human rights. Walhi was established to respond to serious problems such as deforestation, land degradation, flooding, and other natural and man-made environmental destruction that resulted from economic growth and industrialization.

The growth of NGOs in Indonesia can also be seen as a response to the emerging power of the state under the New Order. Issue-oriented NGOs such as LBH, Fordem and Walhi have gained prominence due in part to their efforts to provide alternatives to the society beyond the state's frameworks and strategies of development. There has been a growing realization that the empowerment of civil society is one of the most viable means of ameliorating problems rooted in the model and strategies employed by the state in the process of development.

Thus, the structural approach taken by the LBH in the fields of legal aid provision and human rights protection is aimed at enhancing the people's self-confidence regarding their basic rights. Fordem's efforts to energize democratic impulses through dialogues and building networks of democratic forces in society are intended to keep the drive towards democracy alive and to provide alternative views on the political process beyond the state-sanctioned ones. Walhi's activities in environmental and, later, human rights protection are motivated by the growing concerns over the abuse of natural and human resources by the powerful in society with the support of the state apparatus.

These NGOs have been well received in the society and have built good reputations and extensive networks both domestically and internationally. Their members consist mainly of young, well-educated middle class people and intellectuals. It is not an exaggeration to say that Indonesia's NGOs are one of the backbones of the country's future civil society.

Nevertheless, one should not overestimate the capability of these NGOs. Several constraints hamper both their present performance and their longer-term survival. According to Sinaga (1993, p. 148), Indonesian NGOs' survival is "dependent on their managerial efficiency, leadership styles, the qualifications and dedication of members of their staff, and their social credibility". He notes that Indonesian NGOs still suffer from lack of efficiency in management and are too dependent upon their leaders. Many of the young, educated middle class employees of NGOs lack specific knowledge or other required skills. Worse, there is a tendency for new graduates to join NGOs only because of their inability to find other jobs and then to leave the NGO as soon as they find better opportunities (Sinaga 1993, p. 152; Hannam 1987).

Externally, pressure from the state is the main operational constraint on Indonesian NGOs. Through various regulations and policies, the government has the ability to keep the NGOs in a subordinate position. Also, the government bureaucracy has often made it difficult for NGOs to operate in the more remote regions. The suspicion that NGO activities will lead to social tensions is still strong, creating an atmosphere of distrust both within the government apparatus and among the people.

Financial dependency is another major problem for Indonesian NGOs. As long as this dependency cannot be overcome through self-generated income, the NGOs will be vulnerable to external pressures (Sinaga 1993, pp. 141–48). They do not have "influence to draw funds from public sources or from government revenues", and unlike business organizations, they "lack access to 'customers' who are able and willing to pay the entire cost of the services provided" (Sinaga 1993, p. 141). Dependency on foreign donors is a particular problem for some NGOs, such as LBH.

But despite these weaknesses, NGOs, especially the newer, issue-oriented NGOs, are increasingly looked to by Indonesians as an effective channel for addressing grievances and resolving pressing problems as well as a source of protection and assistance. They appear destined to play a significant role in the empowerment of Indonesian civil society.

Notes

[1] These early NGOs included Budi Utomo, Sarikat Islam (SI), Taman Siswa, Muhammadiyah, Nahdlatul Ulama (NU), and other similar organizations. SI and NU became political parties, while Taman Siswa and Muhammadiyah have remained as social organizations which focus on education, social and religious activities.

[2] Fordem has no organizational structure, although it does have a formal working group (*kelompok kerja*). It has neither a constitution nor explicit membership criteria, although it does have common goals and objectives which serve as standards for those who want to get involved in its activities.

[3] On the power and influence of the office of the president during the formative years of the New Order, see Mas'oed 1983.

[4] The early NGOs under the New Order can be labelled as the "second generation" in David Korten's (1985, p. 1) typology of NGOs. Korten classifies as "first generation" NGOs those engaged in self-help, relief, and charitable activities.

[5] It is important to note that the expansion of the scope of NGO activities was made possible partly by their growing independence from state support. The large NGOs with national and international networks obtained their financial support from external sources such as the World Bank, Novib (Netherlands), IMF, USAID, etc. Also, most of them operated in large cities where the political atmosphere was less repressive than in small towns and rural areas.

[6] The notion of the universality of human rights is still a controversial issue in Indonesia. Although in the 1945 Constitution this notion is generally accepted, in practice the New Order has applied a more particularistic notion of human rights. In this view, human rights is

understood in the context of the specific cultural system of Indonesia, which may not follow the internationally accepted standards. For a detailed discussion of this controversy, see Lubis 1993, esp. Chapter III, passim.

[7] The decision itself was a retaliatory action by the Indonesian Government to a cut-off of development aid by the Dutch Government in the aftermath of the Dili incident in November 1991.

[8] Unless otherwise indicated, most of the information regarding Walhi in this paper is based on Eldridge 1989.

12

Policy Advisory Institutions: "Think-Tanks"

Dewi Fortuna Anwar

> Indonesia is a country and a society which is very much under-
> represented by research institutions, both in absolute terms and
> relative to the size of its population. Furthermore of the few
> existing research institutions, only a small fraction devote at-
> tention to international affairs and even fewer have a policy
> focus. (Soesastro 1991)

Since Hadi Soesastro made the above observation in 1991, the limited
number and scope of think-tanks in Indonesia has not changed very much.
Given the size of the country and its huge population, Indonesia continues
to be poorly represented by research institutions, particularly ones that
self-consciously carry out policy advocacy studies and activities. Moreover, the few that exist are overwhelmingly located in Jakarta, given the
concentration of talent and resources in the capital area as well as its
proximity to the national decision-making process.

CONSTRAINTS AND LIMITATIONS ON THINK-TANKS

The lack of policy-oriented think-tanks in Indonesia is due to a variety of
factors. One of the major constraints is the lack of funding. Currently the
government allocates only about .09 per cent of the national budget to
research, and the nominal amount has tended to decline rather than increase in recent years. Of that small amount, most is allocated for research
in science and technology. Very little money is available for research in the
social sciences, often regarded as a luxury in a developing country and, in
some instances, even perceived as a nuisance.

Nor is private funding easy to come by. It is not yet common for industrialists and entrepreneurs to earmark capital for the purposes of promoting research, although institutions engaged in basic science and technology research may develop links with related industries which sponsor research on certain projects. Moreover, the government does not offer tax incentives to encourage private sector research and development (R&D), as is the case in the United States. There are, of course, a number of *yayasan* (foundations) set up by members of the political and economic élites, but these foundations are mostly involved in social activities.

Foreign funding organizations are also an important source of revenue for research institutions. However, these foundations, mostly American and European, are few in number while the Indonesian organizations soliciting their support are many. The funding agencies, moreover, prefer to give their support to NGOs that deal with specific issues or carry out concrete community development projects and activities, rather than to research institutions or think-tanks which are engaged primarily in intellectual activities with uncertain effectiveness and impact. Moreover, funding agencies must have Indonesian government approval and permission for each of the projects they sponsor. Additionally, strict government regulation forbids foreign organizations from becoming involved in domestic political activities. This means that foreign funding agencies are often reluctant to support think-tanks which carry out politically related activities. For their part, think-tanks also tend to be quite selective in choosing potential donors, to ensure that associations with foreign agencies do not compromise their political standing in the community or their programmes.

Associated with the financial problem is the lack of qualified people who are interested in working in research institutions and/or think-tanks, for the financial reward is usually not very high. Private firms and consultants tend to attract more of the best and brightest individuals, rather than research institutions or think-tanks.

Despite the constraints which have hampered the growth of policy advisory and research institutions, in the past few years a growing number of think-tanks has emerged. The activities of these institutions, such as organizing seminars and publishing studies, have attracted considerable attention. Perhaps most significantly, the association of some of these think-tanks with important social-political forces, and their perceived roles in attempting to influence government policies, are some of the distinguishing features of institutional change in New Order Indonesia.

This chapter examines a number of research institutions and think-tanks operating in Jakarta. These policy research/advisory organizations are generally quite distinct from programme-operating organizations which are involved in economic development, training and other such concrete activities. However, some of the organizations combine both the advisory as well as the programmatic functions. Some are government bodies with clear national mandates. Others are private organizations but draw financial and personnel support from members of the bureaucracy. Some of the think-tanks cannot really be considered formal organizations, for they are only loose forums for communication between like-minded individuals from different occupational backgrounds. However, what these organizations and forums do have in common is that they are all engaged in activities broadly related to public policies. Some of these activities are carried out openly, others less so.

THINK-TANKS IN JAKARTA

Seven institutions and think-tanks will be discussed in some detail. These are:
- Indonesian Institute of Sciences (Lembaga Ilmu Pengetahuan Indonesia, or LIPI)
- Centre for Strategic and International Studies (CSIS)
- Institute for Economic and Social Research, Education and Information (Lembaga Penelitian, Pendidikan dan Penerangan Ekonomi dan Sosial, or LP3ES)
- Centre for the Study of Development and Democracy (CESDA)
- Centre for Policy and Implementation Studies (CPIS)
- Institute for Strategic Studies of Indonesia (ISSI) (Lembaga Pengkajian Strategis Indonesia, or LPSI)
- Centre for Information and Development Studies (CIDES)

Indonesian Institute of Sciences (LIPI)

LIPI has a long background in the relatively brief history of modern Indonesia. It developed from MIPI (Majelis Ilmu Pengetahuan Indonesia, or Council for Sciences of Indonesia), which was established in 1956. According to Government Act No. 6, 1956 MIPI had two tasks: (1) to promote and guide endeavour in the field of science and technology, and (2) to advise the government on matters of science policy. LIPI was established by Presidential Decree No. 28, 1967. In line with the rapid process of development and the increasing need for research institutions to do studies and advise the government on various development-related issues, over time LIPI has expanded in scope and responsibilities. The present LIPI structure is the outcome of amendments following Presidential Decree No. 43, 1985 and Presidential Decree No. 1, 1986.

LIPI is a non-departmental institution (not under any government department) which reports directly to the president. Its tasks *inter alia* are to assist the president in organizing research and development, and to give guidance, services and advice to the government on national science and technology policy.

LIPI is headed by a chairman who reports directly to the president. The chairman is assisted by a vice chairman and five deputy chairmen. LIPI has nineteen R&D centres, fifteen of which deal with basic science and technology research. The other four, under the deputy for social sciences and humanities, are the Centre for Social and Cultural Studies, the Centre for Economics and Development; the Centre for Population and Manpower and the Centre for Political and Regional Studies.

The social science and humanities centres conduct policy research and make policy recommendations. Centre researchers pursue their individual lines of research and academic interests, and teams of researchers also carry out government funded studies which are submitted on an annual basis for approval by the Department of Science and Technology and the National Development Planning Board (Bappenas). Reports are presented at an annual LIPI seminar before they are finally revised and printed in limited numbers for distribution to the authorized government departments, in particular to Bappenas and the State Secretariat. The reports cannot be sold to the general public.

LIPI has a routine budget for personnel and other overheads which is regularly allocated by the government, and a project budget approved annually for particular research projects. The largest of the social sciences and humanities centres is the Centre for Social and Cultural Studies (PMB-LIPI). In 1994 it had 61 researchers and 39 administrative employees. PMB-LIPI's routine budget is Rp596,398,000, (US$271,090); its research/project budget during 1994/95 was Rp967,401,000 (US$439,728). The Centre for Population and Manpower (PPT-LIPI) had 36 researchers and 42 administrative staff. Its annual budget was Rp410,631,000, (US$186,650); its 1994/95 budget for projects was Rp418,001,000 (US$190,000). The Centre for Economics and Development (PEP-LIPI) had 31 researchers and 39 administrative staff, a routine budget of

Rp387,651,000 (US$176,205) and a 1994/95 project budget of Rp499,154,000 (US$226,888). Finally, the Centre for Political and Regional Studies (PPW-LIPI) had 39 researchers and 25 administrative employees, a routine budget of Rp302,583,000 (US$137,538) and a 1994/95 project budget of Rp341,416,000 (US$155,189).

LIPI is only one of several similarly situated and assigned state institutions. Others are the Agency for the Assessment and Application of Technology (BPPT), the National Atomic Energy Agency (BATAN) and the Central Bureau of Statistics (BPS). LIPI, however, has the broadest range of activities, which include policy research in social, political, cultural and economic issues. Finally, most government departments also have their own internal think-tanks, called Litbang (R&D centres). Each of these deals with the specific issues covered by its respective department and acts as a policy advisor for the decision makers in its particular area.

Centre for Strategic and International Studies (CSIS)

CSIS was established on 1 September 1971 as a private non-profit research institution. CSIS had its genesis from the activities of two groups of young Indonesian scholars, one based in Jakarta and one studying in Europe, who had been interacting informally since 1968. These people shared an interest in issues related to strategy and international relations, which were then generally ignored by Indonesian scholars.

The main objective of CSIS is to engage in policy-oriented studies, both international and domestic, which are closely linked to global issues. The Centre does not produce official positions or recommendations on its own behalf. The reports and analyses it publishes bear the names of their respective authors. The Centre is only responsible for their quality and objectivity (Soesastro 1991).

CSIS has numerous international linkages. It has carried out a series of bilateral seminars with various countries, such as France, Germany, the Netherlands, Vietnam and South Korea. It has also been very active in regional and international initiatives. CSIS is a founding member of the ASEAN-ISIS regional network, an association of ASEAN institutes of strategic and international studies established formally in 1989. CSIS has participated in the Pacific Economic Co-operation Conference (PECC) process since 1980, and in the development of the Council for Security Co-operation in the Asia Pacific (CSCAP) established in 1994. CSIS acts as the secretariat for both the PECC and CSCAP processes in Indonesia.

As of April 1990, CSIS had 50 professional staff members or analysts, assisted by 60 administrative and service personnel. It is sponsored by a corporate foundation, Yayasan Proklamasi (the Proclamation Foundation), established in Jakarta in 1971. In 1974 the foundation granted CSIS an endowment to permanently fund its activities. The Centre's annual budget is about Rp2.2 billion (US$1 million). The income from the endowment constitutes its main source of revenue, supplemented by direct private sector donations and assistance from overseas foundations (such as the Asia Foundation and Ford Foundation) for special projects. Receipts from the sale of publications are an insignificant portion of total revenues.

For many years CSIS had close links to the government through patronage by several senior officials. CSIS was founded with the support and sponsorship of Ali Moertopo and Soedjono Hoemardani, two high-ranking army generals and close associates of President Soeharto.

On the key early relationship between CSIS, its official patrons, and President Soeharto, Juwono Sudarsono (1974) has observed:

> Ali Moertopo's close association with President Soeharto as his special operations officer had underscored the need to establish a think-tank capable of providing intellectual and policy support to the government. Soedjono Hoemardani's extensive links with business circles, particularly in Japan, provided the economic underpinning to CSIS' extensive activities throughout the 1970s, making it the premier Centre for international exchange with many important factions [sic] in other ASEAN governments, most notably in Malaysia and Singapore.

CSIS' close association with Ali Moertopo and Soedjono Hoemardani made the Centre's position very controversial in the 1970s. Both generals were influential members of the president's personal staff (known as Asisten Pribadi, or Aspri). Ali Moertopo was a leading member of OPSUS (Operasi Khusus, or Special Operations) which generally acted as a "trouble shooter" for President Soeharto in the early years of the New Order, while Soedjono Hoemardani was often regarded as the president's personal *guru* (teacher) on spiritual matters. Hoemardani's close links with Japan also led to charges that he was an agent of Japan. During the anti-Japanese riot in January 1974, at the time of the visit of Prime Minister Tanaka of Japan, the Aspri came under popular attack and, because of its association with Ali Moertopo and Hoemardani, CSIS drew some of the fire. After the riot, popularly known by the Indonesian acronym Malari (for "the disaster of 15 January"), the president disbanded his personal staff.

CSIS was often portrayed as the "kitchen" where various ideas to strengthen the government's political control were "cooked". Several of the key individuals who founded CSIS played an important role in devizing a strategy for Golkar's victory in the first general election under the New Order in 1971. Some individual members of the CSIS also had a hand in planning the political incorporation of East Timor in 1975/1976. One Indonesian scholar called a number of the intellectuals associated with CSIS "the New Order ideologists" (Kuntjoro-Jakti 1982).

The position and role of CSIS as a think-tank during the seventies was clearly related to the official power and influence of its two patrons, Ali Moertopo and Soedjono Hoemardani. After these two close associates of President Soeharto left the scene, outside observers initially thought their place was filled by General L.B. Moerdani. Apparently this was not the case, but definitely CSIS maintained close relations with Moerdani. Moerdani had been a close associate of Ali Moertopo, having also served in OPSUS. He had a long career in military intelligence and served as commander of the armed forces from 1983 to 1988 and minister of defence from 1988 to 1993. During the 1980s and early 1990s General Moerdani was generally seen as the second most powerful figure in the country after the president.

With General Moerdani's retirement from active government service in 1993, CSIS probably no longer has a direct link to the seat of power, so that its input to policy — and its corresponding effectiveness — has also become more diversified and less tractable. On the other hand, as CSIS Executive Director Hadi Soesastro (1991) pointed out, support for CSIS activities is now more broadly based than before and its position and role have become less controversial. The Centre's reputation today is more that of an institution producing objective and relevant research and information for the public, rather than an organization clearly linked to specific government personalities.

Institute for Economic and Social Research, Education and Information (LP3ES)

LP3ES was established in 1971 by a group of analysts specializing in social and economic issues. This group had established relations with several domestic and international NGOs. From 1971 to 1981 LP3ES received significant funding from various international donor agencies, such as USAID, Friedrich Naumann Stiftung (FNS), Ford Foundation and Swiss Development Co-operation.

Since 1981, however, the intensity of LP3ES' international connections has declined, resulting in an overall reduction in the organization's funding. This is due, in part, to the growing numbers of NGOs competing for the same scarce resources. Today, LP3ES has to seek additional funding from other sources, such as publication sales and government projects. These later two activities generate some forty-two per cent of LP3ES' revenues, with the rest still covered by support from international funding agencies.

LP3ES has a broad range of activities. It not only produces research on various development issues, which qualifies it to be labelled as a think-tank, but it is also directly engaged in a number of development projects, particularly in rural areas. It also carries out polls on various topics, provides consultation and management to regional newspapers, organizes seminars and carries out studies on democracy.

As a think-tank, LP3ES is particularly active on social and economic issues. LP3ES also provides input to the government, specifically through its interaction with the planning agency Bappenas. It has worked with Indonesia's central bank, Bank Indonesia, to design a credit system for weak economic actors, particularly those living in rural areas. LP3ES also publishes books and journals, of which the best known is the monthly *Prisma*.

Since the second half of the 1980s, LP3ES has appeared to be in decline. Several of the founding members, such as Ismid Hadad and Dawam Rahardjo, left to establish their own organizations. Currently most LP3ES researchers are relatively junior. Funding has become a more serious problem. Also, in the early period LP3ES benefited from the patronage of several prominent government officials, such as Prof Emil Salim and Prof Sumitro Djojohadikusumo, the former Ministers for Environment and Finance respectively, which gave it direct access to policy-makers. Today this access has greatly diminished.

Nevertheless, LP3ES remains prominent in community development projects, and its journal, *Prisma*, is still regarded as a premier publication on social, political and economic issues. LP3ES (including its affiliated institution, CESDA, examined below) has 14 researchers and 23 administrative employees. Its routine budget is Rp800,000,000 (US$363,636) annually, while its 1994/95 budget for projects totalled Rp2.5 billion (US$1.136 million).

Centre for the Study of Development and Democracy (CESDA)

The decline of LP3ES as a think-tank and research institution prompted its members to found CESDA in 1992 to carry out research on more general social, political, and economic issues. Although its research activities are autonomous, CESDA is in fact an integral part of LP3ES. CESDA has received financial support from organizations such as USAID and the Asia Foundation.

During its short lifetime, CESDA has conducted various studies on democratization. It has also conducted opinion surveys or polls including for the Department for Environment and television companies. With USAID funding, it organizes training for editors and managers of regional mass media to improve their editorial and marketing abilities. CESDA also publishes seminar papers and books, mostly on democratization, sales from which add to its income.

Institute for Strategic Studies of Indonesia (ISSI)

ISSI was founded in 1989 by a group of alumni of Lemhanas, the National Defence Institute which conducts courses for senior military and civilian officials and members of Parliament. The group established the Foundation for the National Institute for Strategic Studies (Yayasan Lembaga Pengkajian Strategis Nasional), to support the institute. Most ISSI members are senior military officers, active as well as retired. Since its establishment ISSI has been chaired by General (ret.) Rudini, former Minister for Internal Affairs (1988-1993). Its first chief executive was the late Lt. Gen. (ret.) Soebijakto Prawirasoebrata, a former governor of Lemhanas.

ISSI was established as an autonomous research institution to bring together Lemhanas alumni, intellectuals, politicians and other experts concerned with political, economic, social, cultural, and defence issues. The focus of ISSI's interest is the development of Indonesian national resilience and ASEAN's regional resilience. Members of ISSI also try to present their thinking and experience on strategic issues to the government and to the community at large.

One of ISSI's objectives is to act as a bridge between the government and non-governmental organizations, academics and other leading members of the community in dealing with strategic issues. ISSI organizes discussions, produces publications and carries out networking with likeminded institutions. ISSI self-consciously regards itself as a policy advisory institution, for its activities are aimed at improving the quality of the decision-making process.

ISSI receives support from various sources, including contributions from its council of patrons (which has forty-five members), the government, and private domestic and foreign sources. As it now stands ISSI seems to be a rather exclusive "old-boys' club" for retired high-ranking military officers plus a few senior civilian scholars and politicians.

ISSI has 7 full time and 4 assistant researchers, supported by 15 administrative employees. Its routine budget is Rp210,000,000 (US$95,454) annually, while the 1994/95 budget for projects amounted to Rp1,7 billion (US$772,727).

Centre for Policy and Implementation Studies (CPIS)

CPIS is an in-house research institution and think-tank for the Department of Finance which had existed in embryonic form since 1974. However, in October 1986 CPIS was launched as an autonomous institution, funded by the government through Yayasan Pusat Pengkajian dan Pelaksanaan Programme Pembangunan (Foundation for the Centre for Research and Implementation of Development Programmes).

CPIS was established by several of the leading development economists (so-called "technocrats") who directed the Indonesian economy in the first two decades of the New Order, including Prof. Widjojo Nitisastro, Prof. Ali Wardana, Drs Radius Prawiro, Prof. J.B. Sumarlin and Dr Saleh Afif. The Centre was created to provide development planners with information and advice on development issues. It was intended in part to provide an Indonesian alternative to the Harvard Group (which had a contract with the Indonesian Government) as a source of analysis and advice.

As an institution to provide advice on development policy and its implementation, CPIS has been quite productive and effective. It was instrumental in conceiving and realizing various programmes aimed at improving social welfare, particularly in the rural areas. These include the BIMAS programme to educate farmers on how to improve yields, the development of village banking (BANGDES), family planning and the "SD Inpres" project (Sekolah Dasar — Instruksi Presiden, or Presidential Instruction on Primary Schools), which established primary school facilities in remote areas.

CPIS' influence clearly depends on access to key policy-makers. CPIS does not publish its studies or recommendations for use by the general public, and CPIS researchers are not allowed to publish their work independently or voice their opinions publicly. Therefore, the public at large is mostly unaware of the Centre's existence and role. In the past few years most of CPIS' important patrons have retired from the bureaucracy. CPIS has also lost a number of its researchers (one group, led by the economist Dr Rizal Ramli, has set up a private consultant firm known as Econit) perhaps due to its restrictions on outside work. Further, the cabinet appointed in 1993 contained a reduced number of technocrats. Thus it seems likely that CPIS will have less influence in policy-making circles.

In 1994 CPIS had 23 researchers and 11 research assistants, supported by 34 administrative employees. Its routine budget is Rp960,000,000 (US$436,363), and its project budget for 1994/95 was Rp11.4 billion (US$5.2 million).

Centre for Information and Development Studies (CIDES)

CIDES is a research institution and think-tank established by the Association of Indonesian Muslim Intellectuals (Ikatan Cendekiawan Muslim Indonesia — ICMI). The Centre was formally launched on 25 January 1993 in Jakarta.

The establishment of a research institution which can carry out studies and make policy proposals which are in line with ICMI programmes was the brainchild of the ICMI chairman, the then Minister for Science and Technology B.J. Habibie. Minister Habibie served as the chairman of the board of advisors of CIDES. Nevertheless, in its activities CIDES enjoys a considerable degree of autonomy from ICMI.

As its name suggests, CIDES devotes its attention to studies and the dissemination of information on development. CIDES organizes regular dialogues on economic development, domestic politics, foreign policy, and culture, as well as national, regional, and international conferences on development issues.

Human resources development (HRD) is one of the major issues that is given special attention in CIDES, in line with current government policy emphasis. CIDES also develops models of development at the local and national levels to strengthen interdependence between the formal and informal sectors, the traditional and modern sectors, and the rural and urban areas. These models are aimed at strengthening local resources and ensuring a more equitable distribution of development benefits. CIDES also puts emphasis on promoting co-operation among the developing countries, to reduce their dependence on the more developed countries and improve their collective bargaining position in the global community.

CIDES publishes working papers, books, as well as weekly, monthly, bi-monthly and quarterly magazines and journals. These publications are sold to the public at large as a source of revenue for CIDES.

CIDES collaborates with other institutions, both government and private, and with non-governmental institutions from overseas. Many CIDES seminars are also jointly sponsored by *Republika*, a daily newspaper established by ICMI. Among the organizations that CIDES has co-operated with are the Agency for the Assessment and Application of Technology (BPPT), the Departments of Health and Public Works, the Batam Special Authority, UNDP, the Asia Foundation and the Friedrich Naumann Stiftung (FNS). CIDES has also developed special relationships with the Institute of Policy Studies in Malaysia, an institute close to the then Deputy Prime Minister Datuk Anwar Ibrahim, and with Yayasan Mendaki in Singapore, a foundation devoted to improving the welfare of the Malay community in Singapore.

Like LP3ES, CIDES is also becoming increasingly involved in action programmes. For instance, CIDES helped found and acts as secretariat to FOKUS (Forum Komunikasi Usahawan Serantau, or Communication Forum for Regional Entrepreneurs) which brings together indigenous businessmen from Indonesia, Malaysia and Singapore. CIDES is also conducting pilot projects in Bekasi, Cirebon and Lamongan, three areas which are growing into major industrial centres, aimed at ensuring that the weak informal sector is not marginalized by the development of large-scale industries. Such programmes, however, are not seen by CIDES as simply ends in themselves but are intended to have broader policy implications.

Currently CIDES has no foundation or endowment. It receives a regular sum of money from a fund managed by Habibie, but this is only enough to pay for salaries and other routine expenses. To finance activities such as seminars, CIDES has to raise funds from other sources. This is one of the main reasons why CIDES has developed co-operation with many of the organizations mentioned above. Another way of raising revenues is through the CIDES Society. In return for a sum of money members of the society receive notification of forthcoming seminars, discounts on any seminar fees, and copies of CIDES journals.

CIDES has a three-member board of directors, one of whom is the executive director. At the time of writing it had five executive researchers and about ten research assistants, with the number still increasing. There were twenty-one administrative employees. CIDES has a routine annual budget of Rp178,000,000 (US$80,909) and its budget for projects in 1994/95 amounted to Rp2.3 billion (US$1,045,454).

Although CIDES is an affiliate of ICMI, the Centre is not exclusive in character. CIDES seminars are open to the general public and are usually advertised in the mass media. While ICMI activities would probably exclude non-Muslims, CIDES has no such limitations on, for example, the speakers invited to its seminars.

CIDES has been closely associated with B.J. Habibie, but it is difficult to gauge the Centre's influence on Habibie's thinking, particularly given his roles and connections with many other institutions. CIDES' policy input is diffuse, accomplished through its various seminars, dialogues, and publications. CIDES dialogues are usually attended by students, NGO activists, businessmen, government opposition leaders, as well as members of the bureaucracy and the military. The strategy is to develop both vertical and horizontal networks, the first as a means to influence the decision-making process and the second to disseminate CIDES ideas on various development issues to the wider public.

Other Think-Tanks

There are numerous other research institutions and think-tanks in Jakarta that are relatively unnoticed because their activities are still limited or because they deliberately shy away from publicity. It should also be noted that many universities also have research centres and think-tanks, some of which are quite well-developed. Among these are the Institute for Economic and Social Research (LPEM) of the Faculty of Economics at the University of Indonesia, and the Centre for Rural and Population Studies (P3K) at Gadjah Mada University in Yogyakarta. Other universities in provincial capitals likely have research centres which carry out studies for and provide advice to regional planners and provincial officials.

Several other small think-tanks merit brief mention. The Indonesian Chamber of Commerce (KADIN) has an in-house think-tank known as LP3E. LP3E has 18 members from different educational and occupational backgrounds who advise the chairman of KADIN. Dr Dipo Alam, head of the Bureau for Industry and Mining at Bappenas, established a loose forum called the Tawang Alun Study Group (TASG). TASG brings together about twenty individuals from various government departments, academic institutions and NGOs to discuss various aspects of development and produce policy recommendations for the development planning minister/chairman of Bappenas.

Finally, a number of junior military officers, led by Soeharto's son-in-law, the then General Prabowo, in collaboration with several scholars set up the Centre for Policy and Development Studies (CPDS). These scholars included two prominent ICMI activists, Dr Amir Santoso of the University of Indonesia, and Dr Din Syamsuddin from the IAIN, State Islamic Teaching Institute, in Jakarta. Dr Din Syamsuddin is also active in the modernist Islamic social and educational organization Muhammadiyah, as well as being a functionary of Golkar. CPDS regularly organized small group discussions, mostly focusing on domestic political issues. Not much is known about CPDS, however, because it did not publish its studies or advertise its activities.

TYPOLOGY OF THINK-TANKS

This brief survey shows that, although still limited in number, organizations that devote themselves to policy studies and/or attempt to affect policy formulation and implementation are growing in numbers and importance. Although financial constraints remain a major obstacle, there is now a much greater variety of resources for think-tanks to draw upon to support their activities. These include government departments, state-owned companies, private firms, and wealthy businessmen as well as international agencies. Good analysts are still hard to come by, but the steady improvement of tertiary education has also produced an increasingly large pool of well-educated graduates willing to devote their time to research and policy studies.

Policy advisory institutions can be grouped into four major categories, based on their organizations and affiliations. The first is the state-established institutions which are created as part of the government bureaucracy. These organizations are required to provide input to the government, channelled through authorized government agencies. Such institutions include LIPI and the R&D centres in the various ministries.

The second type are think-tanks established by government departments or bureaucrats to provide analysis and policy input formally to the departments concerned, but which organizationally are not part of the state bureaucracy. CPIS is a good example of this second type.

The third type are private institutions which have been established by, or are closely linked to, high-ranking government officials, active as well as retired, such as CSIS, ISSI and CIDES. It should be noted here that some think-tanks initially established with significant government patrons, such as CSIS and LP3ES, are now, for various reasons, less closely identified with particular government figures and increasingly perceived as more independent institutions.

Finally, there are private research institutions neither founded nor closely associated with specific government officials. Such think-tanks can be found at universities, in the private sector (such as the Indonesian Chamber of Commerce and Industry's LP3E), and around a number of prominent NGO activists or counter-élites. The latter group usually draws most of its financial support from international funding agencies.

The establishment of research organizations specifically aimed at providing intellectual and policy input for the government did not begin with the birth of the New Order. As noted above, one of the largest and most important state research institutions, the Indonesian Institute of Sciences (LIPI) started life as MIPI, the Council for Sciences of Indonesia, founded in 1956. Nevertheless, the New Order government enlarged, re-organized and expanded the scope of LIPI. The establishment of LIPI in 1967 and its later development into a huge multi-disciplinary research institution were related directly to the government's increasing need to have detailed and reliable data about development-related issues. The growing scope and increasing complexity of the tasks faced by government ministries also led to the establishment of in-house research and development bodies in most of the government departments.

Thus the initial policy advisory organizations were created by the government and its many functional institutions to meet their own needs. These institutions became an integral part of the bureaucracy, intended to support and strengthen the government and make its various ministries more efficient in carrying out their functions. Their staffs are civil servants, and their projects are mostly funded by the government or by development aid channelled through the government. The growth of this type of policy advisory institution reflects the growing scope and intricacy of the issues that the government has to deal with.

The development of an institutionally separate policy advisory organization within a government bureaucracy, such as the creation of CPIS as an in-house think-tank within the Department of Finance, was also a response to a perceived need for professional and full-time researchers and analysts. The existence of such institutions was seen to overcome at least two major constraints. The first constraint was personnel: departmental R&D centres do not always have permanently assigned analysts since officials tend to be rotated. The second constraint was bureaucratic, for government researchers have limited independence in expressing their views. Hiring outside analysts as researchers or consultants offers a way of providing policy makers with independent policy alternatives.

Like the first type of policy advisory institutions, this second type also exists to facilitate and support the functioning of the government. These think-tanks' findings are the exclusive rights of the government agencies to which they are attached. Researchers in these think-tanks are usually paid more than the regular government employees, but their presence does not contribute significantly to creating a more pluralistic or diversified decision-making process.

Beginning in the early 1970s, one also began to see the emergence of private research institutions. As noted above, private think-tanks can also be divided into three types based on their origins, main source of funding and link to the government or government officials. Two important organizations, CSIS and LP3ES were both founded in 1971. Private think-tanks began to grow in number in the late 1980s and early 1990s.

Unlike the first two types of policy advisory institutions which have been specifically established to provide official input to policy making, the position and role of the private think-tanks are less clear-cut, and vary greatly between organizations. It can be argued that the birth of these private think-tanks is both demand and supply driven. Some have been set up because of a perceived need to provide independent policy alternatives. At the same time, the increasing number of people with higher education and expertise who are interested in public policy has also stimulated the growth of new think-tanks. In the case of ISSI, it seems to have been created mainly to provide several retired high ranking officials and military officers a vehicle for expressing and publicizing their views.

Some think-tanks recruit full time staff. Many of the new think-tanks, however, have a much looser organizational structure. Members of some of these think-tanks come from diverse occupational backgrounds, such as the bureaucracy, the academic world and the NGOs, without leaving their primary jobs. In the case of this second mode of recruitment, the think-tanks act more as a forum of communication for their members. Drawing from their varied expertise and institutional attachments, members of the think-tanks can develop new insights which they can take back to benefit their original institutions. At the same time, the diverse occupational backgrounds of the think-tank members provide the new organizations with important ready-made vertical and horizontal networks.

CONCLUSION

The establishment of private think-tanks by influential government fig-ures, such as CSIS by Ali Moertopo and Soedjono Hoemardani in 1971 and CIDES by B.J. Habibie in 1993, clearly has some political implica-tions. It can be argued that people who are competing for political interests and influence want the best information and policy analysis available. They find it increasingly difficult to affect policy without the support of complex analyses. In this respect think-tanks form a linkage between government and the world of politics.

Besides providing their political patrons with information and analyses, think-tanks may also be used by the patrons as "trouble-shooters" and as a means to canvass popular support for their policy and positions. A think-tank may be asked to carry out activities by its political patrons that cannot easily be done within the strict confines of the bureaucracy. For example, in the 1970s CSIS was asked to prepare the ground for the political incorporation of East Timor, and in the 1980s to host bilateral meetings with Vietnam at a time when the government strictly adhered to the ASEAN policy of putting pressure on Vietnam. The private nature of the think-tank enables members of the military, the bureaucracy and the public to meet as private individuals to exchange ideas and suggest policy alter-natives without bureaucratic constraints.

Think-tanks may also be used by political figures to obtain popular support for their ideas. Such dissemination of views and public acceptance can in turn be used to strengthen the position of the concerned officials within the government. Publication, dialogues, seminars and informal consultations are the most common ways of disseminating information and influencing public opinion.

The development of think-tanks such as CSIS, CIDES, and CPDS, however, is not only due to political patrons, but also to the desire and willingness of the non-official actors to participate. In some cases it is not the patrons that select their followers, but rather the latter that select the government official whom they feel can best promote their political, social or economic interests.

The appointment of the then Minister for Research and Technology B.J. Habibie as chairman of ICMI (Association of Indonesian Muslim Intellectuals) is a good example of this. Habibie was asked to lead ICMI not only because he is a devout Muslim and the most prominent figure in Indonesia's science and technology development to which ICMI is com-mitted, but because the minister was known to have been close to the then

President Soeharto. The initiators of ICMI, students and some leading Muslim intellectuals such as Dr Imaddudin, first approached the popular minister for environment, Emil Salim, to lead the organization. Salim, while supportive, felt that he was too old and suggested that Habibie would make a more effective chairman of the organization. Habibie was at first reluctant to accept the invitation, reportedly saying "I am an engineer and a builder of airplanes, not an Islamic scholar." He is also said to have expressed fears that acceptance might violate the wishes of President Soeharto. Habibie's reluctance was only overcome when the former Minister for Religious Affairs interceded, and a petition was circulated among prominent Muslim intellectuals supporting his leadership (Hefner 1993).

Thus the association of a number of think-tanks with important figures in the government has been used by others to advance their own ideas about society, in order to broaden policy input to the government, and whenever possible to influence the decision-making process. Think-tanks which do not have powerful political patrons may also affect policy changes in a less direct way through publication, seminars, or carrying out policy studies for government departments that are willing to pay for them.

The development of think-tanks has, to an extent, brought into greater prominence some of the different groupings in society. For instance, because a number of scholars at CSIS are of Chinese descent or are Catholic, CSIS as an organization had at one time been perceived by some Islamic groups as reflecting Chinese and non-Muslim (mostly Catholic) outlooks. This perception was especially pronounced in the 1970s and 1980s, primarily because Ali Moertopo was generally credited with the New Order's earlier policy of de-politicizing Islam and circumscribing Islamic activities, as well as the close association between many of the New Order generals and big Chinese-Indonesian businesses.

CIDES is associated with ICMI which is generally seen as a modernist Muslim organization. Part of its agenda is trying to promote the greater acceptability of Islamic mores in the Indonesian polity and in advancing the welfare of the weaker economic actors, the majority of whom are Muslim *pribumi* (non-Chinese) Indonesians. Many of the think-tanks, however, do not have such clear-cut identities as CSIS and CIDES.

The emergence of think-tanks, especially those that cluster around prominent political figures, to a certain extent can reflect power alignments among policy makers and political élites. However, it should also be noted that a number of individuals are affiliated with several different think-tanks simultaneously, thus making some of the distinctions between these organizations less obvious. The similarity of some of their agendas can lead to new alignments or co-operation between certain think-tanks. In cases where personnel overlap the co-operation becomes closer. There is, however, also a division of labour among think-tanks, with each emphasizing slightly different aspects of public policy.

A number of the think-tanks that were earlier associated with important government officials, such as CSIS and LP3ES, no longer enjoy such close proximity to the seats of power after the death or retirement of their patrons. These organizations, however, continue to survive (though with varying degrees of success) by broadening their bases of support, thus diluting some of their former distinctive identities. CSIS nowadays is no longer perceived as a Chinese Catholic think-tank, for many of its staff members are Muslim *pribumi*. The activities of CSIS are also attracting a more diversified audience.

The phenomenon of think-tanks can be seen as part of the larger process of development and elaboration of intermediary institutions, linking the official world with the broader élite and community. The functions of information-sharing, informal consultations, and input of policy views and recommendations, all of which are served by the various publications and dialogue activities of the think-tanks, can be seen as functionally part of the wider political process, and thus as one of the institutional adaptations to the new economic-societal conditions. Nevertheless, it is premature to argue that the presence of think-tanks has really made a significant contribution to the larger political process and outcomes, for their numbers are still limited and many have only been established in the last several years. The case of think-tanks shows that institution-building in Indonesia is still in a highly formative, transitional stage.

CONCLUSION

Conclusion

Richard W. Baker and M. Hadi Soesastro

What broader conclusions can be drawn from these case studies of the relationship between economic growth and institutional change? The interactions are complex and often indirect, and there are important gaps in our information in a number of areas, so it would not be reasonable to expect to identify simple, sweeping lessons. However, a number of observations can be made, and some patterns can be identified in the experiences of the major institutions studied.

Looked at from the perspective of adaptation, the institutions we have examined fall into several clusters along a spectrum from the least adaptive to the most adaptive. The following sections describe this spectrum and some of the specific noteworthy attributes of the various clusters and institutions. In the final section we offer some comments on the interrelationships between the findings of the study and Indonesia's current crisis, as well as some more speculative thoughts on the possible implications for the next stages in Indonesia's economic and political development.

GOVERNMENT INSTITUTIONS: NOT KEEPING PACE

The first cluster of institutions includes those that are formally and explicitly a part of government. Four of the institutions studied fall in this category: the formal political structure, the bureaucracy, the armed forces (ABRI), and (of the three political organizations discussed in Chapter 6) the government political vehicle Golkar.

The common characteristic of all four institutions is that, during the New Order period, each of them has evolved but has not changed in fundamental ways. Indeed, it is arguable on the evidence of the case studies that none of them has fully adapted to the changing external conditions, and in some respects as economic change has proceeded they have been falling further behind the pace. This is not to say that the institutions have not changed over the period; indeed all of them have, and some of the changes have been directly responsive to the consequences of economic growth. Further, the issues facing the institutions in most cases are recognized, including by individuals within them, and a number of proposals have been aired and in some cases tried for overcoming the problems. But the practical results to date have been relatively limited, and the challenges seem to be growing.

Government Structures and Processes

As indicated in Ramlan Surbakti's survey, the primary evolution in formal government processes over the period of rapid economic growth under the New Order government has been one of progressive centralization of the decision-making processes. The executive, and most particularly the presidency, has emerged as overwhelmingly the most powerful and dominant element of government — to the extent that the legislature and the judiciary in effect function as dependencies of the executive. The executive has also seen more elaboration of its structure and processes over this time than the other branches of government. The executive and most of all the presidency have profited most from the direct benefits of economic growth, both in terms of such institutional factors as salaries and facilities and in increased access to funds for patronage to sustain political support.

Surbakti does point to examples of efforts within both the legislature and the judiciary to assert a more independent role in government decision making. He also identifies a number of specific adaptations by the government, both of structure and of policies, over the period. These include steps explicitly intended to meet the needs for social justice, respect for human rights, de-bureaucratization and democratization. However, Surbakti concludes that in most instances the actual changes that have occurred to date have been more cosmetic than real, and that efforts to alter the fundamental power relationships within the government structure have not been successful.

The net result is a government structure that is powerful but whose institutions are not deeply rooted. Personalities and personalistic ties remain far more important in government decision making than structures or formal processes. Even within the presidency, the system appears centred on the person of the president rather than the presidency as a structural institution. Correspondingly, government policies appear to give priority over maintaining stability and control as opposed to fully accommodating (much less stimulating) popular concerns and input. Government institutions and officials do not appear particularly close to the people but rather somewhat distant and aloof.

Such a system is capable of reacting to change (whether economically induced or otherwise) and is even alert to change particularly insofar as this may present challenges to government policy and control. But it does not put a high premium on adapting to change in more fundamental ways, including changes in the structures and processes of government themselves. A major question raised by this assessment is whether this highly centralized, personalized, control-oriented structure is well suited to dealing with the increasing complexity of national life and policy issues under sustained growth. A related question is whether it can ensure continuity of structure and decision-making as leadership changes.

The Bureaucracy

The government bureaucracy (civil service) is arguably the key human institution for the delivery of government policies and services. T.A. Legowo's study notes that one of the New Order's early achievements was to gain control over the bureaucracy and mould it into an effective instrument to implement development objectives and carry out other central policies. At the same time, however, he sees a distance between the bureaucracy and the public, and a lack of social control over the bureaucracy, resulting in a number of dysfunctional characteristics including arbitrary behaviour and corruption.

The study also describes the efforts that have been made, starting in the 1980s, for reform and de-bureaucratization. The need for more change within the bureaucracy is clearly recognized. Legowo's analysis of the reform efforts to date, however, identifies a number of obstacles that make it difficult to achieve the fundamental changes: an impulse to regulate all aspects of national life, a top-down approach, pervasive corruption and an overall emphasis on maintaining power rather than responding to the needs of the society. Ultimately, he concludes, these characteristics reflect the attitudes at the top of the political system.

A fundamental factor behind this conclusion is that the Indonesian bureaucracy remains highly politicized. It is essentially an extension of the political system rather than the kind of neutral, professional instrument envisioned by Western theorists and advocated by Indonesian reformers. It remains to be seen whether the current bureaucratic culture can be transformed into one that is oriented towards empowering and serving the society rather than controlling the society and serving the political leadership.

The Armed Forces

The Indonesian armed forces (ABRI) have remained the most important power base of the New Order government, the "power behind" the regime. But J. Kristiadi's study of the evolution of ABRI over the past three decades indicates that in certain respects ABRI as an institution has been slowly slipping behind the curve of change.

ABRI's share of the government budget has actually decreased significantly over the period, and the shortfall between ABRI's needs and resources continues to be made up in large part by the military's ample access to extra-budgetary sources of income. This situation inevitably has a certain corrosive effect on the professionalism of the military establishment and its ability to discharge its primary defence functions. A more immediate challenge to ABRI's position comes from increasing criticism both on the part of the growing middle class and from some military figures as well of ABRI's institutionalized roles in Indonesia's government, politics and economy. Equally and ultimately perhaps even more important, with increasingly attractive career opportunities in a wide variety of fields becoming available as a result of economic growth, ABRI today faces stiffer competition in recruiting personnel, particularly in the officer corps, than it did in the past. These problems pose serious difficulties for ABRI in continuing to fulfil both its military mission and its perception of its higher national role in the future.

Golkar

M. Djadijono's study describes Golkar as essentially an instrument of government domination of the political process. Although sustained growth has directly benefited Golkar in terms of increased access to financial resources, economic success has not been correlated with increased independence for Golkar as a political actor.

Further, despite the government's evident success in delivering on its overriding objective of economic development, the trend in popular support is not clear. As Djadijono indicates, Golkar actually lost seats (though not many) in the national parliament in the relatively openly contested election of 1992. It is true that Golkar's percentage of the vote was so high in the early New Order elections, because of the heavy pressures brought to bear at all levels, that as a practical matter over the longer term it was almost bound to decline. It is also conceivable, though impossible to prove, that the actual support for Golkar — in the sense of voters who genuinely recognize the government's success and vote for Golkar as a result — may have been a higher proportion of the Golkar vote in the more recent elections than earlier in the New Order period. (The May 1997 election, which ended with a more successful outcome for Golkar but featured a return to more heavy-handed government campaign tactics, is even more difficult to interpret than the preceding election.) But regardless of the response of the electorate, it is very difficult to make the case that Golkar itself has matured or in any sense come into its own as a political institution as a result of the period of sustained rapid growth.

MIXED INSTITUTIONS: MIXED RECORDS

A second group of institutions falls in the middle ground between government and the private sector. It is in itself a diverse group, ranging from state enterprises which are formally part of government to the mass media much of which has no formal link with government. However, in all cases the institutions are both dependent on or regulated by government and involved with the private market and the civil society. The five institutions in the study in this category are: state enterprises, the educational system, the labour movement, the opposition political parties, and the mass media.

The diversity of these institutions is matched by diversity in their experiences with the impact of rapid, sustained economic growth. However, there is a common thread in the studies, which is a certain tension between the interests and capabilities of government on the one hand, and the pull of market and societal forces on the other. Not surprisingly, with economic growth has come a strengthening of the societal side of the equation; reaction from the government side has been more adaptive in some cases than in others.

Public Enterprises

Indonesia's state enterprise sector is caught between two strong but not fully compatible forces. On the one hand, they are either fully or partially owned by the government and are expected to fulfil social and public purposes consistent with the constitutional mandate of state control of the "commanding heights" of the economy. Their government connection also means that they participate to one degree or another in a complex network of political and patronage relationships. On the other hand, their status as enterprises imposes on them the need to function as economic entities, with the requirements of efficiency and competitiveness that come with their participation in markets.

The study by I Ketut Mardjana indicates that the period of successful economic growth has been paralleled by some movement on the part of state enterprises (especially some of the larger ones) in the direction of more effective and independent participation in the market. The driving force here has been recognition by the government that continued economic growth requires more dynamic and competitive enterprises, and that the state enterprises cannot be exempted from this requirement.

But the progress in this direction has been incomplete, and the policy signals from the top have not been consistent through the period. Mardjana documents a pattern in which government support for marketizing and privatizing of the state enterprise sector has been strongest when economic conditions have been the most straitened, whereas in periods of relative prosperity there has been a tendency to fall back onto old habits of looking to state enterprises to fill other national or political needs. The most dramatic recent example of the latter phenomenon is in the high technology area, where government has undertaken the sponsorship of a number of expensive and, to date, non-competitive high technology enterprises in the interest of leapfrogging Indonesia into these cutting-edge economic sectors. As indicated in the study, the wisdom of investing substantial amounts of the nation's limited resources in this effort is a subject of active and sometimes heated debate even before the 1997–98 economic crisis.

Education

Education in Indonesia, as in most countries today, is primarily a function of government. Education has been a major focus of the government's development plans and capital investment throughout the New Order period. However, private institutions are also allowed to operate (under government license), particularly at the university level. And ultimately the educational system must meet the needs of the private sector which is the strongest engine for continued growth and development.

As documented in Onny Prijono's study, in the first phase of the New Order era the government pursued what might be called a supply-led development of the education sector. The major effort was simply to increase the scope and the extent of educational facilities, starting at the primary level and moving upwards. More recently, as sustained economic growth has changed the structure of the economy and the nature of the labour market, development in the education sector has shifted towards a situation which could be better described as demand-led. The question now is how the changing human resource needs are going to be met by the education system, and how overall quality is going to be increased.

A growing gap has been identified between the types and levels of skills possessed by school leavers and university graduates, and the demand for skills in the economy. As part of its response to this situation, in the 1990s the government attempted to engage private enterprise more directly in the educational system, to help make a closer match between the skills being taught and the needs in the job market.

This is clearly an area in which the New Order government made creative efforts to adapt the educational system to the needs of a developing economy. However, there remain significant questions concerning the ability of the educational system to respond to the new challenges. Some of the needs, such as upgrading the quality of teachers, are very difficult to deal with in a short period of time. In other areas the critical constraint is resources; some of the skill areas where the national needs are greatest — e.g., science and technology — are also those where the costs are highest. In the meantime, the educational system continues to produce more graduates with non-technical skills, both at the secondary school and university levels, than the economy is capable of employing. The increasing numbers of young people with heightened but unrealisable expectations could have serious implications for fundamental social stability.

Labour

The labour sector presents a rather different picture of the interaction between economic and social dynamics and government policy. Here, as documented in the study by Sukardi Rinakit, economic change created powerful new forces. Dramatic growth brought rising consciousness on the part of workers, and a desire to improve their own conditions and a greater share of the benefits of development. At the same time, the objective conditions for labour also changed, reflecting both increasing prosperity and structural changes in the economy.

Government policy in the labour sector, however, has been focused centrally on the need for continued stability and control. The only government-recognized formal labour organization, SPSI, is in effect run by the government and is more an instrument of control than an instrument for the articulation of the interests of workers. Government development policy also dictates that Indonesia has to maintain relatively low wage rates in order to remain internationally competitive. These conflicting elements created new pressures and tensions within the labour sector and institutions.

However, the demands created by economic change are simply too powerful to be permanently suppressed. As the workers pursue their more clearly perceived interests, they are already beginning to move outside and around the formal institutional framework that has been set up to represent labour. This is occurring both through attempts to establish alternative labour unions, and at the local level through smaller social welfare or ad hoc organizations, and increasingly through locally-organized industrial actions. Sukardi Rinakit's case study of a strike in Tangerang is an example of the latter phenomenon. This process seems likely to be played out for some time to come.

Thus in the labour sector, significant changes brought about by economic growth have not been matched by adaptive change in the formal institutions. The new forces could well get out of government control, despite strenuous government efforts to maintain control.

Political Parties

As indicated in M. Djadijono's chapter, Indonesia's two New Order opposition political parties were nominally autonomous entities but are both constrained by detailed government-initiated legislation (including security laws that allowed the government to screen and disapprove party candidates in elections) and subjected to regular informal intervention by the government. The government's restructuring and manipulation of the parties unquestionably succeeded in eliminating any chance that the government could be defeated in national elections, and in removing the threat of serious political challenges to its programme. At the same time, unlike the government's Golkar, the parties did not benefit significantly from economic growth in terms of their own financial resources, and were largely dependent on funding from the government, which in turn further increased the government's influence over the parties.

Ironically, however, Djadijono's study also shows that, despite their institutional weakness and vulnerability to government pressure, the parties did nevertheless manage to display some degree of independence both in their election platforms and in their willingness to criticize the political structure and specific actions by the government. These exercises of independence may well have represented efforts by the parties to respond to the changing political interests and needs of society stimulated by the process of economic growth, even though they certainly did not reflect any direct strengthening in the economic (or political) position of the parties themselves.

Further, as with labour, over the long run it was clearly questionable whether, in the context of a dynamic economy and a rapidly changing society, the underlying impulses and interests that are normally channelled through political parties could continue to be contained by the government through the techniques of manipulation and pressure. This was especially true given the fact that, as previously noted, the government's own political vehicle, Golkar, did not provide a genuine substitute channel for popular political expression and action. The rise and continued prominence, despite concerted government opposition, of popular, independent-minded leaders in both the nationalist and Islamic camps (the PDI's Megawati and NU's Abdurrahman Wahid) clearly demonstrated this point.

Djadijono also cites evidence of increasing resort by the public to other channels of political expression, bypassing the ineffective political party structure. These other channels include both use of alternative, officially non-political organizations as well as direct protest actions. Most sobering was the rising incidence in the mid-1990s of violence by the public against government authorities, suggesting serious longer-term consequences of the New Order's emasculation of the political parties and foreshadowing the events of 1997–98.

The Media

The mass media is another hybrid institution. Some major media outlets are run by government organizations (such as the government television network TVRI and the newspapers sponsored by Golkar and the armed forces), but most of the mass media is privately owned. However, the media is also closely monitored and subject to regular if usually informal intervention by the government. In addition, and particularly in recent years, high government officials, members of their families or others close to government have come to own or control many important private media outlets.

Dedy Hidayat's study documents the dynamic growth and changes in the mass media under the impact of the explosive economic expansion of the past two decades. In this sector, market forces (the combination of audience interest and producer profit incentive) have a very direct impact on the content of the product. There is also a constant tension between the interest of the media in attracting an audience through topical and colourful content, and the interest of the government in controlling the national political discourse and maintaining stability. As a result, in Hidayat's phrase, media owners and operators are constantly "reading between the palace and the market".

The record in this sector in recent years has been uneven, with periods of officially-tolerated openness alternating with crackdowns and discipline against members of the media who pushed political criticism beyond the limits of what the government leadership was prepared to accept. The June 1994 cancellation of the publication permits of three magazines, including the major national weekly *Tempo*, was the latest of these crackdowns, bringing to an abrupt end a period in which the government had seemed genuinely willing to tolerate — and even foster — a wider scope of public discussion and critical debate.

Looking to the future, the various tensions between political and market forces, and the conflicting interests and orientations within the media itself, seem bound to continue. Further, it is difficult to imagine that the government, with its limited human and financial resources, will be able (or willing) to exercise constant effective control over the large and still growing number of media outlets in the country, which now include electronic as well as print media. So this is one institution in which the impact of economically-induced change could safely be expected to be significant and continuing.

THE PRIVATE SECTOR: DYNAMIC RESPONSES

The third group of institutions is unequivocally in the private sector. Of the case studies, two fall in this category: private business enterprises and mass social organizations.

The government has both less formal and less continuous control over this group of institutions that those in the previous category. For example, there is no equivalent to the laws governing political party activities or the regulation giving the government the discretion to revoke publishing permits of the print media. However, this does not mean that these institutions are independent of the government. They are affected by a whole panoply of government licensing and other regulations. And beyond the official processes there are a wide range of informal interactions with government. So the difference between this cluster and the previous group of institutions is only a matter of degree. Nevertheless, the qualitative distinction in the nature of their relationships with government is clear enough to warrant placing them in a separate category.

Private Enterprise

The private enterprise sector discussed in Didik Rachbini's chapter is clearly the most dynamic and rapidly evolving of the institutions studied in this project. Unsurprisingly, given that it is an integral part of the economy, this sector has also felt greater impact of the growth process than almost any other. There has been a huge increase in the size and the role of the private business sector, and this sector now provides the main engine driving further economic growth.

Rachbini's study also points to the numerous active linkages between the private economy and the government. Two major but quite different dynamics stand out. The first is the link between government economic *policies* and the growth of the private sector, and the second is the importance of *personal relationships* with government officials to the success of individual business figures and their enterprises.

As detailed by the World Bank (1993) in its study of the "East Asian miracle", the policies of the New Order government have been directly responsible for creating the environment that made possible the high rates of economic growth during its first thirty years. The major examples are the market-oriented stabilization and recovery programme put in place at the start of the New Order period in the late 1960s, and then, equally important, the deregulation policies followed after the economic crisis of the early to mid-1980s. These government policies allowed and facilitated the very rapid growth of private enterprises in the late 1980s and 1990s that brought the private sector to its position as the leading engine of economic growth.

An irony here is that arguably government policy has been most favourable to the development of private enterprise in the periods when overall economic conditions were worst — first the essentially collapsed economy that the New Order inherited from the Sukarno period, and then the severe downturn experienced after the collapse of oil prices in the early 1980s. During the periods of greatest economic success and booms the government has tended to revert to the kinds of dirigiste policies that had characterized the pre-New Order period, including the establishment or expansion of public enterprises as the vehicle for achieving priority economic development goals.

The second dynamic is the long-standing, and continuing, high degree of dependence of the private enterprise sector on links with government agencies and officials. As described by Rachbini, in the pre-New Order period there had been concerted government efforts to encourage the development of *pribumi* entrepreneurs and businesses. The New Order government largely abandoned the official discrimination between *pribumi* and *non-pribumi* business, but nevertheless continued to provide special government facilities and privileges to certain *pribumi* businesses, and a number of *pribumi* businessmen and women participated prominently in the burst of growth under the New Order government. In the case of *non-pribumi*, largely Chinese-Indonesian businesses, links with New Order leaders first established between military commanders and *non-pribumi* businessmen in the 1950s continued and flourished in the New Order period, as did the business firms involved, some of which have emerged as the leading conglomerates in the private sector.

Thus a strong symbiotic relationship developed between business and government. For *non-pribumi* business, official protection was a necessity; for *pribumi* business official patronage was a major source of business opportunities. Those with economic power sought political access, and those with political power sought access to economic resources. So Indonesia's private enterprise sector cannot really be considered autonomous from government. But it is nevertheless both dynamic and, as a whole, highly adaptive to changing economic circumstances and opportunities.

A major trend within the private sector identified in the study is the centralization of economic power through the growth and consolidation of a series of huge business conglomerates (both *non-pribumi* and *pribumi*), particularly in the latter part of the 1980s and the 1990s. Given the close relationships between business and government, and the highly centralized political system, this was not particularly surprising. However, it was a significant phenomenon, and in important respects was made possible by the conditions of rapid, sustained economic growth.

The new importance of the private business sector, and its increasing centralization, also gave new prominence and urgency to a number of issues that remain to be dealt with. Rachbini cites the problem of equity as one important issue, particularly the relative disadvantage of the *pribumi*-dominated small business sector. The duality of the *pribumi* and *non-pribumi* private business sectors is a major, politically sensitive issue that has not been overcome in the years of rapid, sustained growth. The government's own record and position in this regard are ambivalent. The New Order has depended heavily on *non-pribumi* entrepreneurs both for their proven economic skills and as a source of financing for patronage and other purposes. However, it also engaged in periodic high-profile efforts to support *pribumi* business, and to pressure *non- pribumi* business-men to share the wealth with *pribumi* enterprises. As Indonesia becomes increasingly integrated into the highly competitive international economy, the absence of a genuinely integrated, national private sector could be a serious liability.

A separate but related issue is the privileged role and substantial gov-ernment facilities provided to relatives of powerful government officials, particularly the Soeharto family. This in part was a natural outcome of the broader politico-economic context in which official connections are so important to business success. But the question arises as to whether or to what extent the favoured position of certain *pribumi* businesses inhibited the development of the broader *pribumi* business sector. Another question is whether the effort to solidify and protect the position of the favoured enterprises led to other distortions of the political system and institutions, which in turn hindered constructive adaptation to economic change in other national institutions.

At the broadest level, the increasing size and power of the private sector raised the question of who controls whom in the relationships between the private and public sectors. Growing discussion of the need for a law on competition indicated that the need for stronger institutional means of regulating a more complex economic reality was widely recognized. This is a further example of pressures for institutional change resulting from sustained, rapid economic growth.

Mass Social Organizations

For the traditional mass social organizations such as Muhammadijah or the Nahdlatul Ulama (NU), the period of sustained economic growth brought a rather different challenge. For these organizations the challenge was to maintain their own vitality, relevance and independent existence in circumstances of rapid and fundamental societal change.

Douglas Ramage's study focuses on how one leading organization, the NU, went about this task in a deliberate and dynamic manner, consciously developing new roles and activities relevant to the interests of its member-ship while also taking bold steps to preserve its political independence and influence. As Ramage explains, the number of organizations that fall in this category was never large, and the number that has survived the tumultuous history of the Indonesian independence struggle and first fifty years of nationhood is smaller still. The NU case is clearly the most dramatic story of adaptation in recent years. But similar adaptive processes seemed to be underway in other traditional organizations that continue to play active roles, particularly Muhammadijah.

It can be argued that these older organizations had no choice but to adapt if they were to sustain themselves — at least as serious actors — in the new society being created through economic change. But this does not detract from the conclusion that they were among the national institutions most affected by the processes of economic change, and among the most adaptive in their response.

NEW INSTITUTIONS: FILLING GAPS

The final group of institutions is distinguished simply by the fact of its newness. Although there are some historic precursors, most of the organizations in this group that are active today have appeared on the scene in Indonesia only in recent years. Arguably they could be considered the direct products of the period of rapid, sustained economic growth. The study considered two types of institutions in this category: issue-oriented non-governmental organizations (NGOs) and policy-oriented "think-tanks."

At least two quite different reasons can be adduced for the appearance or growth of these new institutions in parallel with sustained rapid economic growth. On the one hand, they can be seen as responses to new needs in the society, reflecting the greater complexity of life and the greater complexity of the issues faced with rising economic levels. On the other hand, they can be seen as a response to problems, including needs in the society that were not being met by the existing institutional framework — indicators of areas where the older, established institutions were having difficulty dealing with the pace and consequences of change.

Non-Government Organizations

Muhammad Hikam's study of issue-oriented NGOs illustrates the ways in which these organizations have moved to fill the niches opened up by the rapidly expanding economy and the changes in the larger society caused by the growth process. The latest generation of NGOs in particular tends to be concerned with helping disadvantaged groups and strengthening the civil society, counterbalancing the growing powers of government and vested interests. These organizations can also be seen as providing a political space for members of the expanding middle class that is outside the mainstream but nevertheless interacts with and can influence official policy.

"Think-Tanks"

Dewi Fortuna Anwar's survey of the think-tanks that have grown up over the past two decades indicates both the diverse affiliations and the variety of functions served by this relatively new (for Indonesia) institutional form. Broadly considered, the think-tanks are an intermediary institution. They help meet reciprocal needs of government officials and policy makers on the one hand, and members of the intellectual élite on the other. Through the think-tanks, policy makers and other powerful figures can draw on broader and less inhibited sources of information and opinion than generally found within government. For lower-level government officials participation in think-tank activities can provide a forum for expressing their own views more openly than is often possible in the hierarchical structure of the bureaucracy, and it also establishes links to external networks that can be useful to their parent organizations. On the other side of the exchange, intellectuals and activists of various persuasions gain at least the possibility of direct access to and influence on government decision-making processes.

Of course both the issue-oriented NGOs and the policy-oriented think-tanks face problems — with respect to their sources of funding, their human resources and, perhaps most fundamentally, the issues of the larger national structure and the organizational and political culture in which they are trying to operate. Because the existing political and social orders are not fully accustomed to dealing with these institutions and may even feel threatened to some degree by them, the newcomers face a delicate task of finding their way and establishing an accepted place for themselves in the overall structure.

However, the very fact that these new categories of institutions have grown up over this time is perhaps the clearest measure of the degree to which the institutions of Indonesian society, economy, and government have been changed by rapid and sustained economic growth. It is quite reasonable to anticipate that, as the economic growth process continues, these institutions will play a progressively more important role in Indonesia's national life.

IMPLICATIONS AND PROSPECTS

All of Indonesia's institutions face profound challenges. The case studies demonstrate shortcomings and dilemmas in every case. Even the most successful adapters to date must maintain and perhaps even increase their rate of change if they are to solve the current issues and be in a position to tackle the next generation of problems. Some of the studies suggest reasonable confidence that the necessary responsiveness will be forthcoming, but even in these cases continued success will not be easy and is not guaranteed.

The most significant concern that emerges from the study is the apparent discontinuity between the response to change on the part of government and government-related institutions and that in the broader society. In critical areas such as political institutions and labour the New Order government continued to place first priority on control and centralized decision making, while the dynamics of development were creating powerful new forces and actors that seemed unlikely to be contained within the existing structures. In other areas such as the economy, ingrained patterns and vested interests increasingly posed obstacles to further growth, increased efficiency, and international competitiveness. The case studies identify changes in government policies and government-related institutions, but the rate of change did not keep up with that of the society as a whole, and the gap seemed to be growing.

The economic crisis of 1997–98 provided a compelling demonstration of the need for greater government attention to these problems. Key economic issues included the drag of large, inefficient, and expensive public enterprises, the negative impacts of government monopolies and favouritism, and the critical need for further deregulation, greater transparency, and more open competition. The pattern of unrest and violent incidents, coupled with a virtually nation-wide series of student and other political protests, confirmed the inadequacy of the existing political and other representative institutions as well as the inability of the highly centralized decision-making system to anticipate problems and ultimately even to maintain order.

As noted in the discussion of economic policy, Soeharto's New Order government had previously demonstrated the ability, when faced with serious economic difficulties, to make politically painful decisions and institute significant reforms. However, this record was matched by a tendency to backslide and revert to old habits when economic conditions became more buoyant. The most fundamental question posed by the 1997–98 crisis was whether this emergency would be the catalyst for effective action by Soeharto's successors on a whole series of major, long-postponed, and increasingly essential institutional changes.

The case studies in this volume do not provide any clear basis for predicting the ultimate outcome of the current crisis, or other future developments. They do, however, offer examples of more and less successful approaches to dealing with the changes brought about by sustained rapid economic growth, as well as a good picture of some of the major institutional issues now facing the Indonesian Government. Indonesia's ability to meet these challenges of change will largely determine how soon — and even whether — the nation will be able to resume and sustain the position it established over a thirty-year period as one of the East Asia's economic success stories and respected regional leader.

Bibliography

Abdullah, Rozali. 1986. *Hukum Kepegawaian* (Civil Service Law). Jakarta: Rajawali Press.

Abdullah, Syukur. 1991. "Budaya Birokrasi di Indonesia" (Bureaucratic Culture in Indonesia). In *Profil Budaya Politik Indonesia* (A Profile of Indonesia's Political Culture), edited by Alfian and Nazaruddin Sjamsuddin. Jakarta: Grafiti.

Agrawal, Nisha. 1995. "Indonesia: Labor Market Policies and International Competitiveness". Paper presented at conference, Building on Success: Maximizing the Gains from Deregulation, Jakarta, 26–28 April.

Alam, Dipo. 1990. "Kriteria Industri Strategis" (Criteria for Strategic Industries). *Warta Ekonomi* 1, no. 22 (26 March): 84.

————. 1993. "Prof Habibie dan Kwik dalam Tekno-ekonomi" (Professor Habibie and Kwik on the techno-economy). *Kompas,* 11 March, pp. 4–5.

Alamudi, Abdullah, ed. 1991. *Apakah Demokrasi Itu?* (What Is Democracy?). Jakarta: United States Information Service.

Alfian and Nazaruddin Sjamsuddin, eds. 1988. *Masa Depan Kihudupan Politik Indonesia* (The Future of Political Life in Indonesia). Jakarta: CV Rajawali in co-operation with the Indonesian Political Science Association.

Ali, Fachry. 1994. "PPP dan Suksesi" (The PPP and the Succession). *Forum Keadilan* 2, no. 12 (29 December).

Ambong, Ibrahim. 1988. "Pemilihan Umum 1987 dan Prospek Golkar" (The 1987 General Election and the Prospects for Golkar). In *Masa Depan Kihudupan Politik Indonesia* (The Future of Political Life in Indonesia), edited by Alfian and Nazaruddin Sjamsuddin, pp. 67–84. Jakarta: CV Rajawali in co-operation with the Indonesian Political Science Association.

Anderson, Michael. 1980. "Transnational advertising and politics: the case of Indonesia". *Asian Survey* 20, no. 12 (December): 1253–70.

Arndt, H.W. 1991. "Higher Education: The Problem of Quality". In *Indonesia Assessment. 1991*, edited by Hal Hill, Political and Social Change Monograph no. 13, pp. 151–54. Canberra: Department of Political and Social Change, Research School of Pacific Studies, Australian National University.

Babari, J. [forthcoming]. *SPSI dan Permasalahannya* (The All-Indonesia Workers' Union and its Problems). Jakarta: CSIS.

―――― and Onny S. Prijono. 1996. "Pendidikan Sebagai Sarana Pemberdayaan" (Education as a Mechanism for Empowerment). In *Pemberdayaan: Konsep, Kebijakan dan Implementasi* (Empowerment: Concept, Policy and Implementation), edited by Onny S. Prijono and A.M.W. Pranarka. Jakarta: Centre for Strategic and International Studies.

Ball, Alan R. 1981. *Modern Politics and Government*, London: McMillan Press Ltd.

Barlow, Hugh D. 1984. *Introduction to Criminology*, Boston: Little, Brown & Company.

Barton, Greg. 1994. "Neo-Modernism – A Vital Synthesis of Traditionalist and Modernist Thought in Indonesia". Paper presented at seminar, Islam and the Challenge of Modernization, held in conjunction with the 29th Congress of the Nahdlatul Ulama, Tasikmalaya, West Java, 1–5 December.

Beeby, C.E. 1979. *Assessment of Indonesian Education, A Guide in Planning*. Wellington: New Zealand Council for Educational Research, in association with Oxford University Press.

Berger, Peter. 1987. *The Capitalist Revolution: Fifty Propositions About Prosperity, Equality, and Liberty*. Aldershot: Wildwood House.

Billah, M.M., A. Hakim, and G. Nusantara. 1990. "State Constraints on NGOs in Indonesia: Recent Developments". *Prisma* 47, pp. 57–66.

Boediono. 1994. "Pembangunan Sektor Pendidikan Dalam Hubungannya Dengan Pengembangan Sumber Daya Manusia Dalam Repelita VI" (The Development of the Education Sector and its Relationship to Human Resources Development During Repelita VI). *Kelola* 5, no. 3 (January).

―――― and Don Adams. 1992. "A Global Analysis of Education, Social, and Economic Change in Industrializing Societies". In *Education, Economic, and Social Development*, edited by Boediono, Walter W. McMahon, and Don Adams. Jakarta: Center for Informatics, Office of Research and Development, Ministry of Education and Culture, jointly sponsored by USAID Educational Policy and Planning Project (EPP).

――――, Walter W. McMahon, and Don Adams. 1992. "25 Year Education Goals for Economic and Social Development in Indonesia". Executive summary in *Education, Economic, and Social Development*, edited by Boediono, Walter W. McMahon, and Don Adams. Jakarta: Center for Informatics, Office of Research and Development, Ministry of Education and Culture, jointly sponsored by USAID, Educational Policy and Planning Project (EPP).

Boland, B.J. 1971. *The Struggle of Islam in Modern Indonesia*. The Hague: Martinus Nijhoff.

Booth, Anne. 1994. "Repelita VI and the Second Long-term Development Plan". *Bulletin of Indonesian Economic Studies* 30, no. 3: 3–39.

Bourchier, David and John Legge, eds. 1994. *Democracy in Indonesia: 1950s and 1990s*. Clayton, Victoria: Monash University Center for Southeast Asian Studies.

BPPT (Agency for the Study and Application of Technology). 1993. *Science and Technology Indicators for Indonesia 1993*. Jakarta: BPPT/ RISTEK (Department of Research and Technology).

BPS (Biro Pusat Statistik, Central Bureau of Statistics) [monthly]. *Indikator Ekonomi* (*Monthly Statistical Bulletin: Economic Indicators*). Jakarta: BPS.

_____ [annual]. *Statistik Indonesia* (Indonesian Statistics). Jakarta: BPS.

Bresnan, John. 1993. *Managing Indonesia: The Modern Political Economy*. New York and Oxford: Oxford University Press.

Buchori, Mochtar. 1996. "The Dilemma of Achieving Improvements in Education". *Jakarta Post*, 7 November.

Budairy, Said, ed. 1994. *Nahdlatul Ulama Dari Berbagai Sudut Pandang* (The Nahdlatul Ulama From Various Points of View). Jakarta: Lakpesdam and Kompas.

Budiardjo, Miriam. 1977. *Dasar-dasar Ilmu Politik* (Fundamentals of Political Science). Jakarta: PT Gramedia.

Bulletin LAKPESDAM (various issues).

Business News (Jakarta). 1995. "Kegiatan DPR Tahun 1995, Dari Proteksi Sampai Disiplin Anggaran" (Activities of the Parliament in 1995, From Protection to Budgetary Discipline). 29 December.

Centre for Strategic and International Studies (CSIS). 1990. *Study on Human Resources Development*. Report prepared for the International Development Center of Japan (IDCJ). Jakarta: CSIS.

Conklin, John E. 1981. *Criminology*. New York: Macmilan Publishing Co.

Crawford, Robert. 1967. "The Daily Indonesian-Language Press of Dja-karta: Analysis of Two Recent Critical Periods". Ph.D. dissertation, Syracuse University.

Crouch, Harold. 1975. "Generals and Business in Indonesia". *Pacific Affairs* 48, no. 4: 519–40.

_____. 1982. *Perkembangan Politik dan Modernisasi* (Political Development and Modernization). Jakarta: Yayasan Perkhidmatan.

_____. 1986. *The Military and Politics in Indonesia*. Indonesian edition, translated by Th. Sumarthana. Jakarta: Sinar Harapan.

Department of Education and Culture 1990. *Educational Indicators: Indonesia*. Center for Informatics, Office of Research and Development. Jakarta: Departemen Pendidikan dan Kebudayaan (Department of Education and Culture).

_____. 1993*a*. *Empat Strategi Dasar Kebijakan Pendidikan Nasional* (Four Basic Strategies for National Education Policy). Jakarta: Departemen Pendidikan dan Kebudayaan (Department of Education and Culture).

_____. 1993*b*. *Peranserta Masyarakat Dalam Pendidikan Nasional* (Public Participation in National Education). Seri Kebijaksanaan (Policy Series). Jakarta: Departemen Pendidikan dan Kebudayaan (Department of Education and Culture).

_____. 1993*c*. *Sistem Ganda pada Pendidikan Menengah Kejuruan* (The Dual System in Secondary Vocational Education*)*. Seri Kebijaksanaan (Policy Series). Jakarta: Departemen Pendidikan dan Kebudayaan (Department of Education and Culture).

Department of Information. 1986. *Indonesia 1986: An Official Handbook*. Jakarta: Departemen Penerangan (Department of Information).

_____. 1991/1992. *Data Oplah dan Peredaran IPPN Tahun 1991* (Data on Publications and Circulation in 1991). Jakarta: Departemen Penerangan RI.

Dhakidae, Daniel. 1981. "Partai Politik dan Sistem Kepartaian di Indonesia" (Political Parties and the Party System in Indonesia). *Prisma* 10, no. 12 (December): 3–23.

_____. 1991. "The State, The Rise of Capital, and the Fall of Political Journalism: Political Economy of the Indonesian News Industry". Ph.D. dissertation, Cornell University.

_____. 1994. "Membunuh Modal Membunuh Kepercayaan" (Kill Capital, Kill Trust). *Bredel 1994*, pp. 48–61. Jakarta: Asosiasi Jurnalis Independen, AJI (Independent Journalists Association).

Dharwis, Ellyasa. 1994. "Dinamika NU Paska Khittah 26" (The Dynamics of NU's Return to the Commitment of '26). *Bulletin Lakpesdam* (September).

Diamond, Larry. 1994. "Rethinking Civil Society: Toward Democratic Consolidation". *Journal of Democracy* (July).

Djadijono, M. 1993*a*. "Merunut Fenomena Demokrasi Indonesia" (Tracking the Phenomenon of Democracy in Indonesia). *Bernas*, 4 November.

_____. 1993*b*. "Unjuk Rasa dan Keterbukaan Politik" (The Expression of Feelings and Political Openness). *Bernas*, 20 November.

_____. 1995. "Menelaah Kemandirian Orsospol" (Assessing the Autonomy of Socio-political Organizations). *Merdeka*, 23 November.

Djanin, M.A. 1992. "Perkembangan Perbankan dan Pembelanjaan Dunia Usaha" (Developments in Banking and Expenditures of the Business World). In *Prospek Ekonomi Indonesia Jangka Pendek dan Sumber Pembiayaan Pembangunan* (Economic Prospects for Indonesia in the Short Term and Sources of Development Financing), edited by M.A. Anwar, Iwan J. Aziz, and Faisal H. Basri. Jakarta: FEUI (Economics Faculty of the University of Indonesia) and PT Gramedia.

Effendi, Sofian. 1989. "Hambatan Struktural Pengawasan Legislatif" (Structural Obstacles to Legislative Oversight). *Prisma* 6: 13–18.

_____. 1990. *Perspektif Administrasi Pembangunan Kualitas Manusia dan Kualitas Masyarakat* (An Administrative Perspective on the Development of Human and Societal Quality). Paper for Social Sciences Seminar (Seminar Ilmu-Ilmu Sosial), Yogyakarta, 16–21 July.

_____. 1991. "Sistem Administrasi untuk Pembangunan Berkelanjutan" (An Administrative System for Sustained Development). *Prisma* 1: 36–43.

Eldridge, Philip J. 1990. "NGOs and the State in Indonesia". *Prisma* 47: 34–56.

_____. 1995. *Non-Government Organizations and Democratic Participation in Indonesia*. Kuala Lumpur and New York: Oxford University Press.

Emmerson, Donald K. 1978. "The Bureaucracy in Political Context: Weakness in Strength". In *Political Power and Communication in Indonesia*, edited by Karl D. Jackson and Lucian W. Pye. Berkeley: University of California Press.

_____. 1983. "Understanding the New Order: Bureaucratic Pluralism in Indonesia". *Asian Survey* 23, no. 11 (November): 1220–41.

Fealy, Greg. 1994. "'Rowing in a typhoon': Nahdlatul Ulama and the Decline of Parliamentary Democracy". In *Democracy in Indonesia:. 1950s and 1990s*, edited by David Bourchier and John Legge. Clayton, Victoria: Monash University Center for Southeast Asian Studies.

_____. 1995. "The Battle for Islam". *Inside Indonesia* no. 42 (March): 9–12.

_____. 1996. "Wahab Hasbullah, Traditionalism and the Political Development of Nahdlatul Ulama". In *Democracy in Indonesia: 1950s and 1990s*, edited by David Bourchier and John Legge. Clayton, Victoria: Monash University Center for Southeast Asian Studies.

_____ [forthcoming]. Ph.D. Dissertation on Nahdlatul Ulama, Monash University.

Fealy, Greg and Greg Barton, eds. 1996. *NU: Traditional Islam and Modernity*. Clayton, Victoria: Monash University Center for Southeast Asian Studies.

Feillard, Andre. 1993. "Traditionalist Islam and the State in Indonesia: Flexibility, Legitimacy and Renewal". Paper presented at conference, Islam and the Social Construction of Identities: Comparative Perspectives on Southeast Asian Muslims, University of Hawaii, August.

Fidhiawan, E. 1991. Statistics degree research report. Statistical Division of the Faculty of Mathematics and Natural Sciences, Bogor Agricultural Institute (IPB). Duplicated.

General Secretariat of the DPR-RI. 1992. *Dewan Perwakilan Rakyat Republik Indonesia Perideo 1987–1992* (The Indonesian Parliament in the Period 1987–1992). Jakarta: General Secretariat of the DPR-RI.

Giddens, Anthony. 1991. *The Constitution of Society*. Cambridge: Polity Press.

Glytsos, Nicholas P. 1989. "Reviewing Global Labor Market Mismatches of University Educated Workers". *Educational Development 9*, no. 4: 299–306.

Habermas, Juergen. 1979. *Communication and the Evolution of Society*. Boston: Beacon Press.

_____. 1981. *Theory of Communicative Action*. Vol. 1. Boston: Beacon Press.

Habib, Hasnan. 1990. Introduction to *Military and Politics in Thailand 1981-1986*, by Suchit Bunbonkarn. Jakarta: LP3ES.

Hadiz, Vedi R. 1993. "Buruh, Politik dan Industrialisasi" (Labour, Politics and Industrialization). *Republika*, 31 December.

Halim, B. 1986. "Badan Usaha Milik Negara (BUMN) dan Efficiency" (State-owned Enterprises and Efficiency). *Majalah Management & Usahawan Indonesia* (Management and Businessman Magazine) (March–April), pp. 12–15.

Hannam, Peter K. 1987. *Promoting Grassroots Development: Some Insight from the Indonesian Non-Government Organizations*. Cambridge: n.p.

Hardi. 1990. "Arti Partai Politik Bagi Pembangunan Nasional" (The Meaning of Political Parties for National Development). *Analysis CSIS* 19, no. 1 (January–February).

Haris, Syamsudin. 1988. "*PPP dan Pemilihan Umum 1987*" (The PPP and the 1987 General Election). In *Masa Depan Kihudupan Politik Indone-*

sia (The Future of Political Life in Indonesia), edited by Alfian and Nazaruddin Sjamsuddin, pp. 85–103. Jakarta: CV Rajawali in co-operation with the Indonesian Political Science Association.

Hatta, M. 1954. *Beberapa Fasal Ekonomi: Djalan Keekonomi dan Kooperasi* (Some Thoughts on the Economy: The Economic Way and Co-operatives). Vol.1. Jakarta: Perpustakaan Perguruan Kementerian P.P. dan K. (Teaching Library of the Ministry of Information, Education, and Culture).

Hefner, Robert. 1993. "Islam, State and Civil Society: ICMI and the Struggle for the Indonesian Middle Class". *Indonesia* 56 (October): 1–35.

Hendrobudiyanto. 1994. "Bank soundness requirements: a central bank perspective". In *Indonesia Assessment 1994*, edited by Ross H. McLeod, pp. 158–70. Canberra and Singapore: Research School of Pacific and Asian Studies, Australian National University and Institute of Southeast Asian Studies.

Heryanto, Ariel. 1993. "Memperjelas Sosok yang Samar" (Clarifying What is Unclear). In *Politik Kelas Menengah* (The Politics of Middle Class Indonesia), edited by Richard Tanter and Kenneth Young. Jakarta: LP3ES.

Hill, David. 1994. *The Press in New Order Indonesia*. Needlands: University of Western Australia Press.

Hill, Hal, ed. 1994. *Indonesia's New Order: The Dynamics of Socioeconomic Change*. Sydney and Honolulu: Allen and Unwin and the University of Hawaii Press.

———, ed. 1991. *Indonesia Assessment 1991*. Political and Social Change Monograph no. 13. Canberra: Department of Political and Social Change, Research School of Pacific Studies, Australian National University.

———. 1987. "Concentration in Indonesian Manufacturing". *Bulletin of Indonesian Economic Studies* 23, no. 2: 71–100.

Hooker, Virginia Matheson, ed. 1993. *Culture and Society in New Order Indonesia*. Kuala Lumpur and Oxford: Oxford University Press.

Himpunan Peraturan Perundang-undangan Republik Indonesia (Collection of Legislative Regulations of the Republic of Indonesia). 1993 and 1994. Jakarta: CV Eko Jaya.

Huckshorn, Robert J. 1984. *Political Parties in America*, 2d ed. Monterey, California: Brooks/Cole Publishing Company.

Human Rights Watch/Asia. 1994. *The Limits of Openness*. New York: Human Rights Watch/Asia.

Imawan, Riswandha. 1990. *Menciptakan Birokrasi Yang Responsive Untuk Pembangunan Martabat Manusia* (Creating a Responsive Bureaucracy for the Development of Human Values). Paper for Social Sciences Seminar (Seminar Ilmu-Ilmu Sosial), Yogyakarta, 16–21 Juli.

IMF (International Monetary Fund). *International Financial Statistics* (annual and monthly). Washington, D.C.: IMF.

International Institute for Strategic Studies. 1995. *The Military Balance 1994/1995*. London: International Institute for Strategic Studies.

Jackson, Karl D. and Lucian W. Pye, eds. 1978. *Political Power and Communication in Indonesia*. Berkeley: University of California Press.

Jones, Sidney. 1984. "The Contraction and Expansion of the *Umat* and the Role of the Nahdlatul Ulama in Indonesia". *Indonesia,* no. 38 (October): 1–20.

Juoro, Umar. 1993. "Implikasi 'Habibienomics' " (The Implications of 'Habibienomics'). *Kompas,* 11 March, pp. 4–5.

Kaisiepo, Manuel. 1994. *"Uang dan Politik: masalah sumber dana Parpol"* (Money and Politics: the problem of funding sources for political parties). *Kompas,* 1 August.

Kantor Menpan (Office of the Minister for Planning). 1993. *Pembangunan Jangka Panjang Tahap I* (Long-Term Development Phase I). Jakarta: Kantor Menpan.

Karim, M. Rusli. 1991. *Pemilu Demokratis Kompetitif* (A Competitive Democratic General Election). Yogyakarta: Tiara Wacana.

Kayden, Xandra. 1978. *Campaign Organization.* Lexington, Massachusetts and Toronto: D.C. Heath and Company.

King, Dwight Y. 1982. "Indonesia's New Order as Bureaucratic Polity, A Neopatrimonial Regime or Bureaucratic Authoritarian Regime: What Difference Does It Make?". In *Interpreting Indonesian Politics: Thirteen Contributions to the Debate*, edited by Ben Anderson and Audrey Kahin. Ithaca: Cornell Modern Indonesia Project.

_____. 1989. "Pengawasan dan Birokrasi di Negara Berkembang" (Oversight and Bureaucracy in Developing Countries). *Prisma* 6: 19–25.

Kolbe, Richard L. 1985. *American Political Parties, An Uncertain Future.* New York: Harper & Row.

Korten, David. 1985. "Private Voluntary Development: Toward the Third Generation". Manuscript.

_____. 1990. "Voluntary Organizations and the Challenge of Sustainable Development". In *People's Participation and Environmentally Sustainable Development*, Asian Coalition for Reform and Rural

Development, pp. 83–109. Metro Manila: Asian NGO Coalition for Reform and Rural Development (ANGOC).

Kuntjoro Purbopranoto. 1959. *Sedikit Tentang Sistem Pemerintahan Demokrasi* (A Little About the Democratic System of Government). Surabaya: Universitas Airlangga.

Kuntjoro-Jakti, Dorodjatun. 1982. "Political Environment for Korean-Indonesian Development Cooperation: An Indonesian Perspective". In *Indonesia and Korea: Policy Issues for Long Term Development Cooperation*. Jakarta: CSIS.

Kuntjoro-Jakti, Dorodjatun and T.A.M. Simatupang. 1987. "Indonesia: Defence Expenditures in the Period of New Order 1967–1985". In *Defence Spending in Southeast Asia*, edited by Chin Kin Wah. Singapore: Institute for Southeast Asian Studies.

Kwik Kian Gie. 1993. "Konsep Pembangunan Ekonomi Prof Habibie" (Professor Habibie's Concept of Economic Development). *Kompas*, 4 March, pp. 4–5.

Lay, Cornelius. 1994*a*. "The Economic Base of Political Parties In Indonesia". Paper presented at research seminar, Financing of Political Parties in Southeast Asia, sponsored by Yayasan SPES [Foundation of the Society for Political and Economic Studies], Jakarta, 26–27 February.

_____. 1994*b*. "Financing Political Parties in Southeast Asia". Faculty of Social and Political Science, Gadjah Mada University, Yogyakarta, July. Manuscript.

Lee, Yok-shiu F. 1994. *Community-based Urban Environmental Management: Local NGOs as Catalyst*. Honolulu: Program on Environment, East-West Center.

Lent, John. 1982. "ASEAN mass communication and cultural submission". *Media, Culture, and Society* 4.

Lewis, Oscar. 1993. "Kebudayaan Kemiskinan" (The Culture of Poverty). In *Kemiskinan Perkotaan* (Urban Poverty), edited by Parsudi Suparlan, pp. 7–11. Jakarta: Yayasan Obor Indonesia.

Liddle, William. 1992. *Partisipasi dan Partai Politik Pada Awal Orde Baru* (Participation and Political Parties at the Start of the New Order). Jakarta: Pustaka Utama Grafiti.

Lubis, T. Mulya. 1979. "Pembangunan dan Hak Azasi Manusia" (Development and Basic Human Rights). *Prisma* 12 (December).

_____. 1993. *In Search of Human Rights: Legal-Political Dilemmas of Indonesia's New Order, 1966–1990*. Jakarta: Gramedia.

Macintyre, Andrew. 1992. *Business and Politics in Indonesia*. North Sydney: Allen & Unwin Pty Ltd.

Mackie, J.A.C. 1990. "Money and the Middle Class". In *The Politics of the Middle Class*, edited by R. Tanter and K. Young. Clayton, Victoria: Monash University Center for Southeast Asian Studies.

Macridis, Roy C. 1988. "Pengantar Sejarah, Fungsi dan Tipologi Partai-partai" (An Introduction to the History, Functions and Typology of Parties). In *Teori-teori Mutakhir Partai Politik* (Current Theories of Political Parties), edited by Ichlasul Amal, pp. 27–31. Yogyakarta: Tiara Wacana.

Magnis-Suseno, Franz. 1991. "Hubungan Kerja Pancasila" (Pancasila Industrial Relations). *Kompas,* 1 May.

Magno, Francisco. 1993. "The Growth of Philippine Environmentalism". *Kasarinlan* 9, no. 1: 7–18.

Makarim, Nono Anwar. 1978. "The Indonesian Press: An Editor's Perspective". In *Political Power and Communication in Indonesia*, edited by Karl D. Jackson and Lucian W. Pye. Berkeley: University of California Press.

Manning, Chris and Joan Hardjono, eds. 1993. *Indonesia Assessment 1993 — Labour: Sharing in the Benefits of Growth?*, Political and Social Change Monograph no. 20. Canberra: Department of Political and Social Change, Research School of Pacific Studies, Australian National University.

Mas'oed, Mochtar. 1983. "The Indonesian Economy and Political Structure During the Early New Order. 1966–1971". Ph.D. dissertation, Ohio State University.

_____. 1989. "Restrukturasi Masyarakat oleh Pemerintah Orde Baru" (Societal Restructuring by the New Order Government). *Prisma* 7: 12–31.

_____. 1990. "Pembangunan Ekonomi dan Peran Serta Masyarakat" (Economic Development and the Participation of Society). In *Beberapa Aspek Pembangunan Orde Baru* (Aspects of Development under the New Order), edited by Ahmad Zaini Abar. Solo: CV. Ramadhani.

McKendrick, David. 1992. "Obstacles to 'Catch Up': The Case of the Indonesian Aircraft Industry". *Bulletin of Indonesian Economic Studies* 28, no. 1 (April): 39–66.

McLeod, Ross H. 1993. "Analysis and Management of Indonesian Money Supply Growth". *Bulletin of Indonesian Economic Studies* 29, no. 2 (August): 97–128.

_____, ed. 1994. *Indonesia Assessment 1994*. Canberra and Singapore: Research School of Pacific and Asian Studies, Australian National University and Institute of Southeast Asian Studies.

McMahon, Walter W. and Boediono. 1989. *Universal Basic Education: An Overall Strategy of Investment Priorities for Economic Growth*, BEBR Faculty Working Paper no. 89–1543. Urbana-Champaign: University of Illinois at Urbana-Champaign.

McVey, Ruth. 1971. "The Post-Revolutionary Transformation of the Indonesian Army". *Indonesia* (Ithaca), no. 11 (April): 131–76.

Mestoko, Sumarsono. 1979. *Pendidikan di Indonesia, Dari Jaman ke Jaman* (Education in Indonesia, From Era to Era). Jakarta: Badan Penelitian dan Pengembangan Pendidikan dan Kebudayaan, Departemen Pendidikan dan Kebudayaan (Office of Research and Development, Department of Education and Culture).

Mills, Edwin S. 1995. *Growth and Equity in the Indonesian Economy*. Background Paper no. 1, The United States-Indonesia Society. Washington, D.C.: United States-Indonesia Society

Moertopo, Ali. 1984. *Strategi Pembangunan Nasional* (The Strategy of National Development). Jakarta: CSIS.

Mohammad, Goenawan. 1995. "Pers Indonesia, Difference" (The Indonesian Press, the Difference). *Media Indonesia*, 12 February.

Mudatsir, Arief. 1985. "From Situbondo Towards a New N.N.: A First Note". *Prisma* 35: 161–77.

Muhaimin, Yahya. 1990. "Birokrasi di Indonesia" (Bureaucracy in Indonesia). In *Beberapa Aspek Pembangunan Orde Baru* (Aspects of Development under the New Order), edited by Ahmad Zaini Abar. Solo: CV. Ramadhani.

_____. 1991. *Business and Politics 1950–1980*. Jakarta: LP3ES.

Nahdlatul Ulama. 1985. *Khittah Nahdlatul Ulama* (The Commitment of the Nahdlatul Ulama). Jakarta: PBNU (National Headquarters, Nahdlatul Ulama).

_____. 1994. *Konsepsi Pengembangan Sumberdaya Manusia di Lingkungan Nahdlatul Ulama* (The Conception of Human Resources Development in the Nahdlatul Ulama). Jakarta: PBNU (National Headquarters, Nahdlatul Ulama).

Nasikun. 1986. "Pemerataan Pelayanan Pemerintahan Dalam Program Pangan Kita" (Equality of Government Service in our Food Program). *Prisma* 12: 24–34.

Nasoetion, Andi Hakim. 1991. "Indonesian Higher Education: Improving Input to Improve Output Quality". In *Indonesia Assessment 1991*, edited by Hal Hill, Political and Social Change Monograph no. 13. Canberra: Department of Political and Social Change, Research School of Pacific Studies, Australian National University.

Nasution, Adnan Buyung. 1994. "Defending Human Rights in Indonesia". *Journal of Democracy* (July), pp. 117–19.

Ndraha, Taliziduhu. 1986. "Birokrasi dan Pembangunan: Dominasi Atau Alat Demokratisasi" (Bureaucracy and Development: Domination or a Tool of Democratization). *Jurnal Ilmu Politik* (Journal of Political Science) 1.

Noer, Deliar. 1973, *The Modernist Muslim Movement in Indonesia, 1900–1942*. Singapore: Oxford University Press.

Nugroho Notosusanto. 1979. "Angkatan Bersenjata dalam Percaturan Politik di Indonesia" (Indonesian Armed Forces in the Political Constellation of Indonesia). *Prisma* 8: 17–34.

_____, ed. 1991. *Pejuang dan Prajurit* (Fighter and Soldier). Jakarta: Sinar Harapan.

Nursyahbani, KS. 1993. "Hak Buruh dan Politik Kekerasan" (Labour Rights and the Politics of Force). *Republika*, 31 December.

Oetama, Jakob. 1987. *Perspektif Pers Indonesia* (The Perspective of the Indonesian Press). Jakarta: LP3ES.

Oey-Gardiner, Mayling. 1991. "Policy-Making in Higher Education and Implications for Equity". In *Indonesia Assessment. 1991*, edited by Hal Hill, Political and Social Change Monograph no. 13, pp. 77–95. Canberra: Department of Political and Social Change, Research School of Pacific Studies, Australian National University.

Organsky, A.F.K. 1965. *The Stages of Political Development*. New York: Knopf.

Pamudji, S. 1990. "Makna Daerah Tingkat II Sebagai Titik Berat Pelaksanaan Otonomi Daerah" (The Meaning of District Governments as the Centre of Implementing Regional Autonomy). *Analisis* 3.

Pangestu, Mari. 1990. "The Role of the Private Sector in Indonesia: Deregulation and Privatization". Paper presented at meeting, PECC Pacific Economic Outlook, Structural Issues, Kyoto, 11–12 October. 1990.

_____. 1993. "The Role of The State and Economic Development in Indonesia". *The Indonesian Quarterly* 3: 253–83.

_____ and Mayling Oey-Gardiner. 1992. *Human Resource Development and Management*. Publication M84/92. Jakarta: CSIS.

"Pertanda Zaman di Wajah Konglomerat Yang Terbesar di Indonesia"

(Signs of the Times in the Appearance of the Largest Indonesian Conglomerates). 1991. *Warta Ekonomi* 2, no. 37 (11 February): 20–65.

Picard, Robert. 1989. *Media: Economics, Concepts and Issues*. Newbury
Park: Sage Publications.

PPPI (Persatuan Perusahaan Periklanan Indonesia, The Indonesian Advertising Companies Association). 1993. *Media Scene 1991–1992 Indonesia: The Official Guide to Advertising Media in Indonesia*. Jakarta:
PPPI.

Pranarka, A.M.W. 1991. "Tinjauan Kritikal terhadap Upaya Membangun
Sistem Pendidikan Nasional Kita" (Critical Views on the Effort to Build
Our National Education System). In *Mencari Strategi Pengembangan
Pendidikan Nasional Menjelang Abad XXI* (Searching for a National
Educational Development Strategy towards the 21st Century), edited
by C.R. Semiawan and Soedijarto. Jakarta: PT Gramedia Widiasarana
Indonesia.

Premchand, A. and P.M.W. Wijayasuriya. 1987. "Indonesia: Monitoring of
State Enterprise Finance". Washington, D.C.: International Monetary
Fund, Fiscal Affairs Department. Duplicated.

Priest, Serano V. 1974. "The Quest for Educational Equality". In *Emerging Educational Issues, Conflicts and Contrasts*, edited by Julius
Menacker and Erwin Pollach. Boston: Little, Brown and Company.

Prijono, Onny S. 1991. "Education and Training in Indonesia's Economic
Development". In *The Impacts of Education on Training and Work in
Indonesia's Economic Development*, Centre for Strategic and Interna-
tional Studies. Publication M74/91 (November). Jakarta: CSIS.

_____. 1993. "Indonesia: The Relationship between Direct Foreign In-
vestment (DFI) and High Level Manpower (HLM)". Paper presented at
Human Resources Development Task Force Meeting of the Pacific
Economic Cooperation Council, Singapore, 28–29 October.

_____. 1995. "Era Liberalisasi dan Dampaknya Terhadap Dunia
Pendidikan" (The Liberalisation Era and Its Impact on Education). In
Refleksi Setengah Abad Kemerdekaan Indonesia (Reflections on a Half
Century of Indonesian Independence), edited by Bantarto Bandoro,
J. Kristiadi, Mari Pangestu, and Onny S. Prijono. Jakarta: CSIS.

_____ and A.M.W. Pranarka. 1979. *Situasi Pendidikan di Indonesia Selama
Sepuluh Tahun Terakhir, Bagian I (Permasalahan)* (The Educational
Situation in Indonesia Over the Last Ten Years, Part I, Problems).
Jakarta: CSIS.

_____ and Mayling Oey-Gardiner. 1991. *The Impacts of Education on*

Training and Work in Indonesia's Economic Development. Publication M74/91. Jakarta: CSIS.

Rachbini, Didik J. 1994. *Politik Deregulasi dan Agenda Kebijakan Ekonomi* (The Politics of Deregulation and the Economic Policy Agenda). Jakarta: Infobank.

_____. 1995*a. Resiko Pembangunan yang Dibimbing Utang* (The Risk of Debt-Led Development). Jakarta: Grasindo.

_____, ed. 1995*b. Negara dan Kemiskinan di Daerah* (The State and Poverty in the Regions). Proceedings of INFID Conference, Paris, April 1994. Jakarta: Pustaka Sinar Harapan.

Ramage, Douglas E. 1995. *Politics in Indonesia: Democracy, Islam and the Ideology of Tolerance.* London: Routledge.

Ranis, Gustav and Francis Stewart. 1994. "Decentralization in Indonesia". In *Bulletin of Indonesian Economic Studies* 3, no. 3 (December): 41–72.

Ranuwihardjo, Sukadji. 1991. "Equity, Quality, and Efficiency in Indonesia's Higher Education System". In *Indonesia Assessment. 1991*, edited by Hal Hill, Political and Social Change Monograph no. 13, pp. 53–57. Canberra: Department of Political and Social Change, Research School of Pacific Studies, Australian National University.

Rasyid, M. Ryass. 1991. "Birokrasi dan Budaya Politik Lokal: Kasus Sulawesi Selatan" (Bureaucracy and Local Political Culture: The Case of South Sulawesi). In *Profil Budaya Politik Indonesia* (A Profile of Indonesia's Political Culture), edited by Alfian and Nazaruddin Sjamsuddin. Jakarta: Grafiti.

Ratam, Waluyo. 1989. "Membudayakan Fungsi Pengawasan Dalam Manajemen Pembangunan Melalui Pengawasan Melekat" (Acculturating the Oversight Function in Development Management Through Close Supervision). *Prisma* 6: 38–48.

Rice, R.C. 1983. "The Origins of Basic Economic Ideas and Their Impact on 'New Order' Policies". *Bulletin of Indonesian Economic Studies* 19, no. 2: 60–82.

Robison, Richard. 1986. *Indonesia: The Rise of Capital.* Sydney: Allen & Unwin Pty Ltd.

Sadli, M. 1986. "Perusahaan Negara dan Masalah Swastanisasi atau Privatisasi" (Public Enterprises and the Problem of Privatization). *Forum Ekonomi* 32: 14–17.

Said, Salim. 1987. "The Political Role of The Indonesian Military: Past, Present and Future". *Southeast Asian Journal of Social Science* 15, no. 1: 16–34.

_____. 1991. *The Genesis of Power: General Sudirman and Indonesian Military Politics 1945–1949*. Singapore: Institute of Southeast Asian Studies.

Salim, Emil. 1991. "Sumber Daya Manusia Dalam Perspektif" (Perspectives on Human Resources). In *Mencari Strategi Pengembangan Pendidikan Nasional Menjelang Abad XXI* (In Search of a Strategy for the Development of National Education for the 21st Century), edited by Conny R. Semiawan and Soedijarto, pp. 18–35. Jakarta: PT Grasindo.

_____. 1993. "Kebijakan Ekonomi di Balik Prospek Ekonomi Indonesia" (Economic Policies Behind the Outlook for the Indonesian Economy). In *Peluang dan Tantangan dalam Sektor Riil dan Utilitas pada Dasawarsa 1990-an* (Opportunities and Challenges in the Real Sector and Public Utilities in the Decade of the 1990s), edited by M. Arsjad Anwar, Faisal H. Basri, and Mohamad Iksan. Jakarta: Gramedia-FEUI (Economics Faculty of the University of Indonesia).

Santoso, Amir. 1994. "Administokrasi dan Demokrasi: Dua Tantangan Pembangunan di Masa Depan" (Administocracy and Democracy: Two Challenges of Development in the Future). In *Pembangunan Politik, Situasi Global dan Hak Asasi di Indonesia* (Political Development, the Global Situation and Basic Human Rights in Indonesia), edited by Haris Munandar, pp. 319–27. Jakarta: Gramedia.

Santoso, Priyo Budi. 1993. *Birokrasi Pemerintahan Indonesia Perspektif Kultural dan Struktural* (The Indonesian Government Bureaucracy from the Cultural and Structural Perspectives). Jakarta: Rajawali Press.

Saxena, A.P. 1986. "Peningkatan Produktivitas Tatalaksana Pemerintahan" (Increasing the Productivity of Government Administration). *Prisma* 11: 47–56.

Schwarz, Adam. 1994. *A Nation in the Waiting: Indonesia in the 1990s*. Sydney: Allen & Unwin Pty Ltd.

Setiawan, Bonie. 1990. "Demokrasi di Pedesaan" (Democracy at the Village Level). *Prisma* 7: 59–72.

Setiawan, Maman. 1991. "Analisis Keseimbangan Persediaan dan Kebutuhan Tenaga Kerja selama Repelita V" (An Analysis of the Balance Between Supply and Demand for Manpower during Repelita V). Paper presented at Technical Discussion on the Development of Human Resources Systems and Policies, Jakarta, 1 June.

Setyabudi, Teguh. 1992. "Potret Pelaksanaan Fungsi DPR" (A Portrait of How the Parliament Carries Out its Functions). *Kompas*, 1 October.

Sihbudi, M. Riza. 1988. "*PDI dan Pemilu 1987*" (The PDI and the 1987 General Election). In *Masa Depan Kihudupan Politik Indonesia* (The

Future of Political Life in Indonesia), edited by Alfian and Nazaruddin Sjamsuddin, pp. 104–19. Jakarta: CV Rajawali in co-operation with the Indonesian Political Science Association.

_____. 1994. "Dimensi Poleksosbud Pembangunan Indonesia di IBT" (Political–Economic–Social–Cultural Dimensions of Indonesian Development in Eastern Indonesia). *Analisis* 4.

Silalahi, Harry Tjan. 1995. "Evaluasi Pemilihan Umum 1992" (Evaluation of the 1992 General Election). In *Pemilihan Umum 1992: Suatu Evaluasi* (The 1992 General Election: An Evaluation), edited by M. Sudibjo, pp. 12–38. Jakarta: CSIS.

Silalahi, T.B. 1994. "Kesiapan Aparatur Negara Dalam Mendorong Otonomi Daerah DATI II" (The Preparedness of the State Apparatus in Accelerating the Regional Autonomy Program). *Suara Pembaruan*, 2 November.

Sinaga, Kastorius. 1993. "Neither Merchant nor Prince: A Study of NGOs in Indonesia". *Sociological Bulletin* 42, nos. 1 & 2 (March–September): 137–56.

Singarimbun, Masri. 1988. "Pencapaian Program Keluarga Berencana di Indonesia" (Achieving a Family Planning Program in Indonesia). *Prisma* 3: 3–15.

Singh, Raja Ray. 1986. *Education in Asia and the Pacific*. Bangkok: UNESCO.

Siregar, Evendhy M. 1992. *Demokratisasi Politik dan Perspektifnya* (Political Democracy and its Perspective). Jakarta: Pustaka "Mari Belajar".

Sitompul, Einar M. 1991. *Nahdlatul Ulama dan Pancasila* (Nahdlatul Ulama and Pancasila). Jakarta: Sinar Harapan.

Sjahrir. 1990. "Kriteria Industri Strategis" (Criteria for Strategic Industries). *Warta Ekonomi* 1, no. 22 (26 March): 85.

_____. 1993. "Habibie, TekTi, dan Teknokrat" (Habibie, High Tech, and the Technocrats). *Tempo*, 3 July, pp. 86–87.

Soebijono. 1991. *The Development of ABRI's Social and Political Function*. Yogyakarta: Gadjah Mada University Press.

Soedjati Djiwandono. 1988. "The Military and National Development in Indonesia". In *Soldiers and Stability in Southeast Asia*, edited by J. Soedjati Djiwandono and Yong Mun Cheong. Singapore: Institute of Southeast Asian Studies.

Soeharto. 1989. *Pikiran, Ucapan, dan Tindakan Saya: otobiografi* (My Thoughts, Words and Actions: An Autobiography). As told to G. Dwipayana and Ramadhan K.H. Jakarta: Citra Lamtoro Gung Persada Ltd.

Soemitro, General (ret.). 1991. *Mengungkap Masalah, Menatap Masa Depan: Sebuah Refleksi* (Acknowledging Problems, Observing the Future: A Reflection). Jakarta: Pustaka Sinar Harapan.

Soesastro, M. Hadi. 1991. "Think tanks in Indonesia: The Centre for Strategic and International Studies". In *Think Tanks and Governance in the Asia-Pacific Region*, edited by John W. Langford and K. Lorne Brownse. South Halifax: The Institute for Research and Public Policy.

_____. 1989. "The Political Economy of Deregulation in Indonesia". *Asian Survey* 29, no. 9: 853–69.

_____, Simandjuntak, and Silalahi. 1988. *Report: Financing Public Sector Development Expenditure in Indonesia*. Jakarta: CSIS.

SPSI (All-Indonesia Workers' Union). 1986. *Buku Pedoman Pelaksanaan Pungutan Iuran bagi Serikat Pekerja* (Guide Book for the Implementation of Dues Collection for Labor Unions). Jakarta: SPSI and AAFLI (Asian-American Free Labor Institute).

_____. 1988. *Anggaran Dasar dan Anggaran Rumah Tangga Serikat Pekerja Seluruh Indonesia* (Constitution and By-Laws of the All-Indonesia Workers' Union). Jakarta: SPSI.

_____. 1991. *Pedoman SPSI* (Guide to the All-Indonesia Workers' Union). Jakarta: SPSI.

SRI (Survey Research Indonesia). 1995.

Sudarsono, Juwono. 1974. "International Studies in Indonesia: Problems in Training and Research". *The Indonesian Quarterly* 2, no. 3 (April): 2–13.

Sudibjo, M. 1994. "ABRI Dalam Jabatan Pemerintahan" (The Armed Forces in Government Functions). Not for publication.

Sudono, Agus. 1977. *Gerakan Buruh di Indonesia dan Kebijaksanaannya* (Labour Movements in Indonesia and Their Policies). Jakarta: FBSI.

Sukardi Rinakit. 1993. "Wage, Cost to Education and Human Qualities". *Suara Pembaruan*, 2 February.

_____. 1994. "Structural Change and Industrial Relations Development in Indonesia". Paper presented at seminar, Free Trade and the Human Face, hosted by the Asia Pacific Office of the International Confederation of Free Trade Unions (ICFTU-APRO). Singapore, 27 November – 3 December.

Suseno, Franz Magnis. 1991. *Etika Politik: Prinsip-prinsip Moral Dasar Kenegaraan Modern* (Political Ethics: Basic Moral Principles of the Modern State). Jakarta: PT Gramedia Pustaka Utama.

Suyanto, Isbodroini. 1991. "Budaya Politik dan Peranan Dewan Perwakilan Rakyat" (Political Culture and the Role of Parliament). In *Profil Budaya*

Politik Indonesia (A Profile of Indonesian Political Culture), edited by Alfian and Nazaruddin Sjamsuddin, pp. 164–89. Jakarta: PT Pustaka Utama Grafiti.

Tashwirul Afkar (Jurnal LKiS). 1994, no. 1 (December).

Tjokrowinoto, Moeljarto. 1987. *Politik Pembangunan: Sebuah Analisis Konsep, Strategi dan Arah* (Development Policy: An Analysis of Concept, Strategy and Direction). Yogyakarta: Tiara Wacana.

――――. 1989. "Meletakkan Mekanisme Pengawasan Yang Efisien dan Efektif" (Establishing an Oversight Mechanism That Is Efficient and Effective). *Prisma* 6: 3–12.

Toh, K.W. 1991. "The Role of the State in Southeast Asia". In *Marketization in ASEAN*, edited by C.Y. Ng and N. Wagner. Singapore: Institute of Southeast Asian Studies.

Tsuchiya, Kenji. 1987. *Democracy and Leadership: The Rise of the Taman Siswa Movement in Indonesia*. Translated by Peter Hawkes. Honolulu: University of Hawaii Press.

UNDP (United Nations Development Programme). 1990. *Education and Training in the 1990s*. Policy Discussion Paper. New York:.UNDP.

UNESCO (United Nations Economic Social and Cultural Organization). 1988. "Education in Asia and the Pacific". *Reviews, Reports and Notes*, no. 24. Bangkok: UNESCO Principal Regional Office for Asia and the Pacific.

Van Bruinessen, Martin. 1991. "The 28th Congress of the Nahdlatul Ulama: Power Struggle and Social Concerns". *Archipel* 41: 185–200.

――――. 1994. *NU, Tradisi, Relasi-relasi Kuasa Pencarian Wacana Baru* (Nahdlatul Ulama, Tradition, and Power Relations in the Search for a New Discourse). Yogyakarta: LKiS.

Vasquez, Francisco. 1983. "Media Economics in the Third World". In *Comparative Mass Media Systems*, edited by John Martin and Anju Chaudhary. New York: Longmans.

Vatikiotis, Michael. 1993. *Indonesian Politics Under Suharto: Order and Pressure for Change*. London: Routledge.

Vriens, Hans. 1995. "The Grandson Also Rises". *Asia, Inc.* (March), pp. 46–51.

Wahid, Abdurrahman. 1991. "Sekali Lagi Tentang Forum Demokrasi" (One More Time, About Forum Democracy). Jakarta, 13 May. Manuscript.

――――. 1994. "Islam, Politics and Democracy in the 1950s and 1990s". In *Democracy in Indonesia: 1950s and 1990s*, edited by David Bourchier and John Legge. Clayton, Victoria: Monash University Center for Southeast Asian Studies.

Wardhana, Ali. 1989. "Structural Adjustment in Indonesia: Export and the 'high-cost' Economy". *The Indonesian Quarterly* 17, no. 3: 207–17.

Warouw. [n.d.]. "The Role of Public Enterprise in Indonesia: The Challenge of Development to Law". Mimeograph.

Wibisono, Christianto. 1988. "Profil dan Anatomi BUMN" (The Profile and Anatomy of BUMNs). Paper presented at Seminar Sehari (One-Day Seminar), "Peranan BUMN dalam Ekonomi Indonesia" (The Role of BUMNs in the Indonesian Economy), Jakarta (Sahid Jaya Hotel).

_____. 1992*a*. "Pasar Besar Oplah Turun" (The Media Market Declines). *Tempo*, 15 February, p. 33.

_____. 1992*b*. "Piramida Pers Indonesia" (The Indonesian Press Pyramid). *Tempo*, 15 February.

Wilson, Graham K. 1990. *Interest Groups*, Oxford: Basil Blackwell Ltd.

Winarno, Ateng and Martin Sallis Say. 1993. *Kabinet Pembangunan VI Riwayat Para Menteri* (Biographies of the Ministers of the Sixth Development Cabinet). Jakarta: Yayasan Metropolitan Suara Karya.

Wirjasuputra, A.S. and A. Rieffel. 1972. *Government-Owned Enterprises in Indonesia*. Jakarta: USAID.

World Bank. 1989. *Indonesia Basic Education Study*. Document of the World Bank (30 June). Washington, D.C.: The World Bank.

_____. 1993*a*. *Indonesia: Industrial Policy — Shifting into High Gear*. Washington, D.C.: The World Bank.

_____. 1993*b*. *The East Asian Economic Miracle*. Oxford: Oxford University Press.

_____. 1994*a*. *Indonesia: Sustaining Development*. Washington, D.C.: The World Bank.

_____. 1994*b*. *University Research for Graduate Education Project*. Report no. 12841-IND. Washington, D.C.: The World Bank.

_____. 1995. *Indonesia: Improving Efficiency and Equity — Changes in the Public Sector's Role*. Washington, D.C.: The World Bank.

_____. 1996*a*. *Higher Education Support Project: Development of Undergraduate Education*. Report no. 15498-IND. Washington, D.C.: The World Bank.

_____. 1996*b*. *Central Indonesia Junior Secondary Education Project*. Report no. 15500-IND. Washington, D.C.: The World Bank.

_____. 1996*c*. *Secondary School Teacher Development Project*. Report no. 15028-IND. Washington, D.C.: The World Bank.

_____. 1997. *World Development Indicators 1997*. Washington, D.C.: The World Bank.

Yusuf, Nasir, ed. 1994. *NU dan Gus Dur* (Nahdlatul Ulama and Gus Dur [Abdurrahman Wahid]). Bandung: HUP.

Zulkarnaen, M.S. 1995. "Pengalaman Walhi Dalam Advokasi Masalah Lingkungan" (The Experience of Walhi in Advocacy on Problems of the Environment). In *Agenda LSM Menyongsing Tahun 2000* (The Agenda of NGOs Anticipating the Year 2000), edited by Aswab Mahasin and Rustam Ibrahim. Jakarta: Cesda-LP3ES.

Index

Abdul Gafur, 188
Abdul Latief, 188
Abdurrahman Wahid, 190, 205, 206, 207,
   208, 209, 211, 213, 224, 225, 226
   civil society ideas, 212
Achmad Siddiq, 207
advertising
   expenditures, 181, 186
   industry, 181
   market, 186
   revenues, 196
Agency for Co-ordination of National
   Development Strategy
   (Bakorstranas), 109, 110
Agency for the Assessment and
   Application of Technology (BPPT),
   237
agriculture, 13, 14, 37
   growth, 14
   rice
      self sufficiency, 13
Agum Gumelar, 117
Ahmad Sumadi, 122
Aisyah Amini, 123
Ali Moertopo, 238, 239, 250
Ali Wardhana, 47
All-Indonesia Workers' Union (SPSI),
   142–43, 144, 261
   effectiveness, 146
   funding, 146
   government control, 144–46
   independence, 146
   membership
      dues, 146
   negative perception of, 142, 143, 144
   objectives, 144
   officials, 144
      educational background, 146
   structure
      unitary, 145
All-Indonesian Workers' Organizations'
   Union, 143
Amir Santoso, 246
Archipelago policy, 41
Arie Sudewo, 105

Armed Forces (ABRI), 99–114, 257–58
   "1945 Generation", 108
   AKABRI, 110–12
      family background of applicants, 112
   Army Command and Staff College
      (SESKOAD), 112
   Bakrotanasda, 63
   budget, 101–7, 258
   characteristics, 100
   corruption, 103
   and democratization, 109–10
   dual function, 101, 107, 108
   economic activities, 103–6
   egalitarian principles, 109
   governors, 82
   "Middle Way" concept, 100
   military equipment, 107, 113
   ministers, 82
   mission, function, and role
      ABRI's perception of, 100–1
      changing social dynamics and,
         107–9
   non-profit foundations, 104, 105
      Yayasan Kartika Eka Paksi, 104
   origins, 99–100
   personnel, 258
      recruitment, 110–12
   political doctrines, 100–1
   in politics, 109, 110
   self-financing, 103–6
      debate over, 106–7
   Taman Taruna Nusantara, 111, 177
   University Ahmad Yani, 104
   value system, 108
Ary Mardjono, 119
Asia
   manufacturing labour wages, 149
Asia-Pacific Economic
   Co-operation (APEC)
   Bogor declaration, 47
Association of Indonesian Cement
   producers (ASI), 67
Association of Indonesian Muslim
   Intellectuals (ICMI), 189, 208, 225,
   243, 245, 249, 250

Association of Indonesian Workers'
    Unions (GSBI), 143

Bambang Trihatmodjo, 33, 187, 196
BANGDES, 242
Bank Indonesia
  credit policies, 23–24, 25
    ceilings, 24
    subsidies, 24
  functions, 20, 22
  saving programmes, 22, 38–39
banking
  competition, 25–26
  deregulation, 25
  interest rates, 25, 26
banks
  state
    credit providing, 26
    non-performing loans, 27
Bapindo
  scandal, 33, 36
Baramuli, 104
Bimantara Group, 185
BIMAS programme, 242
Bintang, 188
Bob Hasan, 188, 189
Bulog, 105
bureaucracy, 257
  accountability, 89, 95
  adaptive, 94
  authoritarian structure, 78
  characteristics, 90
  civil service system, 96–97
    merit-based system, 96
  complaints, 90
  corruption, 81, 88, 89
  decentralization, 92–94, 95
  definition, 97
  depoliticization, 82
  deregulation, 76
  financing, 88
  functions, 84
  institutional development, 83–86
  legitimization, 82
  linked training, 91
  misconduct, 91
  procedures, 95–96

quality control, 90–91
  co-ordinating system, 91
  inspectorates, 91
  internal controls, 91
reform, 81–97
  forms of, 90–94
  need for, 86, 88–90
  phases, 88, 89
  regional autonomy, 92–94, 95
  responsible, 95
  responsiveness, 89, 94
  stabilization, 82
  structure, 95–96
  suitable, 94–95
bureaucratic polity, 197
business
  education and training programmes,
      172–73, 176
  in-house training, 173
    tax deduction, 178
  small, 37

cabinet, 65–68
  decision making, 65–66
  Menko, 66
  structure
    changes, 65–66
capital
  formation, 48
  market
    deregulation, 27
  private, 27–28
cement
  regulated price, 67
Cement Nusantara, PT, 67
Central Bureau of Statistics (BPS), 237
Centre for Information and Development
      Studies (CIDES), 243–45, 250
  agenda, 250
  budget, 245
  CIDES Society, 244
  dialogues, 245
  funding, 244
  personnel, 244
Centre for Policy and Development
      Studies (CPDS), 246

Centre for Policy and Implementation
    Studies (CPIS), 242–43
  budget, 243
  development policy, 242
  funding, 242
  personnel, 243
Centre for Strategic and International
    Studies (CSIS), 237–39, 249, 250, 251
  budget, 238
  genesis, 237
  international linkages, 237
  objectives, 237
  personnel, 238
  reputation, 239
  revenues, 238
Centre for the Study of Development and
    Democracy (CESDA), 241
  activities, 241
  financial support, 241
Chandra Asri petrochemical complex
  foreign borrowing, 66, 67
changes, 5–6
China
  foreign investment, 75
  manufacturing labour wages, 149
civil servants, 83, 84
  expenditure on, 85
  loyalty, 82, 83
  number of, 84
  regional, 94
communist coup, abortive, 2
conglomerates, 26, 27, 31, 32, 34–35, 37
Constitution, 1945, 44
  Article 33, 41, 44, 74
  human rights
    universality of, 231
  judicial review, 72
  presidency, 62, 124
Control Institution for Finance and
    Development, 91
Co-ordinating Ministry of Economic,
    Monetary, Industry and Development
    Control, 91
corruption, 5
Council for Sciences of Indonesia (MIPI),
    235
  tasks, 235

Council for Security Co-operation in the
    Asia Pacific (CSCAP), 237
courts, 71–73
  independence, 72, 73
  salaries, 71
  Supreme Court, 71–72, 73
    appeal cases, 71
Czechoslovakian Civic Forum, 225

democracy, 190–93
Democracy Forum (Fordem), 220,
    224–27, 230
  Cibeureum Accord, 224
  dialogues, 225, 226
  established, 224
  government response, 226
  objectives, 225, 231
  political
    alliance, 225
  reform, 226
  structure, 226, 231
democratization, 76–78
demonstrations, 131, 132–34
Department of Education and Culture,
    169
Department of Environment, 228
Department of Finance, 24, 242
Department of Home Affairs, 76, 117,
    118, 130
Department of Justice, 72
Department of Science and Technology,
    236
Department of Transportation, 46
deregulation, 76
Detik
  closure, 191
development
  sustainable, 89
development plans
  five-year, 84
development policy
  equality, 74
  redistributive programmes, 74
development process
  role of private sector, 89
Development Unity Party (PPP), 115,
    125, 129, 130, 135, 204, 206, 213

financing, 127, 128
leadership selection, 118–19
party programme, 122–23
Dili incident, 190
Din Syamsuddin, 246
Dipo Alam, 245

economic crisis, 4–5, 270
factors, 4
economic development
and strong state, 220
economic equity
concerns, 36
economic issues, 270
economic policy, 265, 270
economy
growth, 2, 88
negative, 1
and performance of political
parties, 115–31
and private enterprise, 13–38
sector growth rates, 14
Guided Economy policy, 42, 56
informal sector, 37
problems, 5
structural changes, 13–14, 140–42
characteristics, 140
Edi Sudradjat, 190
Editor
closure, 191
education, 159–77, 260–61
access to, 160–63
as commodity, 173–75
compulsory, 162
enrolment, 162
curriculum improvement, 164
development
demand-led, 260
supply-led, 260
dual system, 169–70
goals, 169
and enterprise, 170–73
for gifted children, 177
lack of qualified teachers, 164–65
National Education System, 159, 160
objectives, 159

opportunity
equality of, 160
pre-school, 160–61
primary, 161–62
compulsory, 161
enrolment, 161, 175
Presidential Instruction on
Primary Schools, 161, 163, 242
private institutions, 170, 260
problem areas, 159
public spending on, 178
quality, 177
gap, 163–65
high cost of, 164
improvements, 175
relevance
"link and match", 169–70
mismatch, 165–68, 260–61
resources, 261
secondary, 162
enrolment, 162
streaming, 164
tertiary, 162–63
academy, 177
best institutions, 165
College of Higher Education, 177
enrolment, 163, 167
institute, 177
number of institutions, 162, 163
polytechnic, 177
science and technology, 168
types of institution, 177–78
university, 177
training
on-the-job, 169
vocational, 162
Ekspo
closure, 197
election
1992
party programmes, 122, 125
results, 135
1997, 1, 136
results, 135
systems, 77
Ellyasa KH Dharwis, 210

employment
 agricultural sector, 140
 changes, 140–42
 expatriates, 170
 graduates, 167, 176
  supply and demand, 168
 industrial sector, 140
 structure, 141
 unemployment, 150, 167
  graduates, 167
 urban, 140, 141
enterprises
 and education, 170–73
 private, 264–67
  1950s–1960s, 28–29
  1960s–1970s, 29–31
  1980s–1990s, 31–33
  changing faces, 28–33
  conglomerates, 266
  and economic growth, 13–38
  and government, 33, 36
  government policies, 265
  links with government officials,
   265–66
  non-*pribumi* businesses, 266
  pribumi businesses, 265, 266, 267
 public, 31, 32, 41–56, 259–60
  assets, 43, 55
  bureaucratic controls, 46
  contribution to GDP, 41
  contribution to national budget, 41
  de-*étatisme* period, 44
  fields, 41
  forms, 43
  and government departments, 46
  high technology industry, 52–53, 260
  listing, 50
  management problems, 45–46
  market orientation, 49
  neo-*étatisme* period, 45
  number, 43
  objectives, 45–46
  Perjan, 56
  Persero, 56–57
  Perum, 57
  price regulation, 46
  privatization, 49, 50

  profits, 55
  reform, 48, 49–51
  restructuring, 49
  return on investment, 50
  sales, 43, 55
  strategic industries, 51–57
  subsidies, 42, 43
 entrepreneurs
  Chinese-Indonesian (non-*pribumi*), 30
  indigenous (*pribumi*), 28, 29, 30
  Benteng Programme, 28, 29
 environment, 227
 ethnic antagonisms, 1
 exports, 14

Fajrul Falaakh, 207, 211
Fatimah Achmad, 125
Federasi Buruh Seluruh Indonesia (FBSI),
  144, 145
 Serikat Buruh Lapangan Pekerja
   (SBLP), 144, 145
 structure
  federated, 145
Fokus
 closure, 197
Forum for Democracy, 190
Foundation for the Centre for Research
   and Implementation of Development
   Programmes, 242
Foundation for the National Institute for
   Strategic Studies, 241
fund mobilization, 22–23

Gadjah Mada University
 Centre for Rural and Population
   Studies (P3K), 245
Gatra, 188, 189, 192, 198
General Agreement on Tariffs and Trade
   (GATT)
 Uruguay Round, 47
GKBI, 30
Global Jaya Kindergarten and Primary
   School, 175
Gobel, Th. M., 30
Gobel Group, 171
Goenawan Mohammad, 186, 189, 192,
   193

Golkar, 67, 82–83, 107, 115, 125, 130,
    135, 258–59, 262, 263
  autonomy, 129
  Council of Founders, 119
  election
    1992, 258
    1997, 258
  financing, 127, 128
  leadership selection, 119–20, 121
  party programme, 123–24
  popular support, 258
government
  budget, 69, 102
  central
    prerogatives, 92
  central offices, 83
  centralization, 256
  departments
    Litbang (R&D centres), 237
  district
    income sources, 94
  executive branch, 69, 70, 256
  form, 197
  Guided Democracy, 126
  judiciary, 256
  legislative power, 69, 70
  legislature, 256
  ministerial decrees, 69
  revolutionary
    surrender, 100
  structures and processes, 256–57
Gross Domestic Product (GDP), 2

Habibie, Bacharuddin Jusuf, 1, 51, 52, 53,
    189, 198, 243, 244, 245, 249, 250
"Habibienomics", 52
Hamzah Haz, 123, 128
Hardijanti Rukmana (Tutut), 33, 36, 187,
    188
Harmoko, H., 107, 119, 123, 186, 187,
    188, 192, 193, 196
Harsudiono Hartas, 198
Hartono, R., 112
Hasjim Ning, 30
Hasnan Habib, 106
Hatta, 44
  surrender, 100

Hedijati Herijadi (Titiek), 33
Hendropriyono, 117
Hong Kong
  manufacturing labour wages, 149
human rights, 75, 76, 77
  protection, 222, 223
  universality of, 231
Hutami Endang Adyningsih (Mamiek), 33
Hutomo Mandala Putra (Tommy), 33, 36

Ibnu Sutowo, 31
income
  disparity, 38, 74
  equity, 3
  national, 2
  per capita, 2, 3
independence
  struggle, 100
Indonesian Chamber of Commerce
    (KADIN)
  LP3E, 245
Indonesian Communist Party (PKI), 101
  attempted coup, 101
  Harian Rakyat, 180
  union, 143
Indonesian Democratic Party (PDI), 1,
    115, 125, 130, 135
  autonomy, 129
  financing, 127, 128
  leadership selection, 116–18, 121
  party programme, 122, 124–25
Indonesian Environmental Forum (Walhi),
    220, 227–29, 230
  activities, 227, 228
  agenda, 228
  antagonisms with government, 228
  empowerment of civil society, 228
  environmental laws, 227
  funding, 229
  law suits, 227–28
  membership, 227
  networks, 228, 229
  objectives, 227
  organization, 229
  political content, 229
Indonesian Institute of Sciences (LIPI),
    235–37, 247

budget, 236
Centre for Economics and
    Development (PEP-LIPI), 236–37
Centre for Political and Regional
    Studies (PPW-LIPI), 237
Centre for Population and Manpower
    (PPT-LIPI), 236
Centre for Social and Cultural Studies
    (PMB-LIPI), 236
organization, 236
R&D centres, 236
study, 77
tasks, 236
Indonesian Nationalist Party
    unions, 143
Indonesian Press Council, 181
Indonesian Prosperity Trade Union
    (SBSI), 147
meetings, 156
Indosat, PT, 50
listing on New York Stock Exchange,
    50
industrial relations
Pancasila Industrial Relations, 144–45,
    147, 155
See also labour relations
inflation, 24
hyper-, 2
Institute for Economic and Social
    Research, Education and Information
    (LP3ES), 239–40, 241
activities, 240
budget, 240
decline, 240
funding, 239–40
personnel, 240
Prisma, 240
Institute for Strategic Studies of Indonesia
    (ISSI), 241–42, 248
budget, 242
focus, 241
funding, 242
objectives, 241
personnel, 242
institutions, 8
government, 255–59
mixed, 259–64

policy advisory, 233–51
private, 264–68
research, 233
    private, 248
structure, 6
International Monetary Fund (IMF)
    financial support, 4, 5
Inti Indorayon Utama (IIU)
    law suit, 227–28
investment
    domestic, 15, 18–20
        law, 15, 38, 170
        location, 20
        sectoral distribution, 20, 21
        value, 18, 19, 38
    foreign, 15–18, 74–75
        Government Regulation on Foreign
            Investment, 1994, 74
        law, 14, 15, 38, 170
        location, 18
        origin, 18
        in public utilities, 50
        sectoral distribution, 15, 17, 18
        value, 15, 38
    trends, 14–20
Investment Co-ordinating Board (BKPM),
    18
IPTN, PT, 54, 57
Islam
    politicization, 224

Jakarta Stock Exchange (JSE), 27–28
    capitalization, 28
Jakob Oetama, 186
Japan
    manufacturing labour wages, 149
Java
    investment
        domestic, 20
        foreign, 18
Jaya Educational Foundation, 175
Jaya Group, 175

Kedung Ombo Dam
    case, 72
Kompas Group, 185, 186
KOPKAMTIB, 109

Korea, South
  democracy and development, 190
  manufacturing labour wages, 149
KORPRI, 82
Kuntara, 105
Kusumaatmadja, Sarwono, 96

labour, 261–62
  activism, 142, 144, 147
  consciousness, 261
  demand and supply
    by education level, 166
    for graduates, 168
  force, 150
  government policy, 261
  strikes, 148
    causes, 147–50
  unions, 261, 262
  unrest, 139–55
  See also trade unions; workers
labour relations
  government role, 146
  tripartite structure, 146
  See also industrial relations
land
  appropriation, 75–76
    compensation, 76
  disputes, 75–76
leadership change, 1
Legal Aid Institute (LBH), 220, 222–24
  activities, 223
  democratization, 223
  financial contributions
    foreign, 223
  goals, 222
  harassment, 224
  legal aid
    structural approach, 222, 230
  legal reforms, 223
  Network Development Programme, 223
Lembaga Swadaya Masyarakat (LSM),
    217–31
Liem Sioe Liong, 31, 33, 188
Lippo Group, 174
Lippo Village, 174
living standards, 3

Local Enterprise Administration Board,
    104
Lubis, T. Mulya, 142

Madura
  investment
    domestic, 20
    foreign, 18
"Malari" riots, 15, 38, 74, 238, 239
Malaysia
  Institute of Policy Studies, 244
  manufacturing labour wages, 149
manufacturing, 14
  chemicals, 15, 20
  growth, 14
  metals, 15
  pulp and paper, 20
  textile, 15, 20
martial law, 103, 104
Masgobel Educational Foundation, 171
mass media, 179–95, 263–64
  ban, 193, 197
  conglomerates, 181
  and democracy, 189–93
  depoliticization, 182
  diversity, democracy, and market,
    193–95
  dual product market, 180
  electronic, 184–85
  foreign investment, 196–97
  government
    control, 263
    organizations, 263
  growth and economic development,
    180–82
  organizational structure, 182–83
  personnel, 183–84
    graduates, 183, 184
  political affiliation, 182
  publication permits
    cancellation, 264
  radio, 184
  sensitive issues, 195
  structure
    changing, 184–87
  television, 185, 187, 188

vertical political integration, 187–89,
   193
Masyumi, 204
Matori Abdul Djalil, 119
Media Indonesia Group, 185
Megawati Sukarnoputri, 117, 118, 129
   removal from party, 1
Menara Bhakti Foundation, 171
Mercu Buana Group, 171, 172
Mercu Buana University, 171–72
Metareum, H. Ismail Hasan, 118, 119,
   128, 129
middle class, 180, 212
Moerdani, L.B., 239
Moerdiono, 124
monetary reform
   Pakjun 1983, 24–25
   Pakto 88, 25
Muhammadiyah, 201, 203, 267
Mustopha Zuhad, 208, 209

Nahdlatul Ulama (NU), 267
   "164 Foundation", 210
   branch leadership, 212
   economic
      factors, 207–9
      issues, 211–13
   established, 203
   – government relationship, 213, 215
   institutional behaviour
      changes in, 205
   institutional relationships, 213
   LAKPESDAM, 209–10, 211
      Bulletin Lakpesdam, 210
      Post-Pesantren Leadership Training
         Project, 210
   LKiS, 210
   middle class, 212
   modernity, 209–11
   national unity, 214
   objectives, 203
   organizational structure, 202–3
   and *Pembangunan*, 201–14
      adaptation to, 204–5
   Peoples' Credit Banks (BPR), 208, 209

   political background, 203–4
      non-political, 204
      political factors, 206–7
      political party, 204–5
   racial harmony, 212
   relevance, 211
   "Return to the Commitment of 1926",
      205, 207
   values, 212
   youth wing (ANSOR), 206
Naro, H.J., 118
Nasution, A.H., 100
Nasution, Adnan Buyung, 222
National Atomic Agency (BATAN), 237
National Commission for Human Rights,
   75, 77, 130, 190
National Defence Institute, 241
National Development Planning Board
   (Bappenas), 52, 236, 240, 245
nationalization, 56, 104
Nationalization Board, 104
Netherlands East Indies
   social organizations, 201
New Order
   ABRI's role in, 101
   bureaucracy, 81–97
      making of, 81–83
   developmental regime, 61
   economic "miracle", 2–4
   educational development strategy, 159
   "Family State", 145
   industrial relations, 144
   media, 179, 181, 182
   Pancasila, 61
   political
      institutions, 61–78
      stability, 206
      structures, 61
   political parties
      leadership selection, 116
newspapers
   banning, 190, 191, 193
   Basic Norms for Press
      Enterprises, 195
   circulation, 180–81, 186, 195
   Guided Democracy period, 194, 195

number of, 186
See also press
Nico Daryanto, 125
non-governmental organizations (NGOs),
    268
  activists, 219
  activities, 221
  characteristics, 218
  constraints, 230
  development-oriented objectives, 220,
    221
  early, 231
  and empowerment of civil society,
    217–31
  financial
    dependency, 230–31
    support, 231, 234
  issue-oriented, 219, 229
    objectives, 219
  leaders, 218
  members, 218
  under New Order, 220–22
  origin, 218
  political activism, 221
  problems, 269
  role, 219
  state pressure, 230
  strength, 219

oil
  price, 15
    declines, 24, 47, 88
    increases, 45
Old Order, 2

Pacific Economic Co-operation
    Conference (PECC), 237
Pamungkas, Ir. Sri Bintang, 119, 122, 123
Pancasila doctrine, 206
Parliament (DPR), 63, 125–26
  budget, national, 68
  candidates
    screening, 130
  criticism, 70
  functions, 125–26
  legislation, 69, 126
    on political structure, 68

limitations, 70–71
openness, 77
operating funds, 70, 71
power, 68–71
Rules of Order, 70
salary, 71
Pelita, 188
Pelita Harapan School, 174
Pelita Harapan Sentul, 174
People's Consultative Assembly (MPR),
    63, 77
  Broad Outlines of State Policy, 76
    1978, 74
    1993, 74, 127
Pertamina
  financial collapse, 105
'Petition of 50' group, 79, 190, 226
Philippines
  manufacturing labour wages, 149
political expression, 131, 263
political institutions, 61–78
political organizations
  quasi-, 130–31
political parties, 262–63
  autonomy
    financial factor, 126–29
  candidates screened, 262
  election campaigns, 121
  government control, 262, 263
  independence, 262
  leadership, 79
  leadership selection, 116–21
    government intervention, 116–21
    regulation, 116
  management, 116–21
  mergers, 143
  and Parliament, 125–26
  performance and economic growth,
    115–31
  programmes, 121–25
  trade unions, 143
  village level, 130
politics
  regional
    elections, 93
population
  family planning, 3

growth, 3
rural, 161
Pos Kota, 187
Pos Kota Group, 185, 186
poverty, 2, 3, 37
rate, 3
Prabowo, 246
Prajogo Pangestu, 31
Prasetya Mulya Foundation, 172
Prasetya Mulya Graduate School of
    Management, 172–73
Prawiro, Radius, 66
presidency, 62–65, 78, 256
Aspri, 238, 239
checks and balances, 63
factors contributing to powerful,
    62–64
State Secretariat, 70, 71, 72,
    127, 128, 236
succession, 65
terms, 124
press
closure, 77
commercially oriented, 181
freedom, 77, 190–91
publication permits
    1984 regulation, 192
See also newspapers
Press Act
1966, 187
1982, 191
pricing policies, government, 46
privatization, 47, 49, 50
problems, 5
Probosutejo, 188
Proclamation Foundation, 238

reforms
structural, 4–5
Republika, 189, 192
research and development, 168
riot, 1
Rudini, 241
rupiah
crisis
    action, 4
    depreciation, 1

Sahid Academy of Hotel and Tourism, 172
Sahid Group, 172
Sahid Jaya Educational Foundation, 172
Sahid University, 172
Said Budairy, 205, 209, 210, 215
Saiful Sulun, 120
savings
national, 22
separatist movements, 92
Sigit Harjojudanto, 33
Silalahi, T.B., 92
Sinar, 188, 194
Sinar Harapan, 198
Singapore
manufacturing labour wages, 149
Yayasan Mendaki, 244
Sjadzali, H. Munawir, 119
social
equity, 160
justice, 73–74
social organizations, 267–68
roles in society, 201–2
society
bureaucratization of, 84, 86, 97–98
diversity, 193
Soebijakto Prawirasoebrata, 241
Soedarpo Sastrosatomo, 30
Soedarwo, Imam, 146
Soedjono Hoemardani, 238, 239
Soedomo, 145
Soeharto, 2, 36, 62, 63, 64, 65, 67, 68,
    104, 106, 190, 196, 197
on ABRI, 108
children, 32, 33, 36, 64, 187
family, 187, 188
    business activities, 195
    financial resources, 64
    foundations, 64, 78
    fund raising, 105
    military budget, 106
on protection, 54
reforms, 5
resignation, 1
Soerjadi, 116, 118, 124
Soesastro, Hadi, 47, 233, 239
Solidarity Free Trade Union (SBMSK),
    147

Southeast Asian Coalition (SEACON), 228
speech
  freedom, 77
state, strong
  corporatization, 220
  depoliticization, 220
  and economic development, 220
  establishment, 220
state administration
  structure, 87
State Ministry of Development Control
    and Environment, 91
Strategic Industry Management Board
    (BPIS), 51, 52, 53, 54
Suara Pembaruan, 198
Subchan Z.E., 206
Subiyakto, 106
Sudharmono, 90, 127, 130
Sudirman, 100
Sudirman, Basofi, 118
Sudomo, 124, 190
Sudono Salim. *See* Liem Sioe Liong
Sudwikatmono, 188
Sugiarto, 120
Sugito, 105
Suhardiman, 104
Sukamdani Gitosardjono, 187
Sukarno, 2, 63, 100
  economic policy, 42, 44
  fall, 42
  Guided Democracy, 101
  Nasakom, 135
  public enterprises, 56
  surrender, 100
Sumarlin, 208
Sumarno Syafei, 123
Sumitro, 120
Suprayogi, 104
Surya Paloh, 185, 192
Suyono, 106

Taiwan
  democracy and development, 190
  manufacturing labour wages, 149

Tangerang
  strike, 150–54
Tarumanagara University, 175
Tawang Alun Study Group (TASG), 245
Tempo
  closure, 72–73, 189, 191, 198
Tempo Group, 185
Thailand
  foreign exchange crisis, 4
  manufacturing labour wages, 149
think-tanks, 233–51, 268–69
  constraints, 233–35
  financial reward, 234
  funding, 233–34
    foreign, 234
  problems, 269
  typology, 246–48
Tiras, 188
trade unions
  government control, 150
  government's perception of role, 144
  and labour unrest, 139–55
  management
    political background, 143–44
  problems, 142–43

Umar Said, 105
United States, 9
  income per capita, 4
Unity of Indonesian Republic Workers
    (KBRI), 143
University of Indonesia
  Faculty of Economics
    Institute for Economic and Social
      Research (LPEM), 245

Vietnam
  foreign investment, 75
Village Social Institution (LSD), 86
Village Society Resilience Institution
    (LKMD), 86

Wahono, 123
Wanita Indonesia, 188

West Irian
  vote in United Nations, 104
Widjoyo Nitisastro, 14
Wismoyo, 112
workers
  awareness, 142, 147
  child labourers, 147, 149
  manufacturing
    educational levels, 141
    wages, 149
  minimum physical needs, 156
  productivity, 150
  rights, 140, 141
  wages, 147, 149, 150

  regional minimum wage, 147, 149,
    156, 157
  See also labour; trade unions
World Bank, 2, 52
world economy
  liberalization, 47

Yamaha Training Center, 171
Yogie Suardi Memed, 117, 129

Zacky Anwar, 117
Zulkarnaen, 228